ALWAYS CARRY SALT

ALSO BY SAMANTHA ELLIS

Take Courage: Anne Brontë and the Art of Life

How to Be a Heroine

ALWAYS CARRY SALT

A MEMOIR OF PRESERVING LANGUAGE AND CULTURE

SAMANTHA ELLIS

PEGASUS BOOKS
NEW YORK LONDON

ALWAYS CARRY SALT

Pegasus Books, Ltd.
148 West 37th Street, 13th Floor
New York, NY 10018

First Pegasus Books cloth edition January 2026

ISBN: 979-8-89710-028-6

10 9 8 7 6 5 4 3 2 1

Printed in the United States of America
Distributed by Simon & Schuster
www.pegasusbooks.com

For B, *fedwa*

Contents

Note on transliteration

It's quite difficult to transliterate a language which is mainly oral and has been written down in two alphabets, neither of which is this one, but I have tried to follow my instincts and be consistent, and give a flavour of how the language sounds.

Preface

Eeyam al babenjan (Days of the aubergines)

In autumn 2019 I was in a cold London playground, spinning my son on a lurid, primary-coloured roundabout. He was two and a half, near-spherical in his green puffer, hair gleaming in the sun. Another boy jumped on. My son offered him a rice cake and he said, '*Merci*.' His mum told me he went to the nearby French nursery, where children ate *pain au chocolat* in improbably clean dungarees. I told her I'd wanted my son to go there so that he could grow up with two languages like me. 'But you're not French?' she said, confused. 'Why not send him to a nursery for your language?' I replied, 'I can't. My language is dead.'

And then I burst into tears.

Because: my language is *dead*?

To be more accurate, it is dying. This wasn't news, but suddenly it hit me with a force that knocked all the air out of me. Guilt banged at my heart too, because one reason it was dying was that I was not wholly bilingual, I was not doing my best to keep it alive. Too blindsided to say this to a stranger, I scooped my son into his pushchair and left her staring. How could I explain when even *I* found it impossible to grasp that Judeo-Iraqi Arabic, which I heard every day of my childhood, at home, with my family, in my community, at parties and on play dates, a language that felt more present than English, more vivid and more colourful, would soon be gone?

One day the chubby boy I was wheeling away from the park would want to know. Back then he was still grappling with

English, coining his own words – *budund* for playground, *mon* for milk – and struggling to twist his tongue around certain sounds. Sometimes I had to translate him and it came easy because, being second generation, I'd been translating all my life. Judeo-Iraqi Arabic always felt like the real, important language. When I was small I thought English was just a children's language, for nursery rhymes and picture books, a language that wasn't entirely serious. I assumed when I grew up I would be fluent in Judeo-Iraqi Arabic. But although there was a time I understood almost everything, I could never really speak it – and now it was too late. The clock was ticking (it had been ticking all my life) and soon there would be no one to talk to.

As my son clamoured for rice cakes I dredged up a phrase for how this felt. Like living *eeyam al babenjan* (in the days of the aubergines), which means living in a time when everything feels upside down or inside out; 'Like Halloween,' said my mum, 'all the craziness comes out.' I don't know why the craziness comes out in the days of the aubergines, I don't even know when that is, but the rocking, comic rhyme of *eeyam al babenjan* captured the nonsense, the uncanniness, the horror of losing the language I grew up with. It felt comforting to pin it down, to say, *it feels like living in the days of the aubergines*. But as I turned onto my street, it hit me that it was not comforting if the only way I could make sense of my situation was by using a language already living on borrowed time. It felt like looking into a future where I would only be able to say how I felt by awkwardly explaining phrases I didn't fully understand myself.

Home. I bumped the pushchair up the black-and-white steps, and went into a blind whirl of coats, nappies, milk. Then he was asleep, and I raced to my laptop to find out if anyone was saving my language. Someone had to be! It goes back such a long time. Jews first came to Iraq in 597 BCE. Only it wasn't called Iraq then, but Babylonia – and sometimes just Babylon after its capital. Iraq's names are confusing. It has had so many, and they haven't all described the exact same geographical area. Mesopotamia usually indicated what is now northern Iraq (and sometimes also eastern Syria), while Babylonia usually referred to what is now southern Iraq. Later, Arabs often referred to the area between the Tigris and the Euphrates as 'al-Iraq'. In 597 BCE, when the first wave of Jewish exiles came to Babylon, the city was the beating heart of Babylonia, also known as the Neo-Babylonian Empire. Its warrior king, Nebuchadnezzar, muddled things further (if that was possible) by conquering other lands. When he sacked Jerusalem, the capital of the Jewish kingdom of Judah (also known as Judea), he deported many thousands of Jews to Babylon as captive labour to dredge canals between the Tigris and the Euphrates. The Jews spoke Hebrew, but when they arrived, they switched to the local language, Aramaic, and quickly developed a variant called Jewish Babylonian Aramaic. When the Persians conquered in 539 BCE, the language was infused with Persian. And when the Arab Muslim conquest swept across the Middle East in the seventh century, the Jews, like everyone else, switched to Arabic; but they always spoke it differently, carrying over Aramaic and Hebrew words and constructions, so it's a language that feels very ancient, somehow.

In the 1940s, the community's heyday, there were 150,000 Jews in Iraq. There are so few now – single figures – that every time the number goes down, someone reports it, and although it feels ghoulish to check, sometimes I can't help it. With my son's snorty snuffles coming through the baby monitor, I discovered that, at the best guess, in 2019, there were five Jews left in Iraq.

Most of Iraq's Jews left for Israel in 1950–1, in a mass airlift known as Operation Ezra and Nehemiah (for the Jewish prophets) or sometimes Operation Ali Baba, for the woodcutter from *Alf Laila wa Laila*, the *Thousand and One Nights*, who discovers a thieves' den full of treasure and opens it with the magic formula 'open sesame'. It was one of the first airlifts of Jews to Israel, echoed later in the airlifts of Ethiopian and Yemenite Jews. My father left then, but my mother stayed in Baghdad until 1971 when she came to London, where they met. My parents fell in love in Judeo-Iraqi Arabic, but they didn't teach it to me or my brother.

I could blame the health visitor who urged them just to speak English, so as not to confuse us, but my parents also felt it was futile to teach us a language that was not going to survive. By 1975, when I was born, there were only around four hundred Jews left in Iraq, and most of the community had been scattered for more than twenty years. A generation. My parents determinedly spoke to us in English, and read us English books, but all the gossip, all the stories, all the exciting, forbidden grown-up *life* happened in Judeo-Iraqi Arabic. When, frustrated, I decided to try to learn, I listened hard, asked a lot of questions, and when I was nine or so, I suddenly got it. It was like walking through a wall and being on the inside. The words were mine. At first I didn't tell anyone, and had fun understanding and outwitting my parents. Then one day my dad made a joke, I laughed and I was rumbled. Anyway, after that it was even better because my parents could talk to me in what was essentially a secret language, because so few people spoke it in London. (Even fewer now.)

Googling furiously, I suddenly worried it wouldn't count as a mother tongue. The UNESCO definition is the language you speak from earliest childhood, and I spoke English. But some linguists describe, instead, a first language, a home language, a parent language, an arterial language, as if it's in our blood; while the Moroccan author and translator Ghita El Khayat speaks of a 'milk language', spoken by your mother when you are tiny, the language you're sung to sleep in, or soothed in. Judeo-Iraqi

Arabic is all of those for me, the intimate, vulnerable language of safety, of closeness, trust and belonging.

I wasn't even sure what to type into the search engine. I'm calling it Judeo-Iraqi Arabic here, as if its name is known and fixed, like English, or French or German, but I settled on this later. In that first frantic burst of research, I tried and failed to find the right words. At home we called it Judeo-Arabic, but that wasn't quite right because there are other languages spoken by Jews in other Arabic-speaking countries. We also sometimes called it Jewish Arabic or *arabi yehudi* – which has the same issues. Or *haki mal yihud* (the talk of the Jews), as distinguished from *haki mal aslam* (the talk of the Muslims), even though Muslims aren't the only people who speak 'Muslim' Arabic, and Jews – when there were more Jews in Iraq – spoke it too when they were with non-Jews, in shops, on the streets, in business, with officials. Which is why, in my family, we called this Arabic 'real Arabic' as if ours wasn't real, but instead was secondary, not quite legitimate. Some call our language Jewish-Iraqi, connecting it to race and place but not to language. Some say Jewish Iraqi-Arabic which feels more accurate. Some say Jewish Baghdadi (or JB for short, which feels affectionate), or Baghdadi Judeo-Arabic, which isn't quite right because it was spoken by Jews in other parts of Iraq, like Basra, where my grandfather grew up. In Israel I've heard it called *Iraqeet* (meaning Iraqi; English is *Angleet*) but this only works because in Israel most people speaking *Iraqeet* are Jewish, so there's no need to specify a religion or a race. We sometimes call it *arabi malna* (our Arabic) or *haki malna* (our talk), but I couldn't search under these cosy endearments. What *did* come up was Judeo-Iraqi Arabic, on UNESCO's list of endangered languages, which felt as good a name as any.

Then I panicked, because I couldn't find it on UNESCO's World Atlas of Languages. I scoured Iraq for it in vain, and only eventually spotted it in Israel, which was correct if you were counting numbers of speakers because Israel is where most of the world's speakers of Judeo-Iraqi Arabic are today, but emotionally it felt wrong for my language to be mapped to anywhere but Iraq. At least UNESCO called it a language, not a *dialect* as some linguists defined it – this felt diminishing to me, and delegitimising. I wondered what the difference was and found that linguists joke that 'a language is just a dialect with an army', and that this joke was first made about Yiddish. I was often told my language was 'to Arabic what Yiddish is to German', because just as my language came out of the collision of Hebrew-speaking Jews and Aramaic-speaking Babylonians, and then absorbed linguistic influences from all the other people who conquered Iraq, so Yiddish (probably) originated in the Rhine Valley, as a variant of German spoken by Jews, and was inflected with Slavic languages over the centuries. If Yiddish did begin in the tenth century it is a little younger than my language but they have a lot in common. Both languages are Jewish (Yiddish actually means Jewish); both are much loved (Yiddish is often tenderly nicknamed *mameloshen*, mother tongue) and also dismissed or minimised (Yiddish has also been called *zhargon*, jargon); both can be written in the Hebrew alphabet (although mine is written in the Arabic alphabet too); both are earthy, sinewy, witty; and both are at risk. At its peak, just before the Second World War, Yiddish was spoken by many more people than ever spoke my language, up to 13 million worldwide, but around 5 million Yiddish speakers were murdered in the Holocaust, and countless others displaced. The joke about Yiddish being a dialect because it lacked an army was made in 1945. It was never meant to be funny.

I eyed the baby monitor. Naptime was nearly over; I'd learned next to nothing and I hadn't even had a biscuit.

Suddenly it hit me, what I needed to do. I had to make a dictionary! But how could I when we don't even have a fixed alphabet? Judeo-Iraqi Arabic is sometimes written in Hebrew script, sometimes in Arabic, although it has never been written down much. I'd love to come from a great literary tradition, but when Iraqi Jews wrote books they wrote them in *fusha*, which is classical Arabic, and literally means *purest*. And didn't this imply that Judeo-Iraqi Arabic was adulterated, secondary, broken? This is a problem beyond my language. *All* Arabic speakers struggle with the split between *fusha* – or the updated version, Modern Standard Arabic – and their own vernaculars, with the fact that the language of literature, school textbooks, newspapers and technology is no one's mother tongue. Iraqi Jewish writers also often write their books in the languages of the places they were displaced to: mostly Hebrew but English and French as well. No one was going to save my language for its literature. Linguists sometimes argue for endangered languages to be saved because they contain information the world might need, like Cherokee (which now has only 2,000 speakers) where the names for plants, herbs, berries and flowers indicate whether they are edible or poisonous or cure particular diseases. It is alarming to think that a cure for cancer might come from the sap of a tree that only has a name in a language that is going extinct, but it probably won't be in my language. Most of Iraq's Jews lived in the cities. They were urban people. My grandfather did heal people, but with conventional medicine. He was a GP.

UNESCO lists 2,464 languages at risk, and that's just languages. We are living through Earth's sixth mass extinction event. A million *species* are at risk. Did my language really matter? A language that might not even be a language. A language with no fixed alphabet, few books and no cures.

Then again, I hated the idea that we should only save languages that were useful, like stripping them for parts. I didn't want to live in a world where I'd shrug and say *yom assel yom bassal* and no one would know I meant *one day honey, another day onions*. I didn't want to cook a meal and never be told *ashteedek* (long live your hands), I wanted to be able to ask *ash lonek* (how are you? – but literally, joyfully, what colour are you?). I don't believe that flattening us all down into sameness is the way to keep the world beautiful or even alive.

I rang my mother who is better than the internet. Within minutes she sent me a PDF of a dictionary – a dictionary with a love story: an American Ashkenazi Jew married an Iraqi Jew and couldn't talk to her family, so he made a dictionary and circulated it to anyone who wanted it. I laughed when I found that the first phrase he included was *enta ju-an?* (are you hungry?). It's where I would have started too. My mother also sent me a link to an archive, held at SOAS but made by an Iraqi Jew called Eli Timan, who I knew, who lived in London, who was my mother's second cousin. Sometimes the Iraqi Jewish community feels very small.

My son cried out, and I stopped searching, but I didn't stop worrying. Yes, it was a relief to find a dictionary and an archive, because I couldn't have done that work. I only ever had a broken, pidgin, kitchen Judeo-Iraqi Arabic which I pronounced so badly my parents joked *tahki kanni kebba b'thema* (she talks like she has *kubba* in her mouth). I often did have *kubba* in my mouth, the meatballs encased in bulgur, rice or potato, elsewhere called *kibbeh* or *kofte*. I missed it, along with the language, when I left home for university. Later my brother and I both married outside our community. My son is also English and German (through his grandfather) and Irish (through his grandmother). When my family gets together now we generally speak English. Most of my community is like this and in some families the language is already lost. It's not being transmitted, and that's how linguists often define endangerment; if children aren't being taught a language, it will die. Many years ago I used to dream in Judeo-Iraqi Arabic and in the dreams I was fluent, but then I stopped. I felt estranged from it, homesick for it, even though I could still ring up my mother and get her to remind me of the phrase I would say as a party trick when I was a child: *thenbet el kalb, khellooha bel kasba, oo ukeb reb'een yom, tel'ooha oo ba'ada ma'eruja* (they put a dog's tail into a sugar cane tube for forty days, and when they got it out, it was still curly). To think that soon – probably in my lifetime – those words would no longer be alive in anyone's mouth felt desperate.

As autumn turned to winter, it gnawed away at me, the idea that a silence was coming. If the words disappeared, would we lose the stories too? The recipes, the jokes, the curses? Even the (very few) things I have from Iraq seemed suddenly vulnerable because I was already losing their names. How could I pass all this on to my son when it was slipping away? I'd often felt lost in translation but soon I would be untranslatable. I needed to do something, but what?

I started jotting down scraps and fragments. It was early 2020.

Then the pandemic started, and we were *all* cut off from each other. We only saw my family on Zoom and I went weeks without a word of Judeo-Iraqi Arabic. I missed the warmth, the noise, I *really* missed the *kubba*. At Pesach I even missed the Iraqi Jewish Haggadah, which I'd often found confusing because instead of being in Hebrew and Aramaic on one side and English on the other, it had Hebrew and Aramaic on one side and Judeo-Iraqi Arabic, in the Hebrew alphabet, on the other, so hardly any of us could read it. But now I wanted it. I made my own *matzah* because I couldn't get to a kosher shop, I made *kechri* (the rice, lentil, cheese and yogurt dish that will always be my comfort food, a relative of Indian *kichri*, Egyptian *koshary*, Levantine *mujadara* and Yemeni *enjadara*), and we did the Seder over Zoom, my son stuffing the egg (symbolising the cycle of life) whole into his mouth.

It was a brief bright moment, a relief from thinking about

viruses . . . and dinosaurs. My son was obsessed. We collected plastic beasts and bloodthirsty facts. I couldn't bear to think about my language going extinct but he was never happier than when we were talking about extinction. One day he put his favourite T-rex down on the carpet and said, 'He's died.' My heart thudded. I didn't know he knew about death, although that was what we were trying to protect him from, as we stayed indoors, locked down, seeing no one. I hoped he hadn't heard us talk about *the numbers* (we did not say *the dead*). I looked at the prone T-rex and wondered how to meet this minor parenting crisis. But my son was ahead of me, rummaging through his toy box for an ugly, mean-faced Stygimoloch. He put its sharp teeth to the T-rex's body and I thought it was going to eat it, but instead my son blew a kiss. 'I kiss him back to life,' he said, and set the T-rex back on his feet. We did this for days: killed off dinosaurs and kissed them back to life. It felt like hope. And so did this: a three-year-old could name creatures who hadn't walked the earth for millions of years and tell me what they ate and how they lived.

Covid was killing languages as well as people. I read that in the Amazon, two of the last seven speakers of Manoki died. In Chile, Yahgan lost its last speaker. There was a rush to translate medical guidance into what linguists sometimes call 'small languages' because they don't have many speakers, and many of those few speakers were older, poorer, marginalised, in bad health and less able to access good health care, so more vulnerable. In Dudinka, in the Russian Arctic, stay-at-home warnings were broadcast in six languages, five of which were indigenous: Dolgan, Nganasan, Evenki, Enets and Nenets.

One weird pandemic night I read a Canadian study which showed that young Aboriginal people who learned their own languages were much less likely to commit suicide. Its authors argued that learning family languages, native languages, ancestral languages makes us more connected, more resilient, mentally stronger, richer of heart. I hadn't seen my mum in person for three months. I ordered a textbook called *The Arabic Dialect of the Jews of Baghdad: Phonology, Morphology and Texts*. It was by Assaf Bar-Moshe, an Iraqi Jewish academic, whose parents left in the early 1970s like my mother, and who grew up in Israel. He started his linguistics career with Mandarin – until his supervisor told him that while many, many people could work on Mandarin, only a few could document Judeo-Iraqi Arabic. Linguists need a body of words and conversations and stories to work with, so Bar-Moshe started recording interviews with his family. Over the next few months, I worked my way through his transcripts, slowly, like feeling along a wall in the dark. Every time I recognised a word or phrase I cemented it down in my mind, and felt louder somehow, more alive. Although when I looked down the list it depressed me: *harb* (war), *janta* (suitcase), *pasportat* (passports), *qacharchi* (smuggler), *sherta* (police), *edmonu* (they executed him), *khof* (fear). It felt like a found poem about why the language was endangered in the first place.

Iraqi Jews start stories with *Kan wu-ma kan ala-Allah wel teklan* ('It was or it was not, it's in God's hands' – and yes, we do say Allah for God). Other communities say 'It was or it was not' but continue the formula differently; they might add 'in a past long ago' or 'not here not there'. Hungarians say *Egyszer volt, hol nem volt* ('Once where it was, where it was not'), Turks say *Bir varmis, bir yokmus* ('Once there was, once there was not'). It's quite a different vibe to 'Once upon a time', more ambivalent, ironic, doubtful, teasing, more of a challenge, maybe, to whoever is listening, to decide how far they'll suspend their disbelief. It suggests that this is not going to be a story of the everyday. There may be marvels and wonders, or there may not. Judeo-Iraqi Arabic loves these existential axes, rocking back and forth between certainty and uncertainty. We use the rhyming opposites *aku* (there is) and *maku* (there is not) all the time. There's an Iraqi Jewish restaurant in Tel Aviv called Aku Maku. You can use *Ash aku, ash maku?* as a conversation starter – 'What is there, what isn't there?' As I tried to get to grips with this language I could and couldn't speak, that might or might not be a dialect, that had more than one alphabet or none, that teetered on the edge of extinction, I felt like I was rocking back and forth too. I read that one of Iraq's last five Jews had died, a ninety-something woman who was once a teacher at the Jewish school. The obituary included a picture of her taking a register, looking busy and happy. Twenty years back she'd told an interviewer she'd never leave the place where she'd spent the best years of her life. Now there were four Jews in Iraq. A few months later I read that another had died, a doctor. The community was down to three.

It was 2021. My son, four and a half, splashing in the bath, asked what *fedwa* meant. He'd heard my mother call me that. I didn't want to tell him it means 'I would die for you' so I just said it meant 'I love you very much'. 'Why don't you call me that then?' he asked. I didn't know what to say. *Fedwa* felt too dramatic a term of endearment. Although I would. Die for him. I couldn't say it. *Fedwa* carries my family's danger, drama and trauma, which I wanted to leave behind when I became a mother, not to pass on. Although I was born in London, have always been safe from the persecution my family experienced in Iraq, and have never had to face the rupture of leaving my home, I was a worried child and an anxious adult. I imagined trauma gnawing through generation after generation like the caterpillar eating his way through fruit and cake and sausages in *The Very Hungry Caterpillar*, except at the end you didn't turn into a butterfly but a guilt-stricken neurotic with recurrent nightmares. I was determined to break the cycle, because, after all, we were both safe, weren't we?

I wrapped him in the towel which made him look like a tiny dinosaur, with fabric spikes over the hood, and *he* said it. *Fedwa.* I melted. He loved me very much. Although part of me felt worried, again, because it was the wrong way round. I was the grown-up! I was supposed to be saying it to him. But still, *kenna kanehki* (we were talking). We were talking Judeo-Iraqi Arabic. We were talking about love (and also about death). I wanted to know more about why my language was going extinct, and about what else we keep and what we lose, how we decide what to let go of, and how sometimes we don't get to make these decisions, but are swept up by history or politics or fate. I was acutely aware that difficult family stories can weigh us down, but also that, sometimes, our ancestors give us the survival kits we need to be resilient and to heal. It seemed crucial, now, to think much more deeply about all this, about what we pass on, not just as parents (if we become parents), but what we put out into the world, the legacies we leave, the ideas we give, the stories we tell, the contributions we make, the kindnesses we are (hopefully) remembered for, the food we cook for friends. I needed to understand the stories of my culture and community before they were lost or (worse) erased, so I could tell them to my son – and to anyone who cared to listen. I wanted to work out how to be a good future ancestor myself. I wanted to write down the recipes! I wanted to hold the *things* my parents brought from Iraq and keep them safe, and to know their stories, and I wanted to think about what heirlooms I might pass on, what memories, what imprints – and fast. It felt as if a flood was coming. I needed, urgently, to build an ark.

Losing

Ekel qalbi (He ate my heart), or An incomplete list of Judeo-Iraqi Arabic idioms about the heart

At seven I was in a production of Benjamin Britten's opera *Noye's Fludde*. I was playing a duck in my gym kit with a gorgeous headdress (with real feathers!). I was supposed to keep my beak down, but I couldn't stop looking at Mrs Noye, who laughed when her husband came home with a mad story about God and a flood and started building a boat and gathering animals. I mean, you absolutely would. She went on carousing with her friends until her sons dragged her bodily onto the ark, and when she watched those friends drown, she slapped her husband. Hard. She made more sense to me, clinging to her friends, to her world, while phlegmatic, stolid, cowardly Noah didn't even try to save anyone except his immediate family, let alone argue with or beg God for mercy for all mankind. In the *Epic of Gilgamesh*, the ancient epic poem from Mesopotamia which contains a version of the story of the Flood, the Noah figure, Utnapishtim, is even colder, saying, 'I let all my ale, beer, oil, and wine / flow like rivers for the workmen' and 'they drank like it was New Year's!' He gives the shipwright his palace and possessions, knowing he won't live to enjoy them. Did he feel any remorse as he stood on deck in the falling rain or as the waters rose still higher and he retreated inside, his friends and neighbours banging on the ark to be let in, water sloshing against the sides, and the cries got quieter and quieter and then stopped? Did he feel a great, heaving sadness about what he'd lost?

As for me, every time I tried to think about what to put on my ark I was overwhelmed by what was already gone.

I'd already lost so many words, I could barely make a sentence. I couldn't remember the Judeo-Iraqi Arabic words for *cloud* or *seed* or *hope*. The language didn't feel like a river I could swim in any more. Not like when I was small and listening to grown-ups talk, sharing recipes and gossip and secrets and stories, all above my head, and feeling nourished because talk is life and curiosity and empathy and wonder and all at high speed.

So far as I know no one has analysed the speech patterns of Iraqi Jews, but reading linguist Deborah Tannen's analysis of New York Jews talking, I recognised something. Tannen found they talked fast, jumped from topic to topic, told lots of stories emotionally and dramatically and interrupted a lot, but not in a rude way; their 'high-involvement cooperative overlapping', showed interest and kept the conversation moving. They were interrupting to affirm, to sympathise, to underscore. I wanted to talk like this in my language, not to reach painfully for half-forgotten words. I wanted to join the conversation that used to go on around the Formica table in my grandparents' kitchen in Wembley, me sitting underneath the table, maybe three years old, pulling the stalks off parsley, armfuls of it, so my mother and my aunt could make tabbouleh. They called me *mish mish* (little apricot) – many Iraqi families have a *mish mish* and I love that about us – or *fedwa*, of course, or *abdalek*, which literally means 'may I be your sacrifice' or 'your atonement' and comes from the Orthodox Jewish tradition on Yom Kippur of swinging a chicken over your head to symbolically give it your sins so it would suffer for them instead of you. (Poor chicken.) But mostly they talked to each other, joking that someone they knew was *ibn kelb* (son of a dog) or *kelb ibn kelb* (dog, son of a dog), the two generations of being canine making it, for some reason, a bigger insult, or a *zmal* (donkey), or wishing *wakka mazzalem* (may their luck run out). Or exclaiming *rathab Allah!* – literally 'anger of God!', but it is used when you are happy. Or *weh-hu-weh!* which doesn't mean anything, but is just a way of gasping in shock. Or *booma!* which means 'owl', but also means someone is being a fool and is not to be mixed up with *bezoona* which means 'cat'. Or *Wi abel!*, literally 'oh mourning!' If anyone predicts bad things might happen, you say *skitti oo-khalia*, or *shut up and leave it*, because everyone knows words are powerful and talking about bad things can will them into being. If you upset someone they might say *yethrem basal all ras efadi!* (you're chopping onions on my heart!), the Judeo-Iraqi Arabic version of 'you're rubbing salt in the wound' but so graphic it makes you wince. It isn't always said seriously; sometimes it's said ruefully or as a joke. And my mother pointed out it's not just 'my heart' but 'the head of my heart'. Using a heart as a chopping board is such a painful image that specifying the vegetable as well (*and* a vegetable that's particularly associated with stinging and tears) seems excessive. But that's Judeo-Iraqi Arabic for you. It *is* excessive. Wry. Noisy. Vivid. Hot, where English often seems cold. Mouth-filling where English seems empty. Patterned when English seems plain. Or maybe it just felt that way because my family were speaking boldly, confidently, colourfully in their mother tongue, and in English they sounded quieter, meeker, *less*, like the Danish mum who told me at the playground that having to live mainly in English meant 'I've lost my nuance. I'm like a butterfly with no wings, a flower with no petals.'

Under the table, I heard more questions than statements, and most of them were rhetorical. Instead of replying 'yes' or 'of course', you could say *lakan?* (or else?). Asked if you'd put cumin in something, you might say *ash kmoon?* (what? cumin?!), sounding outraged, as if it would be insane to add cumin, as if you'd lived all your life in a world without cumin, as if cumin was not even food, as if it was an insult to be asked. We were allergic to saying *la* (no) – unless we were offered food, when, I absorbed early on, you had to refuse multiple times before accepting, even if you were ravenous, even if the people offering the food were English and didn't realise you were being polite, and gave up offering, and you ended up hungry. This happened a lot when I was a child. The talk came with hands in motion, red-painted nails whizzing, gold bangles tinkling, cigarettes waving, tendrils of smoke curling round and up and mixing with, in my family anyway, the heady scent of Shalimar. Language is not just words; it's intonation, gesture, facial expressions, volume, emotion, *style*.

I wanted to pull my son under that Formica table with me, but no one was sitting at it any more.

I couldn't bring him, either, to sit on the carpet between my grandfather and his friend, who we called *ummi* (uncle) even though he wasn't. Two old doctors, in exile, click-clacking their amber worry beads one by one as they talked, me only understanding half of it, but feeling so, so safe. I wanted that for him too, but my grandfather and *ummi* both died long ago.

I'd never told my son he was cutting onions on my heart. I'd never said, if he tired me out, *ekel qalbi* (he ate up my heart). And actually I couldn't, because that phrase uses a different word for heart, *qalbi*, which begins with the notoriously difficult to pronounce Arabic letter *qaf*, a sound that comes from deep in the throat, from where a dentist's instrument makes you gag. To say it you have to make your tongue touch your soft palate. The name for the Iraqi Arabic languages spoken in the top half of Iraq is *qeltu* Arabic; *qeltu* means 'I said'. In the lower half of Iraq, the languages are *gelet*, which also means 'I said' but is much easier to say. In Baghdad there was a mix but, unluckily for me, Jews mostly spoke *qeltu*. If I mispronounced *ekel qalbi* with a hard K – *Ekel qalbi* – I'd be saying 'he ate my dog'. Which would make me feel *waja'a qalb* (pain of the heart) – which of course I would mispronounce 'pain of the dog'. If I wanted to talk about instinct, how *qalbi qalli* (my heart told me), I would end up saying something even more incomprehensibly canine. 'I cooled my dog,' I would say when I calmed down. 'You have a dog made of stone!' I would say in arguments, or 'You have a black dog'. All this felt like, well, cutting onions on my dog.

I felt defeated. I knew transmitting culture was hard. If I didn't know it before my son was born, I learned it in the delivery room. We'd planned to welcome him into the world with music – specifically with Joni Mitchell's album *Hejira*. We liked its Arabic title, meaning 'exodus' or 'departure', and its hypnotic, swooshy vibe which was soothing but also restless, somehow. Perfect. But at the hospital, the CD player was broken. A nurse offered to play 'a really lovely playlist' over the Wi-Fi instead. We said yes, hoping for something soothing or inspiring.

I gave birth to Pink Floyd's 'Another Brick in the Wall'. The surgeon, startled, stopped, mid-incision, to ask, 'Is this your choice?' We had tried so hard to choose the perfect music to bring our son into the world and he emerged to rage, heavy beats and a rejection of formal education. When I looked at the little stranger, with his scrunched-up face and shock of dark hair, it didn't seem to matter.

Now I wondered if I'd failed before I'd even really started.

I didn't pass on my surname, because it was already lost. It should be Elias, but in the 1960s, in London, my father thought it would be easier to have a name that sounded less Jewish, so he anglicised it. I'd often wanted to change it back, or to take my mother's maiden name, Hakim. In Iraq many families didn't have surnames, but went by their fathers' first names, and Elias only went back one generation. So perhaps it might as well be Ellis, even though it feels distorted, whitewashed, fearful, foreign. My mum called me Samantha after a (British) actress.

Some of my family have English names – because the British governed Iraq after the First World War – or French names because a French Jewish organisation called the Alliance Israélite Universelle ran several schools in Baghdad; but still, my name feels awkward. A friend's partner once said, 'I'm always saying you-know-who about you! Why can't I remember your name?', and I found myself replying, 'Maybe it's not my real name.' The words just flew out of my mouth. Again I toyed with changing my name, or adding an Iraqi middle name. I still haven't but I'm glad my son has his dad's surname, and he isn't (I hope) inheriting my confusions and anxieties along with my name.

Once we got him home, I realised I didn't know any Iraqi Jewish lullabies. My parents didn't either so I sang him to sleep with 'Edelweiss' and 'Moon River'. Now I realised if I was going to pack my ark, it would need some lullabies. So I went to see my grandmother. I was sure she'd know. In her nineties her memory was pin-sharp. I found her wrapped up in a polyester quilt splattered in intense orange flowers. She's always cold here. It's not the climate she grew up in. She told me my grandfather bought the quilt in a market in Baghdad and 'I never liked it! He brought it home and I said, it's too short, it doesn't even cover me! How can I use it? And he was so happy he got a bargain.' I gawped. The bargain quilt *was* short but it was also stuffed and puffy. And she brought it all the way from Baghdad? It must have taken up half her suitcase! She grinned. 'Well, at least I'm using it now.'

My grandmother couldn't remember any lullabies either. It felt shocking to not know a lullaby in my own language, shameful to have to go to the library to find one. Thankfully Sara Manasseh, a musicologist whose ancestors came from Baghdad and settled in India in the nineteenth and twentieth centuries, has collected Iraqi Jewish songs which she performs with her group Rivers of Babylon. The lullabies she found often have a chorus of *dililol*, a nonsense word to lull a child to sleep, but they aren't always particularly lulling. In one, a lonely young mother at the end of her tether tells her son that his enemy is sick and lives in the desert, and, heart-rendingly, calls her own mother to rescue her from her 'exile among strangers'. I think she means her in-laws.

There is one, though, where a mother comforts her son and calls him her eyes. I could sing that. Or later I could sing him the song (not a lullaby) where a mother takes her son onto the roof of their house to cool his drinking water in the night breeze, and starts to worry that bad women can see him. To keep their evil eyes away, she starts trash-talking her son, telling the women he is 'rubbish'. But she loves him too much to keep up the game, and by the end of the song the truth bursts out as she sings that he is as precious to her as cardamom, as cloves, as perfume.

The song I really wanted to sing was the one that's sung at henna parties in the run-up to weddings, by the mother of the groom. It's called 'Afaki!' which means 'Bravo to you!' – but it's deeply sarcastic. The groom's mother taunts the mother of the bride, 'Bravo to you!' because, she says, she's been tricked; she did all the hard work, and now the bride's mother will reap the benefit. (There's no mention of the work the groom's father has done to bring up their child; this is between the mothers.) It's deliciously *mean*, acerbic, passive-aggressive. I imagined confronting my son's in-laws with all the ways I'd tired myself out and laboured, the sleepless nights, the worry, the laundry, the hours in freezing playgrounds, the phonics. And he'd only just started school. There were other verses I could sing about how the bride's mother was cunning, how she *persuaded* or *ensnared* the groom, by sitting her daughter by a wall to attract him, fanning out her hair, or by fanning *him*, or feeding him a kebab or getting him drunk on the anise-flavoured liquor *arak*, or even bewitching him. In Baghdad I could have got a group of women musicians called *daqqaqat* to perform 'Afaki!' with kettle drums and tambourines. But there are no *daqqaqat* any more, so I'll have to sing it myself. It feels important. There's so much encoded in it, all the anxieties around a wedding, hopes and fears for the future, and the strangeness and tenderness of bringing two families together, making people who were once strangers now familiar. Yes, I needed to learn the song.

Hoping to find other people in the same boat (ark), I joined a Facebook group for preserving Judeo-Iraqi Arabic. It had over 80,000 members – surely enough to keep a language going! But I was crestfallen to find that most of them couldn't speak a word. They were mostly the children or grandchildren of Jews who'd left Iraq in 1950–1. Reading the posts, I sometimes felt like we were calling to each other over the pouring rain, the rising flood. They asked the words for *welcome*, for *ashtray*, for *widow*. They posted videos of the Iraqi Jewish diva Salima Murad. Pictures of their families. Pictures of food. So much food, sometimes with recipes, sometimes with anxious questions. 'Why does my *kubba* never stay red?' wailed one, and I felt like I was at their stove, trying to recreate the taste (or colour) of their mother's or grandmother's cooking – painfully aware they had to ask strangers online because their mothers and grandmothers were no longer around. Another asked plaintively, 'Will anyone talk to my father?', explaining that his father was the last surviving speaker in his family, his friends were all scattered or gone, and he had no one to speak Judeo-Iraqi Arabic to. I waited, my heart in my mouth, to see if anyone replied, and I was thrilled when several people offered to visit, call and even cook.

I asked the group about the 'days of the aubergines' because one of my cousins said it didn't mean a time of craziness but 'days of heat', as in hot temper, violence or arguments. Responses were inconclusive, so I went back to my grandmother. She looked at me suspiciously and asked, 'How old are these people?' I blinked. I hadn't thought to ask. She grinned, saying, 'If they're young, they don't remember what it was like before we got air conditioning.' Young people didn't realise how crazy-making the intense heat of Baghdad could be, she explained. My mother said Iraqi summers were so hot you could fry an egg on the ground, and the government lied about the high temperatures 'because there would be riots'. When the Jewish traveller Benjamin of Tudela visited Baghdad around 1160 he described how one of the world's first mental hospitals was built there in 705 specifically to 'keep charge of the demented people who have become insane in the towns through the great heat in the summer, and they chain each of them in iron chains until their reason becomes restored to them in the wintertime'. Maybe the days of the aubergines were a time of madness and violence both. But I also read, in Violette Shamash's memoir *Memories of Eden*, that *eeyam al babenjan* was sometimes said if someone did something a bit crazy, not to condemn, but as a joke and to forgive them; as if to say, in this heat, can you blame a person for going off the rails?

Everything I learned about my language was like this, contradictions and confusion, shreds and patches. There was no agreement on anything, and the language itself was constantly being undermined. If I ever told anyone about a word in Judeo-Iraqi Arabic, they often asked 'Is it a word only in your language?' or said 'But that's in other Arabic dialects too', as if, when a word was shared, it could never have originated with my language but must always have been taken or (I felt the implication) stolen. I found myself having to explain that many words spoken by Iraqi Muslims and Christians weren't specific to them either, because for so long everyone was all mixed up, all talking to each other, and no one knew who'd first said something, it was passed back and forth all the time.

The lack of books didn't help. When I asked people in my community about books in Judeo-Iraqi Arabic, I was told about the translation Saadia Gaon made of the Torah in the ninth century. Gaon was born in Egypt, studied theology in Palestine, then joined one of the two rabbinical academies in Babylonia, a life that is testament to a Middle East more fluid, plural and cosmopolitan than now. I was also pointed, more than once, towards the century-old *Qanun al Nisa,* a book of Jewish law for women. 'Written by a man?' asked my mother. Yes, I said. She laughed. 'Typical.' My language was not like Yiddish, which was saved by its books. In 1980, a young American student called Aaron Lansky realised that American Jews were throwing away their parents' and grandparents' Yiddish books because they couldn't read them, so he started collecting them. His volunteers rescued books from attics, synagogues and schools, building a library (an ark) of over a million books at the Yiddish Book Center in Massachusetts. There were cookbooks, there were sex guides, there were romance novels, there were so many knotty, complex, devastating plays. I browsed their online library feeling wonderment, awe and, frankly, envy. I wished our community had had the confidence to write literature in our language. Let alone sex guides.

The lack of books made me wonder if we ever really valued our own language – and now it was too late. Certainly *I* was. I remembered how my mother used to joke, when I was a teenager reluctant to do the washing-up, *kamet el keslana oo kesret lenjana* (the lazy woman got up and broke the bowl). The lazy woman does nothing, and when she does eventually stir herself to help, she makes a mess. That was me. I was the lazy woman who'd left it too late. In a book about dying languages by linguist K. David Harrison, a last speaker of Chemehuevi, spoken by Native Americans in Arizona, complained that he'd tried teaching it to children but 'when it comes time to do the work, nobody comes around'. Reading this, I felt ambushed by guilt. I was part of the generation that wasn't busting a gut to keep a dying language alive. Again and again, in books and articles about endangerment, I read that people like me were too lazy to learn, that we didn't value our languages or care for them, that we were recklessly letting them die. But after a while, though genetically prone to Jewish guilt as I am, I started resisting these blamey judgements. They didn't take much account of why languages were going extinct, the forces that drove them in that direction; and they didn't seem to care about the people caught up in those forces. I was beginning to see that there was always violence somewhere in the vanishing of languages. There certainly was in mine.

Farhud (The breakdown of order)

It was 2011. I was on the Tube. I was thirty-five, and if people talked about antisemitism in the UK, or even when it happened to me, I was liable to (inwardly) roll my eyes, minimise it, try to ignore it. I was aware, that day, that the far-right English Defence League had been marching in Luton, chanting Islamophobic slogans, and that they'd felt encouraged by the prime minister David Cameron saying multiculturalism doesn't work. When two men wearing EDL badges got on, talking loudly about their rally and how 'Dave's on our side', I was more angry than wary. Until suddenly they were looming over me. In my face. Jabbing their fingers at me, laughing, and saying, 'This train terminates at Auschwitz.'

My heart was pounding, I was frozen in fear and going through my mind was: *How do they even know I'm Jewish?* I was not wearing a Star of David. I had no outward markers of my ethnicity, other than my actual face. Then I thought: *The Holocaust isn't even my trauma!* Growing up, I was always told we were lucky our family was not in Europe, lucky we didn't lose anyone, lucky we did not have to carry the weight of that. And we *were* lucky. We *are* lucky. But when those men were standing over me, spewing hate, they didn't care what kind of Jew I was. They just wanted me dead. Or, at least, terrified.

We stopped at a station, the men opened cans of beer and I saw my chance: I leapt off the train.

To my horror, they followed. One swung for me.

I ducked, and dived back onto the train as the doors closed.

They banged on the doors. I could see the rage steaming off them on the platform, but the train left and I was safe.

When I sat down, shaking, a young Black man apologised for not helping me, saying, 'It's just I think they would have gone for me.' Of course he was right, they probably would have gone for him and I would have hated to be the cause of that. But he *did* help, by saying what he'd said. He made me feel less alone. And suddenly I was aware that the rest of the carriage, the white people, hadn't said anything. Even once the EDL thugs had gone and it would cost them nothing to ask if I was OK, they didn't.

After that I found it harder to shrug off my fear of antisemitism. It became an abject terror that grabbed me in the night, a deep anxiety about being hated, about what the haters might do with that hate. When I got pregnant, I was determined to pass on none of that fear. I wanted my son to feel safe.

So there was one word in Judeo-Iraqi Arabic I *didn't* want to pass on. The word for what happened in Baghdad in 1941, where in two terrible days, around 180 Jews were murdered, countless women were raped, thousands were injured and homes were looted. It was often called a *pogrom* but my grandmother's cousin, historian Sylvia Haim, once asked me, 'Why use the Russian word, *pogrom*, when we have a perfectly good word of our own?' The word was Farhud and it meant the breakdown of order.

I'd known it a long time, because my grandmother was there, but I'd only heard the story piecemeal, over years, interrupted, contradicted. Now I wanted to get it straight in my own head, even if I was not going to tell my son about it. (Was I *really* not going to tell my son about it?) So I went to see my grandmother. We had lunch and talked about *mahasha*, which some people call *dolma* ('I don't use that word,' my grandmother said, 'it's Turkish!'). And then we sat down and I started recording, even though I didn't really want to. I was worried she'd talked about the Farhud enough; she was eleven when it happened, and remembered everything, and there were very few people left who did, so she'd been interviewed about it before, by journalists and for archives. And now by me. Would I upset her? Wasn't this the opposite of what you are supposed to do when someone is traumatised – make them go over it again?

But she was pragmatic, sanguine, even upbeat.

She was born in the optimistic, hopeful Iraq of 1929. For centuries Iraq had been part of the vast Ottoman Empire. Confusingly, the Ottomans didn't call it Mesopotamia *or* Babylonia *or* Iraq but divided it into three *vilayets* or administrative provinces named for their major cities: Baghdad, Basra and Mosul. When the First World War broke out and the Ottomans sided with the Germans, Britain invaded Basra. They were only planning to protect the oil for the Allies' war effort, but started advancing up the Tigris towards Baghdad, and finally took the city in 1917. There was no plan. (Yes. Sigh. Just like later British invasions of Iraq.) Sir Percy Cox, who led the temporary administration, wanted what the British were now calling Mesopotamia again to become a British colony. His eccentric colleague, Gertrude Bell, a traveller, writer, spy and colonial diplomat who my grandfather remembered seeing riding her horse along the banks of the Tigris dressed in white, wasn't sure. She would later argue for independence – and win.

She and T. E. Lawrence had been spies together in Cairo, helping to encourage the Arabs to rise up against the Ottomans in the Hejaz Desert in what is now Saudi Arabia. As the Arab Revolt got going, Lawrence promised the melancholy, moustachioed warrior Faisal (the one Alec Guinness's role was modelled on in *Lawrence of Arabia*) that the British would support Arab independence after the war. This promise would be hard to keep because Britain had also secretly promised the French that after the war they'd slice the Middle East into two spheres of influence, and because in 1917 they'd made yet another promise, in the Balfour Declaration, to 'favour the establishment in Palestine of a national home for the Jewish people'.

Even after the Romans levelled Jerusalem in 70 CE, banishing most of the city's Jews, there were always Jews in what had been first the ancient Jewish kingdom of Israel and then split into the two Jewish kingdoms of Judah and Israel. During the four centuries of Ottoman rule, the Jewish population swelled as the Inquisitions in Spain and Portugal and other persecution in Europe pushed Jews east. Like the Jews of Iraq, Jews in Palestine spoke Arabic and lived side by side with their Christian and Muslim neighbours. It was in Europe, in the late nineteenth century, that Jews started to dream of a country of their own where they would be safe from persecution and pogroms; the word Zionism was coined in Vienna in 1892, taking its name from Zion, which first referred to the hill where King David built his city in Jerusalem and then came to mean the whole ancient Jewish homeland. The early Zionists considered many other locations for a new Jewish country, from Angola to Australia, but from the 1890s Jews started immigrating to Palestine and buying land. They were almost all European; most Jews in the rest of the Middle East were not keen. According to Bell's pugnacious colleague A. T. Wilson, the announcement of the Balfour Declaration 'aroused no interest' among the Jews of Baghdad. 'They remarked that Palestine was a poor country . . . Compared with Palestine, Mesopotamia was Paradise . . . the Garden of Eden.' Many felt, like the mother of historian Avi Shlaim, that 'Zionism is an Ashkenazi thing' and they mostly planned to stay put, although some worried about what would happen with the Ottoman Empire gone and the Middle East in flux. Some Jews anxiously asked the British to govern Mesopotamia directly, while others asked for British citizenship. In 1920, as agreed with the French before the war, both Mesopotamia and Palestine formally became British mandates. *Not* colonies.

A year later, Bell and Lawrence persuaded the British government to make Iraq independent and to make Faisal its first king, even though he'd never been there. In spite of this, Iraqis generally felt affectionate towards Faisal, and Iraqi Jews took to him after he reassured them that 'There is no meaning in the words Jews, Muslims and Christians in the terminology of patriotism, there is simply a country called Iraq and all are Iraqis' and even kissed the Torah at a party Bell breathlessly described in her diary, down to the menu of 'iced lemonade, coffee, tea and cakes and ices!'

It's supposedly ironic that the new country's name meant 'deeply rooted, well watered' in Arabic because Iraq was never rooted, never viable, just an incoherent group of people shoved together. But reading accounts from Iraq in the 1920s and 30s I got the feeling that many Iraqis, including Iraqi Jews, felt they could come together and make their country work. Iraqi Jewish writers composed love letters to Iraq and to Arabic, in *fusha*, and bold, radical fiction about the kind of country they wanted to build, and the injustices they wanted to fight: fiction like Yaqub Balbul's 'True Copy', a searing polemic against honour killing. Jews were part of the government too; my grandmother's grandfather, Reuben Somekh, was an MP. There's a formal picture of him in a *sidara*, the hat King Faisal brought in to replace the Ottoman *tarboosh*; it is dark felt, with a deep fold in the top, shaped a little bit like an overturned boat, or an ark.

But as historian Elie Kedourie (whom I was lucky enough to know when I was a child) wrote, Iraqis also mistrusted this 'make-believe kingdom, built on false pretences and kept going by a British design and for a British purpose', especially after, in 1930, an Anglo-Iraqi Treaty allowed the British to continue controlling Iraqi foreign policy, to maintain a military presence there, and to benefit from Iraqi oil. Two years later, in 1932, Iraq became independent, but British advisers stayed on.

Iraq joined the League of Nations, promising to give minorities 'Full and complete protection of life and liberty . . . without distinction of birth, nationality, language, race or religion' and to protect languages (although the only languages mentioned were Kurdish and Turkish). Some of this talk felt hollow when in 1933 the Iraqi government massacred 6,000 Assyrians. And then the tide started turning against the Jews. Having been semi-colonised by the British along with everyone else in Iraq, the community was accused of being too friendly with the British – as well as being blamed for what was happening in another British mandate: Palestine.

Even though Iraqi Jews were, patently, not trying to emigrate there, Iraqis who were angry about the idea of a Jewish homeland started questioning the loyalty of their Jewish friends and neighbours, seeing them as *not really Iraqi*. When a British Jewish industrialist who supported Zionism visited Iraq in 1928 to learn about fertiliser, Iraqi protesters chanted 'death to the Jews'. When violent unrest erupted in Jerusalem in 1929, over 100,000 Iraqis gathered at the Haydar-Khana mosque and went out attacking Jews. The Iraqi government also started passing discriminatory laws. During the 1930s, especially after King Faisal died in 1933 and his playboy son took over, they banned the teaching of Hebrew in Iraqi schools, banned Zionism, dismissed Jews from the civil service, set a quota on Jews getting further education and made them pay a tax every time they left the country, effectively trapping most of the community – who could not afford the tax – in Iraq.

The 1930s were also troubled in Palestine. Many more Jews arrived, especially from Germany, fleeing the Nazis. The mufti of Jerusalem, Haj Amin al-Husseini, led a violent Arab revolt against the British, who issued a warrant for his arrest in 1937. He fled. Then, on the eve of war, the British abruptly changed direction. They'd been favouring partition but in May 1939 they issued a White Paper that abandoned the idea. Instead, they vowed to create a Jewish national home within an independent Palestinian state, while also massively restricting Jewish immigration and Jewish rights to buy land, Still leading from exile, the mufti rejected the plan.

It is not true that, as Benjamin Netanyahu once said, the mufti gave Hitler the idea of the Holocaust; but he did, notoriously, meet Hitler, who assured him that once he had destroyed Jews in Europe he would move on to 'the destruction of the Jewish element residing in the Arab sphere under the protection of British power', and he did spend much of the war on a lavish salary from the Nazis, recruiting Bosnian Muslims to fight for the Nazis, and broadcasting Jew hate on Radio Berlin. He also wreaked havoc in Iraq.

The country was unstable because King Ghazi, Faisal's son, had just died in a car crash, and since *his* son was only three, a regent – his uncle – was in power. Britain needed Iraq to win the war – to host two airbases, to serve as a land bridge between their troops in India and in Egypt, and for the oil. The Nazis wanted all these advantages too, so they tried to get Iraq to switch sides, broadcasting propaganda in Arabic and cultivating allies, like the mufti. On 1 April 1941, he helped stage a coup that put the pro-Nazi Rashid Ali al-Gaylani in power. The regent fled. Rashid Ali started making overtures to the Germans, the British sent troops to Basra, Rashid Ali besieged the RAF base at Habbaniya and the Anglo-Iraqi War began.

For thirty days, Baghdad's Jews stayed at home, terrified, listening to Rashid Ali and the mufti broadcast antisemitism. Swastikas and violence filled the streets. A mob broke into a Jewish hospital, killing a pharmacist, wounding patients and doctors. The city's British population took refuge in the embassy, camping on the roof and in the gardens, and, according to the writer, adventurer and spy Freya Stark, keeping up morale with alcohol, clock golf and amateur dramatics.

And suddenly, on 29 May 1941, it looked like the nightmare was over.

British troops reached the edge of Baghdad. Rashid Ali and the mufti fled. Jews breathed out for the first time in a month. It was the eve of Shavuot, the festival where we celebrate receiving the Torah by eating cheese, or, in Iraq, *kaahi* (layers of fried pastry) topped with *qemar* (water buffalo milk cream). In Iraq, it was called Eid al-Ziyaara (Festival of Pilgrimages) because there was a tradition of visiting the prophet Ezekiel's tomb. Some Jews dared to leave their homes, hoping they were now safe.

The Iraqis signed a peace deal with the British ambassador Sir Kinahan Cornwallis, who was now ambassador. Then, strangely, he told the British army to ignore their orders to take Baghdad. He was worried it would look like they were recolonising Iraq. He told the troops to wait outside the city until the regent arrived.

In the city, anger grew. Iraqi police and soldiers who had supported Rashid Ali were furious his coup had failed and wanted someone to blame. Along with the Hitler Youth-inspired Futuwwa group, on the morning of 1 June, they started attacking Jews. There was no government to quell the violence. According to the British intelligence officer Somerset de Chair, 'as darkness settled like a mantle over the domes and minarets across the river, the shooting began'. Students stopped a bus, dragged off the Jewish passengers and murdered them. Demobbed soldiers and paramilitary youth groups went on the rampage. They murdered Jews in the streets, and in their homes. They raped Jewish women. No one knows how many because afterwards, if they were able, the women hid what had happened. In Violette Shamash's memoir *Memories of Eden* she writes that pregnant women were raped, their stomachs cut open, and girls' hands were cut off to steal their gold bangles. In Samir Naqqāsh's novel

Tenants and Cobwebs, one character remembers, 'I saw blood flow like a river, and people slaughtered like animals, their carcasses hanging.' In his memoir *Farewell Babylon*, the writer Naïm Kattan describes rioters ululating with joy, and how a friend's uncle was pushed into the bathroom where they held him down 'and slit his throat like a sheep'. The Futuwwa painted red *hamsas* on Jewish homes to direct the mob. There are stories of people smashing up radios to kill the devils in them that were playing Jewish songs. Poor rural Iraqis streamed into the city to join the plunder. Historian Edwin Black wrote that 'Hundreds of Jews were cut down by sword and rifle, some decapitated. Babies were sliced in half and thrown into the Tigris river. Girls were raped in front of their parents. Parents were mercilessly killed in front of their children. Hundreds of Jewish homes and businesses were looted, then burned.'

Someone came to my grandmother's door and said the mob was 'in the market, they are coming this way, you better get out'. A boatman who worked for her MP grandfather had betrayed them by telling the mob this was a Jewish house. Her father had encephalitis and could hardly walk, so she and her mother and brothers half carried him to her aunt's house. When she saw her nephew in a sharkskin suit, my great-grandmother begged him to take it off because it was so bright, so visible, and the rioters were coming.

My grandmother's aunt's Muslim neighbour got out his gun and shot in the air to scare off the mob. Then his family gave all of them shelter – my grandmother's family, her aunt's family *and* several other Jews. 'They were very very good,' she says. 'The woman said, The ill man has to lie on the sofa! Everything for the ill man! And she said, Bring some juice, some yogurt. They treated us very well.'

As the violence went on, no one intervened. De Chair scathingly described how 'eight miles to the west waited the eager

British force which could have prevented all this. Ah yes, but the prestige of our Regent would have suffered!' Stark was unnerved by Cornwallis's calm, and horrified by the 'night of snapping rifles . . . Jews murdered' and reports of people 'wading in blood'. From the embassy roof, she saw Baghdad 'strewn with confetti, the loot lying out on the street. Number of killed will never be known' and was amazed to see 'streams of people going empty-handed eastward, coming back laden with spoil'. Cornwallis laconically cabled London to report 'Sporadic shooting with murderous assaults on Jews seems to have gone on throughout the night'. The passive verb. The word *seems*. He didn't order the troops to go into the city.

By the evening of 2 June, when the governor of Baghdad finally fired on the mob, at least two hundred Jews were dead. Maybe more. Kattan says the chief rabbi posted a notice of mourning for three hundred Jews. De Chair wrote that Cornwallis first told him that 2,000 people, mostly Jews, had been believed to be killed but then revised the figure down to seven hundred. A recently discovered document from an Iraqi Zionist group claims that 120 people died in one hospital alone after injections of poison were administered.

I was trying to work out how many people helped my grandmother's family and we were both getting confused. 'Did he also shoot in the air?' I asked, and 'Who brought the yogurt?' She sheltered with her aunt's neighbour for three days. She went home to find it had not been looted because their Muslim neighbours had also deterred the mob by shooting in the air. She dwelt on who helped them and how they survived. For some Iraqi Jews, the Farhud was the moment that, as Marina Benjamin wrote in *Last Days in Babylon*, they lost 'the illusion that Iraq was a country to which they could truly belong'. For Kattan 'in one night thirteen centuries of shared life and neighbourliness crumbled like a structure of mud and sand'.

In many Iraqi memoirs, the time before the Farhud is described as paradise and the Farhud as the fall. But when I asked my grandmother if it was the end of Jewish life in Iraq, she said, 'No, no. On the contrary . . . it was the beginning of the good life afterwards.' Was she scared? Did her friends talk about it at school? 'No, no, we were back to normal. It was OK. Finished! It was safe again.'

Certainly they were encouraged to forget it. The dead were buried in a mass grave. In Eli Amir's novel *The Dove Flyer*, the chief rabbi explains how the community tried to move on: 'I took care of the orphans,' he says, and, even more distressingly, 'I arranged marriages for Jewish girls who had been raped.' Cornwallis took six weeks to write a report about what had happened. He said there had been 'brutal outrages . . . which all right minded persons will for long remember with shame and horror' and 'The Jews suffered most'. He added that 'a large number of them [the Jews] would emigrate rather than face the risk of another such pogrom if they could only find a country to take them'. But where could they go? Cornwallis said some Baghdad Jews had 'made pathetic attempts' to get visas to India. He didn't say why the attempts were 'pathetic'. In Palestine, the Jewish Agency asked Britain to allow Jews to move there. Cornwallis called the Jewish Agency's report on the Farhud 'too highly coloured', and said one reason that the rioters had not been punished was that Jews had not been willing to give evidence. Some Iraqi Jews just started escaping. In *Tenants and Cobwebs*, a Muslim character rages that the Jews are 'all traitors and bastards . . . All of them are leaving the country. They appreciated nothing.' His Jewish friend thinks (but does not say), 'I pretended not to see what you did in the Farhud' and 'I am not a traitor. How could I betray a homeland containing soil holding the remains of my father and forefathers? This land is made of us . . . I was here in this land before you, twelve centuries before you.' Another Jewish character in the novel marries a Muslim. She wants to live a secular life, but he makes her convert, using the argument that once she's a Muslim her family will be safe, because next time there is a Farhud, 'not even one Jew will be spared, but thanks to you, your relatives will be saved. Isn't that good enough? . . . Why dig up the graves of the dead?' She converts. When her mother visits her, she greets her in the Muslim dialect.

Why my father left

Most of Iraq's Jews – around 125,000 people – left Iraq for Israel a decade after the Farhud, in the space of just a few months. My father was one of them. And I didn't have a clear answer to the question *why*.

It wasn't for lack of trying. For years I read histories of the Middle East hoping to better understand the stories my parents told me, to get context and perspective, to learn more. I often read in vain; my community's story rarely made it into history books. Or we appeared only in footnotes, or spare mentions, without elaboration or context. The Jewish stories that were told were overwhelmingly European. The default Jew was Ashkenazi. There is even a word for this: *Ashkenormativity*, the assumption that all Jews are Ashkenazi, and, with it, the wilful forgetting of other stories. Maybe we are just too complicated, sitting right at the intersection of the difficult and contested histories of both Iraq and Israel. In his landmark study *Enemies and Neighbours, Arabs and Jews in Palestine and Israel, 1917–2017*, veteran *Guardian* Middle East journalist Ian Black almost sounds like he's throwing up his hands as he writes in the preface, that 'Jews who came to Israel from Iraq, Morocco and elsewhere in the Arab and Muslim worlds are another specific element with no exact parallel elsewhere' – and then barely mentions us again in the rest of the 600-odd pages. But it feels important to tell our story because it is not over. Its consequences are still reverberating – and not just for us.

For many, the Farhud was the point of no return, proof that Jews had never been safe in Iraq, and a spur to leave as soon as we had somewhere to go. As Israeli academic Shmuel Moreh puts it, 'The *Farhud* demonstrated clearly that the Jews all over the world shared the same fate and that the holocaust of the Jews of Europe hit them as well . . . The Jews of Iraq therefore understood that the only solution was the Zionist movement.' On the other side of the political spectrum, Iraqi Jewish writer Ella Shohat calls Jews from the Middle East and North Africa Zionism's 'Jewish victims', and Iraqi Jewish historian Avi Shlaim wrote that the Farhud was an 'aberration' and antisemitism 'a foreign import', and Iraqi Jews were otherwise safe, happy and equal until another foreign import – Zionism – made life there untenable.

Our community – even my family – was divided on these questions. And I was divided. I found it hard to steer a path between these wildly different narratives, expressed with such vehemence and volume and, often, in such pain. What I did know, though, was that having a community story that was unsettled for us, and exploited, weaponised and used as a political football by other people, was deeply disorientating and distressing.

One evening my son's friend stayed for dinner. It was Friday so I made challah and my son volunteered, 'We're Jewish. We used to live in Iraq but then the government told us to leave.' When I tried to unpack this, over the fish fingers, he said he thought I'd lived in Iraq too. I hadn't realised he was so muddled, but maybe he was because I was. If I was going to unmuddle him, maybe I had to try to unmuddle myself first, to tell the story as simply and plainly as I could. In a world of contested facts, manipulated history, erasure and amnesia, of rival narratives so opposed that conversation and empathy become impossible, of a language sliding into silence, it felt important to recover and retrieve what I could of at least my family's stories. In Noreen Masud's memoir *A Flat Place*, she writes that some people say trauma is 'untellable' but she believes that 'traumatised people do know how to tell their stories. What's difficult is that often people don't know how to hear them.' It was time to listen.

In Iraq, after the Farhud, most Iraqi Jews did not think of leaving. Some did join Zionist underground groups 'in case there was another Farhud', said my grandmother, 'so we could take care of ourselves'. Her brother was one of them. 'They used to come to the house,' she said. 'A gathering of eight. Each time in a different house. With rifles.' One group, Shabab al-Inqadh (Youth to the Rescue), distributed a pamphlet urging Jews to 'awake', to learn the lessons of the Farhud, saying, 'God did not want a three-day-old baby butchered! God did not want us butchered as sheep!' But most Jews were still not Zionists. Some even campaigned against it. Besides which, it wasn't at all clear that there was going to be a Jewish state to go to.

In Palestine the British stuck to the quotas for Jewish immigration they'd set in 1939, even after the Holocaust made many Jews feel that there would never be safety without a Jewish state, and survivors and other displaced Jews started arriving in the Middle East, seeking refuge. Angry and terrified, Jewish groups launched a campaign of bombings and kidnappings against the British. The British arrested vast numbers of Jews. In 1946, the Irgun, a Jewish paramilitary group, bombed the British headquarters at the King David Hotel in Jerusalem, killing ninety-one and injuring forty-five, an act of terror that accelerated the end of the British mandate. The British turned the problem over to the UN. And when a leaky ship called the *Exodus*, packed with 4,500

Holocaust survivors, came near the coast of Palestine, Britain deported them all back to Germany and interned them there.

No wonder Iraqi Jews mostly got on with their lives. In the 1940s, my dad said, 'Baghdad was a Jewish city,' where on Saturdays the streets were quiet, the shops closed and the synagogues full. The baby of the family, youngest of ten, he lived in a small house built around a tiny courtyard which held a tree and a *tannour*, a clay bread oven; *tannours* have been used to bake bread in Iraq since the third millennium BCE. They cooled their house the old way with an *aqool* ; they'd pour water onto hay or thorn branches, and as the water evaporated, the air would cool. As well as our Arabic and the Arabic he spoke out and about, he knew a little Hebrew, some English, and also French, because he went to a school run by the Alliance Israélite Universelle.

He loved shopping with his father. 'He will buy everything fresh, and if there is somewhere where there are chickens that have been slaughtered already, he is not interested. They have to be fresh. Same thing with fish. He will go to them and say, OK I will have five. So they start to give him fish and he says not them; new. They have to catch them.'

At around the same time, my grandmother accidentally sat on a royal throne. She went to the palace with two of her six aunts, called the Tantes because thanks to the Alliance school they spoke beautiful French. Tante Bertha, a dressmaker, made the princesses' clothes, while Tante Marcelle, who later became a lawyer, taught them Arabic. At the palace, my grandmother said, 'They sat with the princesses. They were laughing and laughing and laughing.' She heard guns and at the window saw soldiers parading and saluting the regent. Excited, she climbed up on a chair to see better. 'It had a step,' she said. I started to laugh. Because I love this story. 'It was a very nice chair.' Her aunt sharply told her to move. 'And later, she said, Aida, do you know what you did?' The nice chair, with the step, had been the queen mother's throne. My grandmother stopped school early and learned dressmaking with her aunt; she still looks at my clothes with a couturier's critical eye and sometimes pinches the fabric where she thinks it needs a dart. She's always right.

In the 1940s there was, still, hope that Iraq could be a diverse, multicultural country. Just about. *Farewell Babylon* opens at a Baghdad cafe where clever, cosmopolitan, bohemian young men passionately discuss Iraq's future. 'In our group,' Kattan writes, 'we were neither Jew nor Muslim. We were Iraqis . . . Except that the Muslims felt more Iraqi than the others.' Two of the men were Jewish, and two were Christian (one Chaldean, one Armenian), but the presence of a single Muslim was enough for them to all start speaking Muslim Arabic. Jews 'had only to open our mouths to reveal our identity'. So to avoid danger, and mockery, the Jews, the Chaldean and the Armenian all code-switch, speaking Muslim Arabic. It's humiliating, it's effortful, but it feels safe. Then, suddenly, Kattan's friend starts speaking Judeo-Iraqi Arabic. Kattan viscerally describes his terror; it makes him feel 'coldly naked . . . frozen'. But his friend keeps speaking Judeo-Iraqi Arabic, refusing to back down, and eventually Kattan joins him. It's a revelation. He feels 'worthy . . . restored . . . We stood there in our luminous and fragile difference. And it was neither a humiliation nor a symbol of ridicule. In a pure Jewish dialect we made our plans for the future of Iraqi culture.' This pride in difference doesn't last, and the book ends a decade later, wearily, disillusioned. Kattan left Baghdad to study in Paris and did not see his parents for five years, when he was reunited with them in a transit camp in Israel. He lived most of his life in

Canada and wrote his memoir not in Judeo-Iraqi Arabic but in French.

In November 1948, the UN voted to partition Palestine. The Jews accepted the deal, but the Palestinians rejected it. Violence intensified as the British prepared to leave and the day after 14 May 1948, when David Ben-Gurion declared the creation of the State of Israel, four Arab nations invaded: Egypt, Jordan, Syria and Iraq. Israel won the war, and took more land, leaving the Palestinians with the Gaza Strip (controlled by Egypt) and the West Bank and East Jerusalem (both controlled by Jordan). 700,000 Palestinians were uprooted; they call it the Nakba (catastrophe).

A year before, the Iraqi foreign minister told the UN, chillingly, that 'the fate of the Jews in Muslim countries depends on developments in Palestine' and called Iraqi Jews 'hostages'. Now the Iraqi government turned Iraqi Jews into scapegoats. They used the words 'Jewish' and 'Zionist' interchangeably. Zionism was made a death penalty offence, hundreds of Jews were accused of passing military secrets to Israel and arrested, or worse, and in Basra, the government arrested Jewish tycoon Shafiq Adas on trumped-up charges of selling weapons to Israel. After a show trial, he was hanged in front of his home, his children watching as 10,000 people cheered, played drums, sang and threw stones, and even more listened to the live broadcast on Radio Baghdad. Adas is often called the Iraqi Dreyfus. He'd been friends with ministers and with the regent but it hadn't helped him. If *he* wasn't safe, who was? In *Tenants and Cobwebs*, one character says Jews are not even buying lentils because the word for lentils is *adas* and they are scared to say it at the grocer's. It was a terrifying time to be a Jew in Iraq, and now that there was a Jewish state to go to, many wanted to leave.

Iraq would not let them go. So they started escaping. A trickle became a flood. The government could not stop them all. Their policies would have to change. It is fiercely debated by historians whether anyone seriously considered a population exchange, where Iraqi Jews would go to Israel while Palestinians went to Iraq. Certainly in 1949 the British Foreign Office bloviated that if this did happen, 'Iraq would be relieved of a minority whose position is always liable to add to the difficulties of maintaining public order in time of tension.' It's quite shocking to read that Britain thought Iraq needed to be *relieved* of a community that had been there for thousands of years, contributed to the new state, written many of its songs and its poems, helped to make its laws, loved Iraq and loved other Iraqis too, who were their friends and neighbours. It's also hard to read that, at the same time, Israel was making conditions about receiving Iraq's Jews, the Israeli foreign minister telling the British Foreign Office, 'Israel could not in any circumstances agree to receive the Iraqi Jews as penniless displaced persons.'

But that was what happened. In March 1950, Iraq decreed a *taskeet*, a law of denaturalisation, which allowed Jews to register to immigrate to Israel so long as they gave up their Iraqi citizenship. 'Everybody was dreaming of what was going to happen in Israel,' my dad remembered. 'They couldn't really imagine what it would be like.' He went to sign the registration document with his parents and, within a week or so, 'we could not go to school, the school was closed. And everything stopped.' By the end of April, around 50,000 Iraqi Jews had registered to leave. Then a bomb was thrown into a cafe full of Jewish customers eating their first bread after Passover, injuring four people. More bombs followed, including a grenade at a synagogue. A seven-year-old was killed, twenty others were injured, two of whom later died. Even more Jews decided to leave.

From the beginning, there were rumours that the bombs were planted by the Zionist underground to scare more Jews into signing up to leave. In 2023 Avi Shlaim claimed he could prove it, but his evidence felt flimsy, relying on the testimony of one elderly friend of his mother's (who even he said was inaccurate when it came to other stories) and on an unsigned, undated page which he believed was part of a longer report by Iraqi police. The same police who tortured a Jewish man into confessing to planning and planting the bombs, and who hanged two Jews for it. Shlaim reached nearly the same conclusions as those patently corrupt and antisemitic police, which felt, at best, unsatisfying.

I don't think I'll ever know for sure if the Zionists planted the bombs. I am going to have to live with not knowing. What I do know is that the possibility is very painful for my community and the fact that we are still arguing over it is, in itself, harrowing.

In March 1951, when the denaturalisation law was about to expire and 125,000 Jews had registered to leave, the Iraqi government met in secret and passed another law: they would seize property, money and assets from all 125,000 Jews, as well as any Jews who had already left Iraq. The law came into force overnight, leaving many Iraqi Jews destitute and starving, relying on charity as they waited for the planes to come. On the mass airlift, Jews were allowed to take just 50 dinars (around £50 today) and a single suitcase each. My father's passport was stamped 'forbidden to return to Iraq', and he got on a plane so packed that 'there were people just sitting on the floor'. A few hours later, he and his parents were in a tent in a transit camp in Israel.

Historian Peter Sluglett calls all this 'a shabby, squalid and deeply tragic story, of betrayal, manipulation and doctrinaire opportunism'. I didn't want it to be that. I didn't want to tell that story to my son. It didn't feel like a story you could learn from. There was no arc. (Although there was an ark: those planes, with everyone squashed into them, clutching their scant possessions, not knowing what would happen next.) Instead there was mess and sadness and pain. I was going to have to learn to live with that too.

Mizrahi

My father started his life in Israel in a tent with a dirt floor. This came as a shock to his parents but, he shrugged, 'They had no choice. Because there were so many people. There was no one to complain to.' Many immigrants were sprayed, straight off the planes, with DDT, supposedly to reduce infection. In *Equal and More Equal*, a novel by Sami Michael, who was born in Iraq and arrived in Israel in 1949, there is a description of the visceral humiliation for a family of Iraqi Jews who arrive in their best clothes, and 'in five short minutes the new homeland turned my father from an energetic man in the prime of his life to an old broken abject fool . . . Before we got our bearings, a white cloud of white DDT powder enveloped [him].'

In 1951 the 130-odd *ma'abarot* (transit camps) housed a quarter of a million people, mostly Jews from Arab lands and North Africa; in all, around 800,000 Jews would migrate to Israel from Iraq, Egypt, Iran, Syria, Turkey, Algeria, Sudan, Yemen, Morocco, Tunisia and Libya. The authorities, who were mostly Ashkenazis, lumped them all together and called them *Mizrahi* Jews. The word means 'eastern' in Hebrew but is used for Jews from places which are west of Israel like Egypt and Morocco, but not for Jews from Russia, which *is* east of Israel. It's also a way of flattening out the differences between, say, Iraqi Jews and Yemenite Jews, Kurdish Jews and Moroccan Jews, Tunisian Jews and Libyan Jews. Sometimes, instead, we are all described as *Sephardi*, differentiating us from Ashkenazi Jews because we practise Judaism the way it was practised in Spain and Portugal, but this isn't very accurate either because not everyone is religious. Some call us *Arab* Jews which does feel radical and polarity-busting, but doesn't really feel logical when describing Jews from Iraq, who were there long before the Arab Conquest. Really we should call ourselves 'Middle Eastern and North African' but who has the time?

The camps were hard and desperate places. Most people were in tents, some were in ramshackle huts made of tin or asbestos. At least one *ma'abara* was a former British army camp, still ringed in barbed wire. They were overcrowded, noisy, with severely limited water and electricity, toilets shared between hundreds, and diseases were rife. It was unbearably hot in summer, cold and wet in winter. There is a drawing of a camp in Sarah Sassoon's *Shoham's Bangle*, a very moving picture book about a family of Iraqi Jews arriving in Israel, but when I read it to my son, my dad looked over my shoulder and said drily, 'It was not that luxurious.' The *ma'abarot* were supposed to be temporary, but like many Iraqis, my dad's family 'were at the end of the queue' for a permanent home. His father was a clerk and accountant in Baghdad but in Israel he found that 'for every job like that, there were ten people waiting'.

And then there was the food. 'It was all for Ashkenazis,' my dad said, grimacing. I read him accounts of Jews from Arab lands and North Africa gagging at meals of jam and greasy, undercooked herring, and he laughed and exclaimed, '*Dag meluah!*' (literally salt fish, in Hebrew). I didn't ask him the word for herring in Judeo-Iraqi Arabic. There probably isn't one. Why would there be? 'We were not used to it,' he said. 'We couldn't take it.' The transit camps only served Ashkenazi food because the (mostly Ashkenazi) authorities thought it was more nutritious and modern. Food discrimination was government policy; during Israel's long austerity regime, from 1949 to 1958, the government set the rice ration at just 250 grams per person per month. Iraqi Jews resorted to buying rice on the black market, substituting semolina for ground rice in *kubba* or making do with *p'titim*, nicknamed 'Ben-Gurion rice' after the prime minister, which were balls or rice shapes made of wheat dough extruded through a mould, cut and toasted. The fact that they looked like rice made their taste all the more unnerving.

Worse even than all the herring were the educational opportunities. My dad did not like the camp's ramshackle school, so he went to the city, all by himself, at just eleven, and bravely talked his way into a better one. That winter it rained and rained, the camp was all churned-up mud, and everyone was ill. A school friend's parents felt sorry for him and offered to let him live with them, maybe even to adopt him. 'But I was a bit too proud,' he said, 'to be taken like that. I told him no.' A year later, he 'did something naughty', and went to the secondary school and persuaded them to let him in too, jumping a whole academic year, in a new language, while living in squalid, stressful conditions.

In 1964, before he became synonymous with the dad in *Fiddler on the Roof*, Chaim Topol starred in the satirical film *Sallah Shabati* as a (similar) dad in a transit camp. Topol's Sallah is swarthy, sloppy and lazy, prefers drinking arak and playing backgammon to working, can't remember how many children he has and greedily wants to marry off his daughter to a fat taxi driver, not a handsome (Ashkenazi) kibbutznik; when she defies him, it's presented as a victory for the melting pot. *Sallah Shabati* is notorious for its negative, stereotypical portrait of Mizrahi Jews, but what (just about) saves it is the way it also takes potshots at the Ashkenazi establishment, and its cathartic portrait of Sallah's struggle for a permanent home. In the end, he games the system by protesting *against* the public housing he longs for, and grins as he's forcibly evicted from the camp and taken to a proper home. Shimon Ballas's novel *The Transit Camp* also ends with a protest, where Mizrahi Jews clash violently with police over the preventable death of a baby. This feels like a gesture at the rumours that were swirling round the *ma'abarot* that babies and children were being stolen from Yemenite (and some Iraqi) families, who were told they had died, and given to childless Ashkenazi couples. For a very long time no one would admit to this, but a few years ago, an Israeli government minister who led an investigation into the 'Yemenite Children Affair' said the abductions were 'not a hallucination'. They happened.

The *ma'abarot* were where discrimination against Mizrahi Jews began – it would continue, as delineated by Rachel Shabi in *Not the Enemy*. In 1971, some Mizrahi Jews even formed an Israeli Black Panther movement to fight back. Inspired by the radical African American organisation, this small group of young Mizrahim started protesting the ongoing discrimination that kept them in poverty or in prison. When the police arrested them for distributing leaflets, and then arrested those protesting the arrests, they had coalesced into an angry, dynamic movement. They wrote a Passover Haggadah rewriting the story so that the Jews were desperately trying to leave Israel, not Egypt. They redistributed food, Robin Hood-style, and in Operation Milk in 1972, they took milk bottles from the doorsteps of wealthy homes and gave them to the poor, leaving a note explaining why. They had a gift for communicating boldly what was going wrong, and it worked: in 1972, the Israeli government started reforming the police and passed what was known as the 'budget of the Panthers', spending more money than ever before on social welfare. Their consciousness-raising functioned as what historian Sami Chetrit called a 'mass workshop for rehabilitating an oppressed identity'. It's partly down to them that Mizrahim are more visible in Israel today. And nowhere is the takeover more complete than in Israel's restaurants and in its kitchens. It's now actually hard to get Ashkenazi food in Tel Aviv, unless you go to dark, retro Keton, the 1940s haunt of writers, musicians and actors whose names are marked with plaques on the chairs, where you can eat *kreplach* and chicken soup and, if you want to, even herring.

My Arabic is mute

The other thing that happened in the *ma'abarot* was that Iraqi Jews started to lose their Arabic.

I've lost my Judeo-Iraqi Arabic to English, which is one of the most notorious of what linguists call *predator languages* or *killer languages*. That makes it sound like the little languages are weak and unfit to survive and the big languages merely blunder in, hungry. I was glad to find my deep discomfort with this rhetoric brilliantly articulated by linguists Mark Turin and Aidan Pine who pointed out that the conversation around *endangerment* and *extinction* implied 'an apparently agentless process in which language loss is both inevitable and naturally occurring' – but also elided the courage and resilience of people trying to keep their smaller languages alive. Some people call the languages that push out others *bully languages*, which makes more sense. There are reasons that over half of us speak just thirteen of the 7,000-odd languages spoken or signed in the world right now, and many languages are at risk because of genocide, forced migration, forced education, suppression and racism. English didn't go from 4 million speakers in 1600 to 2 billion now by accident or luck; in *Decolonising the Mind*, the Kenyan novelist Ngugi wa Thiong'o calls it 'spiritual subjugation'. Technology is accelerating this narrowing down; Google and Facebook operate in only a hundred languages or so, making it hard for smaller languages to survive in our extremely online world.

English isn't the only 'bully language', of course. During the Cold War, the Ukrainian linguist Jaroslav Rudnyckyj coined the word *linguicide* to underline that the Soviet suppression of his language was unnatural, deliberate, even murderous. In Turkey, the Kurdish languages were so systematically suppressed that for eighty-five years the letters Q, W and X (which appear in them but not in Turkish) were banned. Through most of 2005, long before the ban was reversed, I went every week to a community centre in north London to watch six-year-olds learn to speak Kurmanji, one of the four Kurdish languages. The BBC had commissioned me to write a radio play set in the community. I was happy to be there, having grown up on stories about how the Kurds, like the Jews, were persecuted in every country they lived in; how they had also asked for a country in the British and French carve-up of the Middle East, but were still waiting; how they had helped many Jews escape Iraq. At the centre I learned about a shocking incident in London in 1996. A group of Kurdish refugees were rehearsing a play which Harold Pinter had written after visiting Turkey. *Mountain Language* is about people from the mountains forbidden to speak their language, and the Kurds felt deeply affectionate towards it. During a rehearsal in Finsbury Park the police burst in and arrested the refugees at gunpoint. They seized the prop guns they had borrowed from the National Theatre, held them for many hours in the back of a van and, in an almost unbearable reprise of their experiences in Turkey and of the theme of the play they were rehearsing, the police insisted they spoke only in English. I did not realise, when I was researching all this, that I was also trying to comprehend how my own language was endangered. I do now.

The bully language that mainly pushed out Judeo-Iraqi Arabic was Hebrew. This feels strange given that Hebrew so often appears in stories about endangered languages as a happy example of a language revived from the dead.

Except during the time Hebrew was supposedly extinct, it was in continuous use for praying for more than 3,000 years. Jews knew how it sounded, how it felt in the mouth. At least,

Jewish men did. Jewish women usually didn't know more than a few blessings off by heart, which is why they found the switch to Hebrew harder. It was certainly hard for Devora Ben-Yehuda, the wife of the man who is supposed to have revived Hebrew nearly single-handedly. Her husband Eliezer dreamed that Hebrew would connect Jews from all over the world, and in 1881, on the boat to Palestine, he told her that once they got there that was all he'd speak, even though she didn't. The people he accosted in Hebrew when they arrived were probably surprised – just as a Catholic priest might be surprised if you greeted him in Latin – but some of them managed to stammer out replies. Hebrew had long been used as a common language by Jewish merchants, connecting speakers of Yiddish and the various Judeo-Arabic languages with speakers of Ladino, also called Judeo-Spanish, or Judezmo, the language spoken by Jews in Spain and Portugal, and then later all over the world as they fled the Inquisition. It was also used by poets, and by rabbis, especially in the Hasidic movement of nineteenth-century Ukraine.

Even so, Eliezer and Devora were criticised and mocked for speaking Hebrew when they had other languages in common, and when their Hebrew was, apparently, not that good, involving a lot of signs and pointing and painfully stilted conversations. The criticism reached a crescendo when they tried to bring up their son as the first Hebrew-speaking child. They isolated him so he didn't hear other languages, got a male dog and a female cat so they could practise the genders, and coined new modern Hebrew words for things that didn't exist in the ancient, sacred language, like *doll* and *bike* and *jelly* – later setting up the Hebrew Language Academy to do this on a bigger scale. When he was still silent at three or even four, Devora must have been under pressure to give up her husband's plan; the story goes that Eliezer found her singing to their son in Russian and yelled at her (or, some say, smashed a table) and that's when the boy said his first words, '*Abba! Abba!*' (Daddy! Daddy! in Hebrew).

At that point it wasn't a given that the Jewish state's language would be Hebrew – or that there would even be a Jewish state. In 1897, when Devora and Eliezer's son was fifteen, the Jewish world was pulling in different directions. The World Zionist Organisation was founded in Basel, while in Vilna Jews founded the Bund, the Yiddish socialist party; that same year the Hebrew literary journal *Ha-Shiloah* was first published in Odessa, while the Yiddish daily, the *Forverts*, first came out in New York. It wasn't just Hebrew vs Yiddish; it was also Zionism vs *doikayt*, which means 'hereness' in Yiddish and was a commitment to staying where you were and to living a radical, joyful diaspora life, to not needing a homeland. Also, that fateful year, a vast cache of writing in Judeo-Arabic discovered in a synagogue in Cairo was transferred, wholesale, to Cambridge. A *geniza* (hiding place in Hebrew) is a store for any papers or books that are too worn out or damaged to be used, but too sacred to be thrown away because they contain God's name. The Cairo Geniza was a treasure trove of stories of medieval Middle Eastern Jews, and Iraqi Jewish scholar Ella Shohat has written that its dislocation from Cairo to Cambridge anticipated the displacement of Jews from Arab lands.

Meanwhile, in Palestine, Yiddish-speaking immigrants who wanted to get on with their neighbours (including the Arabic-speaking Jews who had lived in Palestine for generations) created Arabic-Yiddish phrasebooks and dictionaries. A book with the startling title *Arabic Elements in Palestinian Yiddish* charts the ways these Ashkenazi Jews stretched their Yiddish to accommodate words and phrases from Arabic. Many Zionists assumed that if a Jewish state did transpire, its language would be Yiddish. But Hebrew's champions promoted it as virile, strong and independent while they called Yiddish the weak, frightened language of the shtetl. The Language Defenders Battalion, formed in 1923, attacked theatres performing Yiddish plays, burned down news-stands that sold Yiddish newspapers and fought Yiddish speakers. There's a famous picture of a group of young Yiddish speakers staring at the camera wounded and furious, their heads bandaged up. Yiddish lost half its speakers worldwide, maybe more than half, to the Holocaust, which in Yiddish is called the *khurbn* (destruction). Then in 1949, Israel made suppressing Yiddish official policy, banning Yiddish theatre and periodicals. In the Soviet Union, the Yiddish speakers who had survived the war also found their language violently suppressed; 12 August 1952 is known as the Night of the Murdered Poets because thirteen stars of Yiddish culture were shot by firing squad on Stalin's orders.

By the time Jews started arriving in Israel from the Middle East and North Africa, the fight for Yiddish was lost. As for Arabic, Israel designated it an official language alongside Hebrew but, perhaps inevitably, it came to be seen as the language of the enemy. So just as Yiddish speakers and Palestinians had to learn Hebrew in a hurry, so did Arabic-speaking Jews, and they were often shamed for their accents and for slipping into Arabic; Shohat describes feeling embarrassed even at kindergarten when she unwittingly spoke Arabic, and going home and trying to force her grandmother to speak Hebrew. Even the pronunciation of Hebrew changed, guttural sounds flattened out so it sounded more Ashkenazi (and less correct). Ben-Yehuda would have disapproved; he considered Arabic a 'sister' to Hebrew, and turned to Arabic to coin new words in Hebrew, on the basis that 'The roots of Arabic were once a part of the Hebrew language . . . lost, and now we have found them again!' When, in 2018, Israel dropped Arabic as an official language, the Israeli newspaper *Haaretz* wrote that he would be 'turning in his grave'.

Language loss haunts memoirs and fiction by Iraqi Jews, which, severed from my language, I can only read in translation. Sara Shilo's novel *The Falafel King is Dead* was described as 'untranslatable' when it came out in Israel because it was studded with Arabic, Judeo-Arabic and Mizrahi street slang, drawing on her family's linguistic profusion; her father is Syrian Jewish and her mother Iraqi Jewish. One of her characters laments, almost briskly, 'They brought us all here as new immigrants. Mixed us a bit and poured us onto the baking sheet. We hadn't even cooled off from the oven, along came the knife of Hebrew and cut us in two pieces: one that corrects how we speak, and one that gets corrected.' In the documentary *Forget Baghdad* (the other major documentary about my community is called *Remember Baghdad* – which says it all really), some Iraqi Jewish writers describe how it felt when the 'knife of Hebrew' came for them. Shimon Ballas, born in 1930, left Iraq at twenty-one with a language he called his suitcase, a suitcase he carried with him wherever he went. In Israel his friends called themselves the Circle of Fans of Arab Literature, and agonised over how they were supposed to continue writing. If they kept writing in *fusha*, they'd only be read by other Arabic-speaking Jews, because it was becoming difficult and even dangerous for people in Arab countries to read books by Israelis. If they switched to Hebrew, they'd lose their fluency, familiarity and ease – and only other Israelis would be able to read them in the original. It was an impossible conundrum. When Ballas eventually decided to write in Hebrew, he worked hard to immerse himself in it, to become fluent, but one night couldn't resist reading a bit of Arabic. After he put the book down to try to sleep, he felt as though the words were attacking him, coming at him for sleepless hours, like a waking nightmare or a seizure – or, as he interpreted it, his mother tongue avenging itself for being rejected. His near-contemporary, Sami Michael, chose to write in Arabic. He claimed that Mossad approached him to spy for them and when he said no, they recruited his brother-in-law, Eli Cohen, who became a legendary spy, working deep undercover in Damascus, where he was even appointed deputy defence secretary. A recent miniseries about Cohen suggested that even before he became a spy, he felt torn between two cultures and two languages, unable to be fully at home in either. As for Michael, he was so exhausted by constantly having to justify his decision to write in Arabic that he just stopped. For twenty-five years. When he picked up his pen again, he wrote in Hebrew. My community breathlessly read his hit novel *Victoria*, fascinated by its Iraqi Jewish heroine finding her way in an extended family in Baghdad at the turn of the last century – and stunned by its scenes of rape and incest. *Victoria* is peppered with Judeo-Iraqi Arabic idioms, translated into Hebrew so they feel deliberately awkward, out of place, uncanny. But there's one tantalising scene where Victoria and her girl cousins find a paper aeroplane on the roof. They can't read, so they ask their rabbi, who is also a healer. He is enraged to find that it compares healers to prostitutes. In the original Hebrew text, Michael writes the Judeo-Iraqi Arabic in the Hebrew alphabet – so Hebrew speakers can sound it out but only Iraqi Jewish readers can understand it – and then translates it into modern Hebrew. This is how my language exists on the page now, as a snippet of scurrilousness written on paper folded into an aeroplane and flown onto a roof, found by people who can't read it, translated by someone who is outraged about it, and printed in a book in such a way that not everyone can fully access it. It *still* feels raw and vivid, mischievous, alive.

The saddest interviewee in *Forget Baghdad* is Samir Naqqāsh who arrived in Israel at thirteen in 1951, but refused to switch to Hebrew, saying 'A Jew who writes in Arabic presents all kinds of problems to everyone, yet I am simply continuing to write in my own language.' I often felt I presented problems to people even by talking *about* my language let alone (if only!) talking in it or (beyond the realm of possibility) writing books in it. I was ashamed that I read Naqqāsh in translation. Most people do. His decision to continue to write in *fusha*, laced with lots of salty Judeo-Iraqi Arabic, meant that he was barely read in the original in his lifetime, and only started to find a bigger readership in translation. What is striking about his novel *Tenants and Cobwebs* is how it refuses to be pinned down to any voice or opinion; instead Naqqāsh keeps spinning his kaleidoscope of characters, so that every single one is eventually challenged or contradicted by another. It is bewildering at times, but it is also exhilarating.

I didn't suffer the first generation's wrenching loss, but I wrestled with how I felt about it. It was helpful to find it expressed by the poet Almog Behar who is second generation too. Born in Israel in 1978, Iraqi on his mother's side, Turkish and German on his father's, Behar heard Arabic as a child but by the time he wanted to learn, it was too late for his family to teach him. One of his poems calls his Arabic 'mute', 'throttled' and 'scared', while his Hebrew is loud, confident, comfortable . . . and 'deaf'. My Arabic is all these things too, and I wondered if my English was 'deaf', if I was always going to be missing something by writing in a language that wasn't fully mine. Writing that, I felt absurd. Of course English was mine. It was the language I grew up in, the language of all my friendships and relationships, the language of my child. I studied its literature at university. I wrote in it. But it nagged at me that it wasn't my milk language, and maybe it would always feel cold in my mouth, always lack intimacy and heft.

Why my mother didn't leave

My mother was making me coffee in a pot. No: she was making me *kahwa* in a *dallah*, a curvaceous copper pot that was comforting to hold.

For each of us, she put in half a teaspoon of sugar (it should have been a full teaspoon, if we were doing this properly, but we worried about our teeth), a *finjan* (a small coffee cup) of water, and a loaded teaspoon of coffee. She added a quarter of a teaspoon of ground cardamom. The coffee sat on the top, and she stirred it in as she turned on the hob, fairly high. She put the pot on, stirred again. When it started to simmer, she stirred one more time. Then she waited. When the coffee started to rise, she took it off the heat until it subsided, then put it back on. When it rose again, it was ready. She spooned the *boza* (bubbles) into each cup first then poured in the rest. It smelled like my childhood.

The *dallah* wasn't from Iraq. I wish we had a *dallah* from the Souq al-Safafeer, the copper market that has been on a narrow lane off Rashid Street since Abbasid times, where coppersmiths beat hot, shimmering copper into pots and pans and jugs and lamps that look like Aladdin's, and the hammering and clanking is so loud you have to talk in signs. I fantasised about going there to buy a *dallah* and a *hawan* (a copper pestle and mortar) to grind my spices, but the *souq* has been nearly silenced by the war and the pandemic. As we drank our coffee I put my voice recorder on to ask my mother why she didn't leave in 1951. In fact, she was *born* in 1951. My grandmother was pregnant with her when she said goodbye to her parents, brothers and many of her friends. They would stay another twenty years.

At first they stayed because my grandfather was not a Zionist; because he thought things would be hard in Israel; and because he hoped that once the airlifts were over, things would calm down for the Jews who stayed. There were only around six thousand of them; the community had shrunk so dramatically that most histories of Iraqi Jews end here. My mother grew up in a Baghdad no one would ever call 'a Jewish city'. In her Iraq, it was often uneasy to be Jewish, so she never went to the hanging gardens or the ziggurats or even the copper market. Much as I'd have liked to imagine her in a romantic old Baghdad, my mother's city was modern. Modernist. At seven she moved into a house in the Al Masbeh area of Baghdad (*masbeh* means swimming pool) designed by the architect Kahtan Awni who had studied under Frank Lloyd Wright, all on one level, with not a garage but a *carport*, and patterned metal screens, based on traditional wooden lattice ones, which kept it cool, and which a magazine at the time called a marriage of East and West.

Lloyd Wright came to Baghdad himself in 1957. He flew over the city with the king, Faisal II, who wanted an opera house on an island in the Tigris. By the time he delivered his design (complete with ziggurat-shaped car parks and a statue of Aladdin), the king was dead. My mother's nanny screamed, 'They killed my son, they killed my son!' She meant the 23-year-old king, who had been so young when his father died that he'd become a sort of national son. Cecil Beaton even went to Baghdad to photograph him looking sad in shorts. He still looks a bit unfinished in the pictures taken of him in Britain, at seventeen, grinning anxiously at the queen who was just a few years older. He was the inspiration for Prince Abdullah in the *Tintin* comics. He loved anything new, and invited Werner March to build the Iraq Museum, and Le Corbusier to build the Baghdad Gymnasium. He wrote a book about judo and self-defence called *Ways to Defend Yourself*, and had copies printed to give to everyone he met. But judo didn't help when revolutionaries broke into the palace, ordered him and his family up against a wall and machine-gunned them down, and dragged the mutilated body of his uncle, once the regent, through the streets.

After the shock and violence came a new prime minister, Abd al-Karim Qasim. While he was in power, my mother learned to swim in the Tigris, which was more the kind of story I wanted to hear. In the holidays they went to a sports club with a pool and swam, played ping-pong and had 'the most delicious plate of crisps you'd ever had in your life, they cook them on the spot, with lashings of tomato ketchup'. She had left her Jewish primary school for the American high school, where for most of her time she was the only Jew. She had had typhoid *and* paratyphoid, and survived. She loved maths. She wore miniskirts. Her father was a GP who specialised in TB and had an X-ray in his surgery, the first in Baghdad outside of a hospital. He was always getting crazy gifts from his patients. One day he came home with a gazelle. 'Tell me about the gazelle,' I asked my mother and she said, 'Oh, her! We didn't know what to do with her. So we put the gazelle on the roof, thinking she was going to be contained. Well, she jumped.' Which was the end of the gazelle.

My Iraqi Jewish friends and I sometimes play Iraqi Jewish cliché bingo with books and stories about our community. Will they mention the river? Compare life in Baghdad to paradise and mention the garden of Eden? And of course, the biggie: sleeping on the roof. But I was not immune. When I was a child I loved hearing about my family sleeping out on their roofs in the summer. At school I drew a picture of them sliding off a pitched roof as they drifted into dreams and my mother laughed because of course the roofs were flat. I've told my son these stories too, they are picturesque – and old-fashioned. By the time my mother was born, many Jews had stopped sleeping on the roof.

'What for?' said my grandmother, puncturing the romance. 'We had air con!' My mother and her brothers sometimes did because, she said, 'We needed to try it!' They saw shooting stars and were convinced they were UFOs. So far, so exciting. But one time, she said, 'we heard gunfire in the distance and it was, oh, go back to sleep, it's another revolution'. Why didn't they go into the house? 'It was such an unusual occurrence that we were allowed to sleep on the roof that we had to milk it!' Later she saw Qasim's bullet-ridden corpse on TV. It was 1963 and the Ba'ath Party had seized power for the first time. She was twelve.

We finished our coffee so we put the saucers on top of the *finjans* and slowly turned them over. Then we waited, and we talked about the 1960s.

When I was growing up, I never heard about the Jews in Iraq in the 1960s from anyone except for my family. In 2003, when Iraq was all over the newspapers and everyone had an opinion, no one mentioned the Jews. We were old news – but also not old enough. Journalists were obsessed with Iraq's *ancient* history, repeating the phrase 'cradle of civilisation' as a sort of mantra against the destruction. However, a lot of people were reading a 1989 book called *Republic of Fear* by Kanan Makiya, whose father, Mohamed Makiya, was another modernist architect who fled Iraq because the Iraqi government accused him of the 'crime' of being a Freemason, but returned when Saddam invited him to build in Baghdad. Kanan went along too and started trying to find out what was happening in Iraq. The result was *Republic of Fear*. The book was controversial for making a case for regime change – Makiya even told George Bush that Iraqis would greet the Americans with 'sweets and flowers' – but it was important to me because it was the first time anyone outside our community told the story of what happened to the Jews who were still in Iraq in the 1960s.

Makiya argued that the Ba'ath Party 'assiduously cultivated' antisemitism, that hating and persecuting Jews was not a sideshow or an afterthought but central to their policy. They had failed to hold Iraq at their first attempt, and they were trying to get back in power when, in 1967, the Six Day War began and changed everything: for Israel, for the Palestinians and for the Jews of Iraq. That May, Egypt closed the Straits of Tiran to Israeli ships and moved its forces close to the border, evicting UN peacekeeping troops. Together, six Arab states, including Iraq, moved over 230,000 troops towards Israel. Iraq's president vowed 'to wipe Israel off the map'. The Jews in Iraq were terrified for themselves and for their families and friends in Israel where mass graves were being dug in playgrounds and parks in anticipation of what might happen – and they couldn't exactly ring them up to see if they were OK for fear of being seen as fifth columnists.

Some historians have argued that Egypt and the other Arab states were just sabre-rattling, that diplomacy could have avoided war, but certainly most Israelis and Jews around the world felt that Israel faced possible annihilation, and that was what they were being openly threatened with. On 5 June 1967, Israel made a pre-emptive attack, bombing Egyptian planes on the ground. By day six they had captured Gaza, the West Bank, the Sinai Peninsula, parts of East Jerusalem and the Golan Heights, and that evening, a ceasefire was agreed. Israel was safe – or seemed safe – but it's haunting now to read Israeli novelist Amos Oz warning, three months after the war ended, 'We are condemned now to rule people who do not want to be ruled by us . . . I have fears about the kind of seeds we will sow . . . in the hearts of the occupied. Even more, I have fears about the seed that will be planted in the hearts of the occupiers.'

Within a week of the war, the Iraqi government arrested one hundred Jews. This was a popular strategy across the Middle East. Egypt rounded up and imprisoned around six hundred

Jews. Tunisians rioted against Jews in the streets, and burned a synagogue to the ground. Syria confined its Jews to their homes for several months. There were pogroms in Libya. The World Jewish Congress begged the UN to help the 'Ancient Jewish communities' who were 'being subjected to terror and intimidation', adding, 'These defenseless people remain in jeopardy.' My mum was sixteen.

Rage at the outcome of the war was a major factor in the Ba'athists seizing power again, in 1968. This time they wanted to tighten their grip on the country and, Makiya writes, to 'reverse the trauma of defeat' in the Six Day War. They did it by giving Iraqis someone to blame. They cut the phone lines to every Jewish home and recruited 3,000 secret policemen to watch the Jews – 'one spy for every adult Jew' Marina Benjamin has pointed out. My mother remembered them in their trademark grey Volkswagen Beetles. 'You knew who they were because they had big moustaches.' They weren't just sinister, they were omnipresent, as implied by the title of Mona Yahia's autobiographical novel, *When the Grey Beetles Took Over Baghdad*. After 1968, my mother said, 'we would just go and do whatever was necessary and come back home and lock the door and that was it. The fear was always there. I would go to school and come back. There was no life. There wasn't going out.' School became increasingly difficult for Jews. The Ba'athists were very interested in education. Yahia's young heroine is horrified by the blood-and-soil racism at school. She starts to feel that even her language is turning against her, and goes through her schoolbook erasing the word *watan* (homeland), 'eliminating one *watan* after the other, delicately, like a soldier dismantling bombs in a minefield', then starts 'unlearning Arabic' altogether. Even though a friend warns that her memories will be scattered, her heart divided, she rejects Arabic. Yahia wrote her book in English.

My mother finished school but was not allowed to go to university. So, in limbo, she spent a year going to special maths classes at the Jewish school. Some friends and relatives escaped Iraq by going north, where Kurds smuggled them across the mountains over the border into Iran, but my mother's family stayed. Then, as a PR exercise to try to prove they were not discriminating, the government let a handful of Jews go to university. My mother was one of them. She even got her picture in the paper. By then there were so few Jews left in Iraq that when another student demanded to know her religion, and she reluctantly said she was Jewish, the student screamed and turned my mother round to see if she had a tail. Things were getting harder for women, too. There were no more miniskirts, said my mother, because 'we had the police checking if girls were wearing miniskirts or anything revealing. And I remember clearly one girl was wearing a miniskirt and a policeman was running after her to spray her legs with paint, and she ran, and she was running, and she was run over, and she died.'

One day someone came to the house and said my mother's cousin was going to be on TV that evening. She didn't know this cousin. She didn't even know her father had another brother, but now she learned he'd married a Muslim woman and fallen out with his family, and that now his son – who was only seventeen – was going to be put on trial, accused of being a Zionist spy. He was obviously not a Zionist spy. He was a Muslim, he'd had no contact with the Jewish side of his family; perhaps he didn't know they existed either. Alongside thirteen others, nine of them Jewish, he was part of a show trial that convulsed the country and consolidated the Ba'athists' power.

Makiya writes that people went 'berserk', listening to broadcasts of each day's proceedings and panicking about car bombings that were happening all over Baghdad and being blamed on the Jews – even though sometimes the state media reported them before the bombs had actually gone off, even though there were only around 2,000 Jews left in Iraq, a tiny, terrified community, all of whom had actively chosen not to go to Israel. It wasn't about truth; it was political theatre where the accused were, Makiya says, 'deployed like mannequins', or, in the words of Max Sawdayee, an Iraqi Jew whose horrifying account is called *All Waiting to be Hanged*, the 'poor "actors" of the scene', the whole thing stage-managed by Saddam Hussein and designed as a macabre spectacle that would create what Makiya calls 'a new kind of fear', first among the Jews and later for everyone in Iraq. In court, the defence lawyer apologised for having to defend spies and asked for it to go on record that he 'would not like to see them go unpunished'. When they pleaded not guilty, the court laughed.

On 27 January 1969, the radio blared out, 'Today is your feast! The day of your joy and happiness! The day on which you have gotten rid of the first gang of despicable spies! Iraq, your beloved Iraq, has executed, has hanged, has settled the account with those traitors! You great people of Baghdad and Basra, get free, move, go to your Liberation Squares to see with your own eyes how the traitors are hanged!' Sawdayee thought 200,000 people went to Baghdad's Tahrir Square, 'red, excited, smiling, laughing, walking fast, running, jostling'. Many more watched on TV. The men and boys were hanged on scaffolds spread across the square. They were barefoot, visibly tortured (Yahia's young heroine is confused that some of them are wearing gloves, and her friend tells her it's because their hands have been chopped off), wearing signs stating their religions and their supposed crimes. The crowd danced, cheered, sang, spat at the corpses, threw stones at them, grabbed and hit them. My mother's cousin, Jamal Hakim, was forced to lie and say he was eighteen because even in Ba'athist Iraq children could not be executed *legally*. It was reported all over the world. In the

New York Times, an Iraqi Jew warned that his friends and family left in Iraq 'face extinction', while his wife, in tears, said, 'Our Jews would gladly leave but they are not allowed to.' In the UK, *The Times* called what had happened 'savagely medieval' while the *Guardian* said it was 'barbaric'. The foreign minister made a rather mild statement that they had taken 'the question up informally with the Iraqi Government on humanitarian grounds, urging clemency and pointing out the effect on Iraq's reputation abroad. We very much regret that the Iraqi Government felt unable to show clemency.'

When I was a teenager, visiting the Anne Frank Museum in Amsterdam, my mother suddenly burst into tears and rushed out into the street. We followed, worried, and she told us she'd seen a picture of her cousin on the wall, part of a display on antisemitism around the world. 'I just didn't know it was going to be there,' she kept saying.

By 1969, she was desperate to leave Iraq. 'Every day there was an argument,' she said. 'We want to leave, we want to leave.' Her father still refused. One time, my mother's little brother went to take a steak from the fridge and, said my grandmother, 'the cook went berserk. He started to shout.' She and my grandfather rushed into the kitchen and he grabbed a knife and threatened to stab my grandfather. 'I stood in front of him and took both his hands. I said shame on you!' But Jews in Iraq had become fair game, and he only stopped threatening my grandfather when a neighbour intervened. Even after this, my grandfather wouldn't leave. Even though his family kept telling him, 'Everybody is gone.' In 1970 they finally persuaded him. They would try to escape by going north, pretending they were going on holiday, and at the village of the Kurdish leader Mullah Mustafa Barzani they would say they wanted to cross into Iran and he would smuggle them out. They bought a Seiko watch as a present for

Barzani and set off in a taxi. 'We were very quiet,' my mother said. 'We didn't speak much.'

On the way into Erbil they were stopped at a checkpoint and asked their name, and when my grandfather said Hakim – not a Jewish name – they were allowed to pass. But on the way out they were arrested. At the police station, they found they weren't alone. Several other Iraqi Jews were there, frantically flushing jewellery down the toilet or tearing up money, so they could say they weren't escaping, just on holiday. My grandmother hid their money in the toilet cistern and quickly had to retrieve it when they were told they were being moved. They were driven back to Baghdad, overnight, bumping along in small buses, and taken to a building that had once been a Bahai temple. 'This massive massive massive room,' said my mother, with a stage at one end, and chairs on a rake and – she burst into tears when she told me – *nooses*.

I've had nightmares about this room, but this was a new detail. 'We all sat down,' she said. 'Nobody spoke. It was the most scary thing.' There were over a hundred people in the room. One was a baby. One was ninety-six. Hours passed. And then the door suddenly opened and the *mukhabarat*, the secret police, screamed out the name of a young man. 'He was gone for quite a while,' my mother said. 'And suddenly the door opens and he walks back in. And the door is shut. And none of us dare to do anything and we are looking at him. And he just walks. And he goes on the stage, and he goes in the middle, and in front of everybody starts to take off his shirt. So we see that he was not actually scarred. But he was electrocuted.' Then he joined his family and told them what had happened and it was whispered, family to family, across the whole room.

Late at night they shouted the name of a young woman. 'She got up and she could barely walk. It was obvious what they wanted from her at ten o'clock at night.' My grandfather turned to my mother and promised, 'If they come and call you, and somebody tries to hurt you, scream as loud as you can and I will try to come and save you.' After some time, the young woman came back. More whispers. They were interrogating everyone, on their own, or by family, or in twos or threes. My mother was taken off with her father. They asked her if she wanted to leave the country. She said 'yes'. I was a bit stunned by the courage of her reply. There was a lot of screaming and some violence. They pulled her hair. They hit her. They made her stand on one leg. After they had interrogated everyone, things got a bit easier. They were allowed to wash with a bucket of water. It was filthy. 'This is why for the rest of my life I cannot bear to have dirt around me. I wash my hands a million times a day.' Me too. My first word was 'dirty'.

Once, a guard gave them all a watermelon. I was told this story as a child, probably because it was less scary and horrible than the other stories about prison, but it stuck with me, and for many years I thought watermelon was prison food, and I could not eat it. Another time, my mother and some friends were huddled under a blanket when someone passed them an ice cream to share. Also under a blanket, they dried out the money my grandmother had hidden in the cistern, note by note.

On the nineteenth or the twentieth day, they suddenly started releasing families, one by one, until it was just my mother's family left. The interrogator asked my mother again if she wanted to leave Iraq. She said 'yes I would like to go and study' but the interrogator wrote down, instead, 'no I love Iraq, I don't want to leave'. And they went back home.

After that, my mother said, 'we kind of went on'. She went back to university, my grandfather went back to work, they stopped trying to escape. She heard of one family who tried to escape three times and were caught every time, and taken to the infamous Qasr al-Nihaya (Palace of the End). It was a royal palace that had been converted into a prison. My mother is not sure if it was the same palace she went swimming in. My grandmother is not sure if it was the same palace she sat on a throne in.

Two months later, someone knocked on the door in the middle of the night. When they went to look, no one was there, but there was a stone on the ground holding down an anonymous message from someone who said he was a patient of my grandfather's and that my grandfather's name had come up and he was going to be arrested. Soon afterwards, he was. The police said they just wanted to ask him some questions and he'd be back in two hours, but when he didn't come home my grandmother went to the prison with a blanket and 'cigarettes because he used to smoke like mad'. She dropped off food every day. (Some of the other prisoners' families didn't dare, so my grandfather shared his blanket, his food, his cigarettes.) She found a lawyer who would get him out for 5,000 dinars, but that was impossible because Jews were only allowed to get 100 dinars out of the bank every month. Every Wednesday she went to see a government minister who phoned the prison and asked, 'What's happening about Albert the old?' (There was another, younger, Albert there too.) Every Wednesday they always told her he was about to be released. He wasn't. Amnesty International started campaigning for the release of my grandfather and thirty-five other Jews in prison in Iraq, in a report which also said the tiny community 'lives in fear and suffers extreme economic pressure'. For the three months my grandfather was in prison, my mother slept on the floor because, she said, 'How can I have a bed if my father didn't have a bed?' She visited once but one of the guards saw her and threatened my grandfather, 'The minute you leave this prison I am coming to marry your daughter,' so she didn't go again. The reason given for my grandfather's incarceration was vagrancy and urinating in the street, even though they arrested him in his house.

When he was released, my grandmother said, 'He lost everything. He wasn't the same man. He used to go to work but he wasn't there.' It was 1971. Some months later, they finally got permission to leave thanks to one of my grandfather's patients. They went to London.

Turning off the recorder felt like coming up for air. The Jewish Ukrainian Australian author Maria Tumarkin writes that 'traumatised people . . . do not experience time as linear' because they remember the bad things that happened so intensely, so viscerally, that 'The past enters the present as an intruder, not a welcome guest'. These were my mother's traumatic stories, not mine, but I recognised the intruder. I'd met them before, had the feeling of *there and then* exploding into *here and now*.

We shooed the past away with a jolt of the future. It was time to tell our fortunes. We lifted up the *finjans*. Most of the coffee dregs had drained into the saucers, and what was left had made patterns and shapes. My mother smiled. 'Now we tell stories.' When we looked at my cup, I saw myself climbing a volcano. Lava pouring down, panic rising in my throat. But my mum saw me dancing. She pointed out the dancer, and I saw her too, her dress flaring in the ecstatic whoosh of her movement, her hair lifting. She looked like joy. Like power. Could she be me, in the future? Could I be her? My mum laughed at me, looking so serious. These were just stories.

Masgouf, or All the foods I'll never eat

Sometimes the trauma surfaced unexpectedly, when we were talking about things that seemed safe. Like the famous Iraqi fish dish *masgouf*. It goes back millennia, to ancient Sumerian recipes where fish is 'touched by fire' then 'placed on the fire', to a plate with the remains of *masgouf* found by archaeologists in the ruins of Ur in southern Iraq, where the Jewish prophet Abraham was born. In a 1930s book racily titled *We Married an Englishman*, American identical twins Ruth and Helen Hoffman go to Baghdad with Ruth's engineer husband and marvel: 'No wonder this part of the world had become the cradle of civilisation when its inhabitants could think up a dish like this.'

Years ago my mother's cousin was reminiscing about how in Baghdad the fish was caught, stunned, cleaned, splayed open and impaled on stakes over fire in what the *LA Times* once called a 'violent alchemy'. It was marinated in rock salt, and sometimes also in date syrup, tamarind, turmeric and coriander. The fire was made of wood from apricot, citrus or eucalyptus trees, which released oils as they burned, giving the fish a sweet, smoky taste. After an hour or so, the fish was put on the embers, skin down to crisp it up, then served with bread, lettuce, lemon and, of course, *amba*, the iconic Iraqi Jewish mango pickle. *Masgouf* evoked a whole world, of sitting in the glamorous restaurants on the east bank of the Tigris, on Abu Nawas Street, watching the sun set over the river as the *masgouf* cooked; or making a day of it, swimming in the river and stretching out to dry under a palm tree, eating dates; the world of the Iraqi folk song 'Balini-b Balwa' (He Plagued Me with a Plague) about being smitten with unrequited love, so painful that the singer moans that even the fish cry for him. *Masgouf* also brought down Saddam Hussein. Even in hiding, with American forces searching every inch of Iraq for him, he couldn't do without his favourite dish and ordered one of his minions to dig a pond and stock it with the right kind of fish. When the Americans found the pond it led them to Saddam's bodyguard and finally to his hiding place in Tikrit.

Of all the stories my mother tells about Baghdad, my favourite, and my son's, is the story of her learning to swim in the Tigris. My mum! Learning to swim! In the Tigris, river of legend. My son listened, agog, to how Hai el Sebach (Hai the Swimming Teacher) rowed her and my grandmother out on the river, and once they were out of reach of land, he threw her in. 'She came up like a turtle,' said my grandmother. 'And she used to laugh and we all used to laugh.' He threw her more than *once*? 'Of course!' said my grandmother, sounding more relaxed than I would be if someone threw my child into a river. 'Was it fast?' he asked, so I showed him a video of the Tigris and his eyes popped. 'It's a thousand mega speed!' Once she'd got the feel of bobbing up in the water, my mother actually learned to swim wearing a lifebelt with cork floats in it. I saw one once, in Eastbourne of all places, on a bitingly cold day that made me feel absurdly Iraqi Jewish as I shivered and watched my son make sandcastles in persistent drizzle, while my friend laughed and said, 'This is what British seaside memories are made of.' When the cold had fully seeped into our bones, we retreated to the lifeboat museum, and there it was: an old canvas lifebelt, with pockets holding fat squares of cork. I showed my son how they would remove the cork floats one by one until my mother was just swimming. In a *river*. She's still a stronger swimmer than I'll ever be.

Swimming in the Tigris is at the heart of Miriam Halahmy's

children's book *A Boy from Baghdad*, inspired by her husband's life. Her young Jewish hero longs to swim for Iraq at the Olympics, but when he moves to Israel he is shocked by his first attempt to swim in the sea. In the graphic novel *The Wolf of Baghdad*, Carol Isaacs, a second-generation Iraqi Jewish cartoonist, is transported by music to Baghdad, where she sees a child swimming in the Tigris . . . and he's a ghost. Everyone she sees is a ghost, the ghosts of her family, haunting the city that used to be their home. No Iraqi Jews are swimming in the Tigris now. Or none that aren't ghosts.

Ghosts walk the pages of almost every Iraqi Jewish book I have read. Marina Benjamin describes going to Iraq in 2004, looking for small cigarette-shaped indentations in the doorposts of houses where there had once been mezuzahs, the small decorative cases containing tiny parchment scrolls with Jewish prayers on them. The mezuzahs were gone, their silver cases stolen long ago, leaving 'empty spaces and silent traces'. In Leon McCarron's book *Wounded Tigris*, Jewish ghosts haunt his journey along the river. He is shown locked-up homes with peeling paint, waiting for Jews who will probably never return to them. Shown a wardrobe, he is told it belonged to Jews. 'It seemed little to remember a people by,' he writes. 'Without the wardrobe, though, perhaps there'd have been nothing at all.' Beside the tomb of the prophet Ezra there is just 'an empty space that had once been a synagogue'.

Masgouf is always made with *shabout*, a large freshwater carp only found in the brackish waters of the Tigris and the Euphrates. Grey, slimy and bewhiskered, you would not eat it for its looks. In an essay with a title I find strangely irresistible – *Names for the Fishes of the River Tigris in Baghdadi Judeo-Arabic and in Zakho Jewish Neo-Aramaic* – linguist Ephraim Nissan tried to reconstruct Judeo-Iraqi Arabic names for fish, in the wake of what he called my community's 'harrowing end'. The *shabout* is probably the same as the *shibuta*, which ancient Iraqi Jewish rabbis salivated over, recommending it for Rosh Hashanah, Jewish new year or literally 'head of the year', when the tradition is to eat foods expressing a desire to be the head and not the tail. Some Jewish sages said the head of the *shabout /shibuta* tasted just like pork – although *how did they know . . .* ?

At the school gate, talking to a couple of other mums, I felt a pang. They were both Greek, and about to go to Greece for the summer, to swim and eat spanakopita with their families and for a moment I imagined saying we were off to Iraq for the summer, to swim in the Tigris and eat *masgouf* with our cousins. But we couldn't go to Iraq and our cousins were not there and my mother's cousin had said, 'Who would eat *masgouf* now? The river is full of bodies. Saddam threw his torture victims there. If you fish, you bring up an arm or a leg.' His words made me feel unsteady. I put my hands flat on the table, breathed, and waited for someone to say it wasn't true. No one did. Saddam Hussein's henchmen really did dump bodies in the river, and, later, so did other factions; and, gruesomely, the *shabout* fish started eating the corpses. There was a rumour that some Muslim clerics put a fatwa on eating *shabout*. Even if they didn't, *masgouf* is tragically tainted.

So is the Tigris. Long ago, before it was a graveyard for people, it was a graveyard for books. When the Mongols sacked Baghdad in 1258, they threw so many books into the river that some say it ran black with ink, and others say the books clogged up the river, forming a bridge so heavy that it would support the weight of a man on a horse. The books were taken from the Bayt al-Hikma (House of Wisdom), the dynamic, diverse library and academy that had made Baghdad the intellectual capital of the world, the jewel of the Abbasid caliphate, which had been going strong since 750. I am embarrassed to admit I know most about the Abbasids from the *Iznogoud* comics by *Asterix* writer René

Goscinny, illustrated by Jean Tabary, where the grand vizier, five foot tall in his pointy slippers, is constantly scheming to BE CALIPH INSTEAD OF THE CALIPH!

Even if the Tigris recovered from the more recent horrors, it has also been devastated by climate change, pollution, dumping of chemical waste and sewage, ill-advised dam schemes, mining gravel and sand from the riverbed and by desperate Iraqis using dynamite to fish. Some have even said it's drying up, and that in a horrible future, Iraq will no longer be 'the land of two rivers'.

The toxic combination of climate change, political oppression and bad policies is also why I'll probably never get to eat another food, *khreet*, a dayglo-yellow street snack made out of reeds from the marshes in southern Iraq, in the flood lands of the Tigris and the Euphrates. The reeds were used for boats once, round boats called *guffas* made of woven reeds coated with pitch to make them waterproof. The great Assyriologist Irving Finkel thinks Noah's ark was a giant *guffa*, and that the gopher wood of the Torah might have come from the Assyrian word for reeds: *giparu*. In his translation of a recently discovered clay tablet, part of another Babylonian epic telling the story of the Flood, which is even older than *Gilgamesh*, dated to (incredibly) eighteenth century BCE, its hero Atrahasis is told:

> 'Wall, wall! Reed wall, reed wall!
> Atrahasis, pay heed to my advice,
> That you may live for ever!
> Destroy your house, build a boat . . .'

This might mean that he lived in a reed house which he tore down to build his ark. Before there were bridges across the Tigris in Baghdad, there were *guffas* strung together in a line to form a bridge which you crossed by stepping from boat to boat.

There are still reed houses in the marshes where I've always wanted to go; to punt a sleek, narrow canoe slowly through mazy paths made by water buffalo treading through the tall green reeds, to see flocks of migrating birds reflected in the wide-open water.

Khreet is made by gathering reeds when they are fat with yellow pollen, stripping off the pollen, drying it out in the hot sun, mixing it with sugar and steaming it in a pot sealed with marsh mud until it clumps. Apparently it tastes crunchy, chalky and a little bit sweet. It is particularly associated with Iraqi Jews, but no one really knows why. Iraqi food historian Nawal Nasrallah wonders if it was because the baby Moses was saved by being put in a basket of reeds, a theory I love even though it probably isn't true.

When Saddam Hussein crushed the 1991 Shia uprising, the surviving rebels fled to the marshes. He followed them and drained the marshes to just 7 per cent of their former size. Millions of birds changed their migration routes or nearly went extinct, and the reeds had fewer and fewer places to grow. When Hussein was ousted, the Iraqi government and the UN worked to recover the marshes, and some Marsh Arabs took matters into their own hands and simply tore down dykes and embankments. It is working. The birds are returning. Reeds are growing back. But it is taking a long time.

In 2021 a friend of mine, artist Eloise Moody, asked my mother for a shirt. She was working on an installation at the London Wetlands Centre in Barnes, tracing the migration routes of birds visiting the wetlands and finding people from the places the birds came from, asking each for a shirt she would make into a windsock and exhibit. A lot of birds come to Barnes from Iraq, so I introduced Eloise to my mother. When Covid restrictions lifted, my mother, my son and I went to see her shirt fluttering with the others in the wind above the marsh. *The Drift* was beautiful. The windsocks looked like birds and, all together, like a murmuration. But it also felt desperately sad because while the birds could go back, the people couldn't.

At least, we couldn't. We can't.

It has always been a criminal offence in Iraq to have any connection with Israel – a law clearly targeted at Iraqi Jews who mostly had a connection to Israel whether we wanted to or not. In 2021, at a conference in Erbil, Iraqis asked their government to make peace with Israel, and also to open the door for Iraqi Jews to visit, to reconnect, to heal. My mother's friend, journalist and activist Linda Menuhin, even spoke at the conference, if only via Zoom. It was a moment of real hope – which was instantly dashed. The very next day, some participants got death threats and the government threatened to imprison all three hundred of them, called the conference illegal and started making arrests. Some of the participants, understandably, took back what they'd said and apologised. A few months later, the Iraqi government doubled down, making it not just a criminal but a death penalty offence to have any association with Israel.

Sometimes I tell people this, and they scoff that of course I could go to Iraq. There are ways. I would just have to be careful, or brave, or careful *and* brave. Journalist friends have offered to find me a fixer, a driver. I know one Iraqi Jew who defied the law – and maybe there are others. Maybe the law is just political theatre, because they haven't executed anyone yet. But I don't want to be the test case. I don't want to risk my life. Maybe I could go to Iraq and escape death, but I couldn't go to Iraq and feel safe. I couldn't go and speak any Arabic because even with my shockingly bad accent, they'd still know I was Jewish the moment I opened my mouth. And even in English I wouldn't be able to say why I was there. It would be a terrified, furtive, dangerous, silenced way to visit Iraq where, towards the end, my family lived terrified, furtive, dangerous, silenced lives. It doesn't feel like it would be healing or nostalgic, not a homecoming or a holiday, more a plunging back into the horrors my family fled from in the first place.

And anyway, it isn't just about going back *there* but about going back *then*. To eat *masgouf*, to eat *khreet*, I'd have to make a journey in time as well as space. I'd have to go back to the Iraq of my parents or grandparents. I'd have to reverse what has happened, not just to the Jews but to all the Iraqis, and to the country itself. And I couldn't do that.

For a long time the weight of this made me feel like it was futile to even bother building my ark, let alone loading it with what I could save of my language or my culture. What was the point when we couldn't go back? Why learn the words for things and places I would never see? Reading *Lose Your Mother*, Saidiya Hartman's extraordinary account of going to Ghana, I started to become unstuck. Hartman didn't go to Ghana to reclaim her African heritage, as others had, inspired by Alex Haley's *Roots*. She understood that return was impossible, that 'For me, the rupture was the story'. But instead of being crushed by the rupture, she made a value out of reckoning with the slave trade, and trying to understand how it still affects the descendants of enslaved people. The rupture was the story for me too, and it felt useful to strive to understand how the past still affects my community, and not just my community, because the story is bigger than us now – not least because Mizrahi Jews and their descendants make up more than half the Jewish population of Israel. Our stories are not being told enough, and even when they are told, a refusal to listen seems to go to the heart of the way the Middle East is so polarised, why its conflicts seem so intractable, why communication feels so impossible. So many times I've said I am an Iraqi Jew and been questioned about it, told 'you mean you're mixed' or 'which parent is which?' or just 'how weird', which actually was refreshing because it was often what the other comments really meant. My friend Marina Benjamin once said that when she was studying Arabic in London, the other students couldn't compute her identity. They found the idea of an Iraqi Jew a 'logical impossibility'. Worn down by this kind of conversation, I once wrote an article saying being Iraqi Jewish sounded like an oxymoron – and regretted it. My identity only sounds 'weird' or 'wrong' or 'oxymoronic' if you see the Middle East in binary terms, and if you assume that the default Iraqi is Muslim, which doesn't just leave out Jews but also Christians and other faiths. At a discussion in London in 2003 about Iraq's future, representatives of various groups were invited to explain their identities to the audience, but when it came to the Shia representative's turn, he joked that he didn't need to, because he came from the majority. I wasn't the only one who found this horribly uneasy. I wished I had an identity I could be carefree enough to joke about, but in its absence it felt important not to dwell on what was lost but to keep talking about what was still here. Ideally in Judeo-Iraqi Arabic.

The Flood might still be coming but I had my ark, and now it was time to fill it with everything I might need for my journey.

Keeping

How to pack an ark

I wanted to learn from Noah now, to focus on what I was keeping, not what I was losing. One evening I described my son as 'half Iraqi Jewish' and my friend Rachel said, 'No, he's Iraqi Jewish *and*' and it made me feel excited about the idea that identity-making could be creative and joyful, about adding rather than taking away. That he could keep and save, not lose. That, faced with a vanishing world, he could stand on the ark and whatever he needed would just come to him, two by two, like in the song, *hurrah hurrah*.

No one knows how all the animals were supposed to have squeezed on. We read picture books which show giraffes poking their heads out of the roof, and elephants squirting water at dolphins leaping behind. Creationists often try to make the numbers work by arguing that the fish swam in the flood waters and the birds flew above, so it was just the mammals. I once visited a creationist zoo near Bristol with a scale model of the ark, with plastic dinosaurs marching up the gangplank along with a zebra paired with a horse – because, they claimed, evolution never happened, and everything that *had* existed still did. To prove this, there was a map of dinosaur sightings in the UK. There was also a poster offering marriage counselling, explaining that, just like Noah and his wife on the ark, modern couples might sometimes feel cooped up and overwhelmed by their caring responsibilities. I started wondering if the song focused on the animals arriving, because it was so neat, so soothing, compared with the rest of the story, the horrific Flood, the loss of life, the loss of a world. Compared with all that, the idea of Noah and his wife counting the animals as they come aboard was as relaxing as those Instagram reels of influencers, packing perfect capsule holiday wardrobes. But in real life, decisions about what to take or leave aren't made that way.

After Russia invaded Ukraine, I read playwright Natal'ya Vorozhbit's account of the imperfect, painful decisions she made about what to take as she fled. She took her daughter, her mother and their cat. Money and ID, and her rings because she remembered that people in books always took jewellery. She regretted leaving her photos, her new moisturiser, her plants, which would die, and the food in her freezer. She wrote that she also left behind her heart. And she *couldn't* take her husband or her daughter's father, because they had to fight for their country. She couldn't take her friends, the film they had been making, or the chestnut trees about to bloom. She couldn't take the theatre she was about to open. All her choices were impossible and most weren't even choices.

I thought (too much) about what I'd take on my ark if I had to leave in a hurry. I imagined it as just one suitcase, like my dad was allowed, along with all the Jews who left Iraq in 1950–1. Authorities even specified what had to go in the suitcases: three summer outfits, three winter outfits, one blanket, six pairs of underwear, socks, sheets, one wedding ring, one watch, one thin bracelet and no more than 50 dinars. No photographs – although some people managed to get them out. I couldn't think of anything my dad had from Baghdad or his childhood, and when I asked him, he said, 'Hardly anything that I can remember. A box for tobacco but I don't know whether I kept it. I remember I had a small knife. And they told me you can't take this with you. The people, the customs. Because they said it could be dangerous. So they took it from me.' This happened a lot. To get anything precious out of the country, Iraqi Jews stuffed it into chickens, or sewed it into the hems of their clothes. One woman baked her jewellery into a cake to get it out of Iraq, telling no one, not even her family, so the only person taking the risk was herself. At the airport, an official was unexpectedly kind, and the woman had to watch, in silent horror, as her husband gave him the cake to say thank you.

Nothing else apart from – maybe – a tobacco box? I asked my dad. 'Nothing,' he said. No keepsakes, no talismans, no heirlooms, no toys, no books, no childhood treasures, no junk. I think about how even for an overnight trip my son crams his backpack with soft toys, favourite pencils, special stones, treasured books, and imagine my father as a child getting on a plane to a new country with next to nothing. I have never seen a photograph of him in Baghdad. I have no idea what he looked like as a child. His whole world exists only in memories and in words – in a language that is going too.

My mother and her family took more. They were each allowed twenty kilos of luggage. Some of their choices seem bizarre, like my grandmother's massive orange quilt. A tape of Beatles songs my mother had recorded off a pirate radio station. Nothing unique, just songs that could be listened to any day of the week, but we played it till it wore out, and loved it for the story. She also packed a wooden box with a rather louche picture of Scheherazade. Some jewellery, including a gold heart with (the story goes) a dent my mother made in it when she was teething. Two rolling pins, wooden, very thin and better for pastry than any others I have used. A blouse my great-grandmother crocheted from a *Vogue* pattern maybe a century ago, which I used to just about be able to squeeze into. Three kohl pots, in the shape of a peacock and two trees, which I have purloined from my mother, the only things I have from Baghdad. The yellow ID card they were forced, like all Jews, to carry in the sixties. Hardly any photographs because in Iraq in the fifties and sixties it became more and more dangerous for Jews to say they had family in Israel. Even though everyone knew that 125,000 Iraqi Jews had gone there. It must have seemed insane not to be able to mention it. My grandmother told me, 'I burned so many photos. If they had my brothers in them or my mother. Because if people asked me where they were, what could I say?'

In the wake of this erasure, the pictures we did have felt like evidence, proof *we were there*. With my mother I pored over the slim pile. A group shot of my grandfather's family in Basra, with his father in the centre wearing a *tarboosh*. One child, sitting on the lap of a great-uncle I never met, was caught in motion, blurred in the act of (possibly) turning to hug his father. My mother guessed he might have been her father's brother, who died at only seven. I liked the pictures of my grandmother's wedding, smiling like a supermodel in a sheeny white dress, surrounded by bridesmaids with flowers in their hair and a pageboy in a sailor suit. In some of the pictures she's on the arm of her handsome moustachioed brother in a gleaming white jacket; she must have hidden those. I loved the one of my mother in a pretty ruffled dress, being held by her father on a carousel horse at the Luna Park fairground, because they both look so happy, so normal; it could be anywhere. So could the one of my grandmother posing next to her gramophone, impeccably manicured, in a pencil dress, and the bit of flickering cine film of my uncle's bar mitzvah, the women swishing about in fabulous sixties dresses. But there are two of my mother in front of the great arch of Ctesiphon just outside Baghdad, which couldn't be anywhere but Iraq, and which capture something unequivocal about her time there. She's all sixties glamour – big hair, shift dress, insouciantly knotted silk scarf – and behind her is the ancient arch, 1,700 years old, gorgeous and ruined, a vast brick parabola, the widest single span in the world, which is all that's left of the ancient city.

What went on their arks – let alone what was left of what they packed, decades on – felt so scant and meagre. Fragments to shore up against our ruins. Reading an essay by an archivist called Terry Cook titled 'We are what we keep', arguing that the physical objects we choose to hold on to, and to pass on, end up defining us, I felt depressed. If my family were defined by what they kept hold of, well, there wasn't much.

The three *mak-halas* (kohl pots) sit on my windowsill, next to where I write. For years they sat on my mother's dressing table and I sat on it too, swinging my legs, watching her blow-dry her hair, and moving the peacock's tail up and down with a satisfying click. The kohl pots were mass-produced, not valuable, but they assumed an outsized importance in the years after my mother brought them here. She never used the kohl because, she said, it was made of lead and could be poisonous. She taught me to say *ghadoo y kehlooha wu emooha* (they came to put kohl on her eyes and instead they blinded her), which is supposed to mean that you try to do good but it backfires – but if the kohl was poisonous, maybe it could actually blind you. So I never tried it. Even though I really wanted to. It felt like a portal to the past, a way of painting myself back into the photographs from Baghdad; to make myself look like someone who could have been at those parties, or the party in the film *Baghdad Twist* by Iraqi Jewish film-maker Joe Balass, built around a flickering home movie of a wedding in Iraq in 1965, with partygoers dancing the twist, in saturated Super 8 colour, or day-tripping to Ctesiphon with my mother. I wanted to claim my true inheritance: a winged eye. I wanted to look like Scheherazade on her way to save the women with her stories. I wanted to be invincible.

I didn't want to get poisoned, though, so I did some research. The first thing I learned was that, long ago, Iraqi Jews smeared kohl on their newborns' eyelids to protect them from *eyn ra'ah*, the evil eye. I felt stabbed by guilt. What kind of mother doesn't protect her child from the evil eye? My mother didn't paint my eyelids but she did pin so many lucky charms to my Babygro that they weighed me down, and, later, sewed salt into the hems of my clothes. Before I had my son I was clear I wouldn't pass this on. I didn't want him to grow up scared, to believe that there really was a dark force roaming around looking for jealous people, so it could go into their eyes and curse anyone they looked at. I read studies showing that superstitious people were more likely to also be anxious, depressed and obsessive-compulsive; after all, there wasn't much difference between always putting salt in your pockets or carrying a blue stone and, say, washing your hands a certain way or counting to a certain number before doing it. At what point did compensatory compulsions, as psychiatrists call them, stop being harmless ways of soothing anxiety and start creating anxiety about whether you could influence the future? This felt dangerously close to believing that you could worry yourself safe, alert to every possible danger, prepared for every kind of risk. I didn't want my son to be a worrier.

I'd tried to break the chain before – to stop believing in the evil eye – and failed. I was twelve. We were going to a henna party for a cousin who was getting married, and my mum wanted to sew a sachet of salt into the hem of my dress, as usual, to ward off the evil eye, but this time I said no. I didn't believe in it, I thought it was ridiculous, I'd be fine. But at the party, while we were dancing and putting dark, sticky henna on the bride's fingers, someone came too close with a candle and my hair caught fire. After that I carried salt. Or I wore a *hamsa*, which in Iraq I would have called a *kaf* for the palm with the lucky blue stone at its centre. When I found out I was pregnant on holiday in Kefalonia, I went straight to one of the touristy seaside shops and bought a bracelet made of knotted blue string with a small blue eye. I felt safer once it was on, and I didn't take it off until the anaesthetist made me. As I read my way through my pregnancy there were so many books about how different cultures bring up children, from *Our Babies, Ourselves* to *French Children Don't Throw Food* and *Battle Hymn of the Tiger Mother*; I imagined writing *Iraqi Jewish Children Always Carry Salt*. I thought I would steer clear of superstition, but when my son was born early and small – just three pounds and fifteen ounces – and I stroked his tiny foot as he lay in his incubator, scrunched up and scrawny, covered in wires, blue under the light that was treating his jaundice, fed by a nose tube, I wanted him to know I was there, not just me and his dad but all the family and the ancestors too. I wanted a ritual. I wanted him to be protected. I said the Jewish prayer for new things, *Shehecheyanu*, which thanks God for granting us life and sustaining us and bringing us to this season, which felt right, because I felt glad and amazed to have been granted this new life, to have been sustained to this season.

Our rabbi suggested a blessing specifically for babies who 'burst forth early surprising the midwives' which I loved, especially because it came from Ritualwell, a clever feminist group which creates and curates new Jewish rituals for 'Jews and fellow seekers'. Browsing their website I found rituals for people and experiences that had been excluded; like re-entering life after rehab, mourning a relative when you are estranged from your family, and even having your first shame-free orgasm. As I said the words to my baby, I cried, feeling reconnected, but also innovative, and awakened to wonder. Meanwhile, outside the hospital, my mum was zigzagging through north London to buy sweets and nuts for the decorated bags called *shashsha* which Iraqi Jews send to friends and family to welcome babies into the world.

When we moved a few months later, I realised I'd amassed more protective objects than I knew. A big blue glass evil eye a friend brought me from Turkey. A brass *hamsa* woven with red thread another friend brought from Israel. The mezuzahs, which are religious, not superstitious, but occupied the same psychological space. In a daze of early parenthood, I grabbed my hammer and started putting them up, until every room was protected. I put up the evil eyes too, hedging my bets, and tucked my *afsa* into my jewellery box. In Iraq I might have pinned this Iraqi amulet to my son's clothes. It is beautiful, made of gold strands woven around two oak gall nuts, with a gold *hamsa* hanging down from it, a blue stone in the middle. Sometimes I wore it on a chain to parties and sometimes I thought it brought me luck. I *did* resist trying to ward off evil by stringing garlic or a wolf's tooth, possibly plated in yellow gold, around his neck, an older Iraqi Jewish tradition.

And of course I didn't paint his eyelids with kohl, even though it was supposed to protect children. I was glad I'd listened to my mother's warnings when I learned that lead-based kohl is banned in the US after a case where a mother put a Nigerian kohl called *tiro* on her child – who ended up in hospital with lead poisoning. She'd only been trying to protect her child. But then I read that not all lead-based kohl is dangerous. When scientists tested samples from ancient Egyptian kohl pots they found that they contained a *good* form of lead which boosted the body's production of nitric oxide and revved up the immune system, so it *did* protect, maybe not against the evil eye but against infection and flies and dust and sand and sun. What tipped me into actually deciding to try the kohl (on myself if not on my son) was reading that traditional Middle Eastern kohl isn't made out of lead at all, but out of cloth, soaked in olive oil and burned down to ash, so it goes a dark, smoky, velvety black. This was probably what was in my mother's pots, not lead at all. I decided to try them.

I opened the peacock first, taking the stick out gingerly. But when I put it to my eyelid, there was nothing. I tried again, jabbing the stick hard into the pot and pushing it around. Again, nothing. Not a speck. I tried the big tree then the little tree. But it was no good. There was no kohl left. I felt bereft. I had a perfectly adequate Rimmel pencil in a jam jar. I could get traditional Arab kohl online and refill the pots. But I had counted on that kohl being there and it was gone. Just another loss.

When I told my mother, she explained, for the first time, how she got the kohl pots. She'd been leaving Iraq. She'd gone to say goodbye to her university friends and mentioned that she wished she had a kohl pot to take with her. That evening one of her friends shocked her parents by turning up (a man! at the house!) with the three kohl pots as a parting gift. They'd gone straight into her suitcase. She'd never used them to get ready for parties. She'd barely gone to any parties in Baghdad. The parties had only ever existed in my imagination. The kohl pots's story had always been about leaving and losing. Maybe they'd never even had kohl in them in the first place. As I put the sticks back in the pots, I wondered if maybe we're not what we keep but what we lose. Except that I still had them, and somehow they managed both to carry the sadness of what was lost, and also to be consoling, chunky in my hands, a comfort, kohl or no kohl. I made a promise to myself to look after them, to (one day) hand them down, with the patina of memories that made them precious, so they would go on gathering meaning for generations to come. They might be almost all I had from *there* but at least I had them, at least they were *here*.

In the British Museum

I was in the British Museum gazing at an Iraqi kohl stick (the pot was lost) from the Abbasid era, so sometime between 749 and 1258. It was tiny. Seven centimetres long and so corroded that no one can be sure if it is bronze or brass. It was mottled with green rust, chunkier and bumpier at one end (perhaps to make it easier to hold) and tapering down at the other. I came because I wanted some lineage (grand as that sounds) for my *mak-halas*, and because it occurred to me that I'd been worrying so much about what my family had kept and saved that I'd nearly forgotten that museums, like archives, were supposed to do this *for* us, for everyone, and on a bigger scale. And not just things; the British Museum was driven by 'a deep belief in objects as reliable witnesses and documents of human history', as if the artefacts could talk. In *The Museum Makers*, Rachel Morris writes 'it is the dance between things and their stories that matters', that this is 'the magic of museums'. In Judeo-Iraqi Arabic – in common with some other Iraqi languages or dialects – the same word, *hkiyi*, is used for both *story* and *thing*, as if to underline the ways they are connected. So what stories were being told about the kohl stick? Why was it in London? And why was it on display in the Iran room when it was found in Samarra, near Baghdad? And how did I feel about it?

I wasn't the only person asking these sorts of questions. The British Museum, the world's first national public museum, once revolutionary for opening its doors to women, people of colour and the working class, is now loud with debate about whether some (or even most) of its artefacts should be returned to their countries of origin. In 2020, the museum confronted its difficult origins by taking the bust of Hans Sloane, whose epic, omnivorous collection of 'curiosities' started the museum, off its pedestal and putting it in a display cabinet that gave some context about his murky past. Some of his curiosities were stolen from or gathered by slaves in Jamaica during the time that, as a doctor, he also 'treated' sick slaves to force them back to work by, for example, applying a pan full of burning coals to a man's head and lighting candles at his hands and feet. His collecting sprees were funded by his wife's money, which came from slavery. As a child visiting the museum I knew nothing of this. Later I vaguely knew that Nana Mouskouri was campaigning, in her signature big glasses, for the return of what I was taught at school to call the Elgin Marbles, after the man who took them, but are now called the Parthenon Marbles, after the place he took them from.

No one was campaigning for this kohl stick to go back. It was not a cause célèbre like the Marbles, or the bronzes seized from Benin in Nigeria in 1897, in what Dan Hicks, in his pointedly titled book *The Brutish Museums*, calls an act of colonial, capitalist greed and ultraviolence; or the many human remains from all over the world, which were where the debates about return first started, with communities asking for the right to bury their ancestors at home, so their graves could be visited, their deaths mourned, their ghosts put to rest. Here, I was complicit. Although hugely sympathetic to the calls for return, I also spent hours in the 'mummy galleries', the busiest in the museum, with my son furiously sketching, asking gruesome questions, and clamouring for mummy key rings, mummy magnets, mummy pencil cases, and badges that said 'I love my mummy'.

Although the kohl stick doesn't appear on any lists of contested objects, it does contribute to a mind-blowing statistic: the museum holds more Iraqi antiquities than any museum outside of Iraq. I'd seen *Detectorists*. I knew you couldn't just take what you dug up. So how had all these artefacts got here? I set out to trace the provenance of just the one kohl stick, hoping its story would help me pin down my feelings about why it was here and whether it should stay. From a trip to the museum's Iraq Study Room, I learned that it was excavated in Samarra by the German archaeologist Ernst Emil Herzfeld, and acquired by the museum in 1921, a date which made my ears prick up because it was a pivotal year for Iraq, when the country went from being governed by the British to having its own king and a promise of independence. So if the kohl stick was acquired at the start of the year, it might have been an entirely British decision, but if it was later then Iraqis might have been involved or at least consulted.

By 1921, Europeans and Americans had been excavating for a century in what was then Mesopotamia, part of the vast Ottoman Empire. Western archaeologists sneered that the Ottomans only cared if they dug up gold, and thought priceless carvings and tablets were just 'stones'; but they also complained that the Ottomans constantly stalled and disrupted excavations, tied archaeologists in red tape, and tried to stop them taking antiquities. It seemed they very much cared. The Western archaeologists said Iraqis didn't care either, but that didn't square with the passion and commitment of the only Iraqi archaeologist of the period, Hormuzd Rassam. He described his team of Iraqi diggers finding a carving of the lion-hunting, enemy-torturing, book-devouring Assyrian king Ashurbanipal and joyously, spontaneously bursting into song and dance. They cared.

When Rassam, whose family were Chaldeans, descended from Assyrians, uncovered Ashurbanipal's face, he was encountering his own long-lost king. And yet, although he was excavating near his home, and it was his story, his heritage,

Rassam couldn't just dig. He had to tangle with three separate colonial powers first. He needed a permit to dig from the Ottomans; he needed permission from the British (because they and the French had divided Iraq into separate digging zones) as well as sponsorship from the British Museum; and then he had to dig secretly, by moonlight, to avoid being stopped by the French, because he realised that what he was looking for was in 'their' zone. Even though Rassam's finds – over 50,000 of them – went to the British Museum, it didn't stop the British press calling him 'a foreigner in an Englishman's position', as if it was more natural for English people to excavate Iraq than Iraqis. It's painful to read how Rassam contorted himself to fit in, studying at Oxford, converting to Christianity, declaring he'd rather be a chimney sweeper in England than a pasha in Turkey, joining the British Foreign Office and, when his Iraqi diggers got anxious about who was profiting from their work and that they might be desecrating their ancestors' graves, cajoling them back to work, by joking that the graves they were digging might belong, instead, to their forefathers' mortal enemies.

After all this, the museum turned on him. They sent a sly young man called E. A. Wallis Budge to Iraq to investigate Rassam, and he claimed Rassam was selling off his best finds, leaving the BM only 'rubbish'; that the overseers were Rassam's relatives and also thieves (because, SIGH, it's not at *all* a racist trope that everyone in a foreign country is both related and criminal). Rassam sued for slander. He won, but he was left with colossal legal fees and frozen out by the museum, while Budge had his fees paid by friends, and scored both a promotion and a knighthood. Rassam died in 1910, his name still mud.

When, four years later, the First World War started, and Britain invaded Mesopotamia, the archaeologists came too. By 1917, the British Museum was excavating there, and in 1918, Budge's old assistant was using prisoners of war as forced diggers, which some British diplomats thought was a bit much, raging that archaeologists were 'always trying to "suck" us', and that it was 'improper for the British Museum to send out people to pillage Mesopotamia under cover of the military occupation'. And then the museum demanded a huge cache of antiquities they hadn't even excavated themselves – including, I *think*, the kohl stick.

Herzfeld, the archaeologist who had dug it up, was a dapper polyglot known for documenting his digs in meticulous watercolours and photographs. He kept on excavating until the British were nearly at the gates of the ruined Abbasid city, and then rapidly packed what he could into ninety-odd cases, and fled. (This wouldn't be his last displacement. Although he considered himself a Christian, he had Jewish grandparents and years later would have to leave Iran too after an antisemitic Iranian minister accused him of stealing antiquities; and then, when he went home to Germany, the Nazis forced all academics of Jewish descent out of their jobs, so he had to leave again, for London.)

The British army didn't know what to do with the antiquities he'd left in Samarra. The British War Office Trophies Committee decided they were spoils of war and wanted to just take them, but diplomats at the India Office and the Foreign Office objected. The army, confused, transferred the cases to the office of the British high commissioner, Percy Cox, and that's when Gertrude Bell had a peek. Maybe she spotted the kohl stick. It was the kind of thing that would have intrigued her. She was mad for archaeology – and for beauty. She wrote so much in her letters home about clothes and cosmetics that when they were published after her death, she was mocked for being silly and frivolous. But she could be fierce when she wanted to be. After looking at the cases, she fired off a memo arguing that Britain should safeguard Mesopotamia's antiquities, not by sending them to London but by building a museum in Baghdad. But the British Museum said only they could properly look after the Samarra finds. Leaving them in Iraq would be, they said, 'cruelty to antiquities'.

In the end, Winston Churchill and T. E. Lawrence ignored everyone and shipped the antiquities to London. The Foreign Office were annoyed, but Cox was pleased, admitting that the sudden decision, taken just before the Iraqi government took over, meant that 'to discuss them . . .would be unnecessary'. This made me quite angry.

It probably made Bell angry too, because she continued to advocate for Iraq's antiquities. She impressed the new king, Faisal, so much with her love of Iraq's history that he made her Iraq's first director of antiquities. In 1924 she got a law passed to protect them, and two years later she opened the Iraq Museum. But she couldn't fight for it to house the Samarra antiquities because that same year she killed herself in Baghdad, maybe because of unrequited love (for Cornwallis? for Faisal? there are so many theories), or maybe because she didn't want to retire to Britain, as Vita Sackville-West reported after visiting her – 'what should she do in England, eating out her heart for Iraq'.

Bell's successor (also British) was caught smuggling treasures out of the country, and the Iraqi government expelled him and vowed to protect 'the treasures which the grandfathers left as a bequest to their grandsons'. Faisal's director of education Sati al-Husri wanted to use archaeology to bring the country together. This set him on a collision course with Britain – and with Agatha Christie's husband.

Christie had come to Iraq to heal a broken heart and she fell for dashing British archaeologist Max Mallowan. She probably didn't first snog him on a dig after he told her a god made the Tigris by ejaculating, as happens in the entertainingly schlocky film *Agatha and the Curse of Ishtar*. But she did fall in love with archaeology; 'The lure of the past,' she wrote, 'came up to grab me. To see a dagger slowly appearing, with its gold glint, through the sand was romantic.' She discovered a knack for joining fragments and used her face cream to clean ancient ivories. She married Mallowan – and promptly wrote a novel about an archaeologist killing his wife! *Murder in Mesopotamia* also has a subplot about stolen artefacts, but it's all quite high-spirited, unlike what actually happened when Mallowan was accused of taking artefacts he wasn't entitled to.

It was 1933, the digging season was over and it was time for what Christie called 'the burning moment of "The Division"' where, in 'agony', the British Museum would divide the finds with the Iraq Museum. Iraq had just become officially independent, in 1932, and for the first time, they asked questions about what was leaving the country. The British Museum, furious, demanded 'some explanation . . . some kind of apology', Mallowan left Iraq in high dudgeon, and the British Embassy muttered that al-Husri was drafting a new 'rabidly nationalistic' antiquities law, even though all he was doing at that point was enforcing Bell's law properly. A year later, he upped the ante by asking for the Samarra antiquities too. The museum grudgingly said they'd send them 'now that a Museum exists' –as if they'd only just noticed the Iraq Museum, which was eight years old – but of the ninety-odd cases they'd taken, just two came back, containing only 'archaeological junk'. The best pieces had been scattered among other Western museums, or stayed in London. Including, *probably*, the kohl stick.

These are the thickets you have to slash your way through to decolonise museums. And Iraq wasn't even a colony, just a mandate, and not for very long. I asked my mother what she thought about this when she was growing up in Baghdad, and she shrugged. 'It was hard to study history because the textbooks kept changing every time there was a new government.' Whenever I asked about Iraq, the answer was bigger than the question.

Having worked out how it might have got here, I was very clear, in my head, that the kohl stick should go back. But my heart felt differently. If the kohl stick was in Iraq, I couldn't see it. No Iraqi exile could. Not the Jews; not the many other Iraqis who left because of the war with Iran; not the Assyrians persecuted by Saddam Hussein, and then again by Isis; not the Shias and Kurds who left because they fought Hussein in the First Gulf War and then he turned on them; not any of the many, many Iraqis who left after the US-led invasion in 2003 and the chaos that came after; not the Yazidis displaced by Isis's genocidal campaign in 2014; not the Iraqis who were still arriving in the UK in small boats; not any of the women who went to school with my mother (the only Jew in her class) and who left for many different reasons over many years, so that, as far as we knew, not one was left in Iraq. Some could go to Iraq to visit. But most, like me, could not. It was a comfort, a connection, to be able to visit this tiny fragment of Baghdad in Bloomsbury. It felt important to hold both ideas at once – that the kohl stick *should* return, but it might be important to Iraqi refugees that it did *not*.

Other other other

I don't know why the kohl stick was exhibited in the Iran room. Just like Judeo-Iraqi Arabic appearing in the wrong place on the endangered languages map, it seemed that everything I searched for fell down the cracks of other people's classification systems. We didn't fit. An Iraqi Jewish friend said that when she filled in forms, 'I just tick OTHER OTHER OTHER until it lets me write what I am.'

There was another artefact in the Iran room which was dug up in Iraq, by an Iraqi (Rassam of course). The Cyrus Cylinder was filed under Iran because the proclamation on it was dictated by the founder of the Persian Empire, Cyrus the Great, when he conquered Babylon in 539 BCE. In his proclamation Cyrus made the radical promise to return stolen treasure and also, amazingly, to reverse forced migration, to allow *people* to go home. My people. Babylonian Jews.

The cylinder didn't look particularly significant. It was just twenty-three centimetres long, cracked and battered, and over a third of it had chipped off. It looked like a corn on the cob someone had taken a messy bite out of. But it came with a big story. A very contested story.

Cyrus conquered Babylon apparently without a fight because the Babylonians were so happy to be freed from tyranny. (And yes, this sounds uncomfortably like other, more recent claims about 'regime change' in Iraq.) Apparently Babylon's ruler, Belshazzar, chose not to defend his city but instead to throw a massive party. Right in the middle of it, he got a shock: God's hand appeared out of thin air and started writing on the palace wall.

It was a big moment for Babylonian Jews. The only person who could read the writing was one of us: the prophet Daniel. He'd been deported to Babylon from Judah by Nebuchadnezzar along with so many other Jews. For most of them, this exile was humiliating and miserable. As Psalm 137 goes, 'By the rivers of Babylon, there we sat down, yea, we wept, when we remembered Zion.' The psalm is a messy, splintered shriek of anguish, a trauma response not *entirely* captured by the Boney M version, 'Rivers of Babylon'. In the psalm, the Jews are tormented by their captors sadistically taunting them with requests for them to sing their songs. Instead, they vow to remember Jerusalem and have revenge fantasies about Babylonian children being dashed against rocks. The loss of the tiny kingdom of Judah must have felt like the end of the world or at least of their people. The Jews had clung to Judah in 727 BCE when the Assyrians had conquered the other Jewish kingdom, Israel, and deported its population, known as the Ten Lost Tribes, who vanished from history. (Although there are many, *many* theories, conspiracies and myths.) When they had first been forced to go to Babylon in 597 BCE, they'd at least been able to take comfort in the fact that Judah still existed, just, under the nominal rule of a Jewish puppet king, Zedekiah. But when he'd rebelled, Nebuchadnezzar had ravaged Judah and besieged Jerusalem, starving its inhabitants for eighteen months before burning down the city, raping and murdering Jews, and deporting another 20,000 to Babylon; looting the Temple dreamed up by King David, and built by his son King Solomon, seizing its gold and silver vessels and the sacred Ark of the Covenant; violently breaking it down so that it tumbled into the valley.

Nebuchadnezzar's sack of Jerusalem was the start of the diaspora, the scattering, of Jews all over the world, but it was also the start of a way of being Jewish, of holding on to Jewish joy, in other places and other ways. While the Jews deported from Israel by the Assyrians disappeared, the Jews deported to Babylon remembered who they were. It was in Babylon that scribes and rabbis whose names are lost collated the Five Books of Moses, forging an even clearer sense of identity for the exiles. In Babylon, too, Jews developed new laws and rituals to carry on being Jewish without a temple. They pioneered a way of being Jewish that was portable.

But instead of just pining to return, the prophet Jeremiah told the exiles to 'Build ye houses, and dwell in them: and plant gardens, and eat the fruit of them. Take ye wives, and beget sons and daughters; and take wives for your sons, and give your daughters to husbands, that they may bear sons and daughters . . . And seek the peace of the city . . . for in the peace thereof shall ye have peace.' In other words, stop weeping and live. Connect with your neighbours! Marry! Have babies! Grow veg! Many of the Jews exiled to Babylon took heed, embracing the fabled city glowing with lapis lazuli, Nebuchadnezzar's signature colour, the glazed bricks echoing the blue of the river and the sky, a city so magnificent that the goddess Ishtar was said to wander its gorgeous streets for the sheer pleasure of it. Many found interesting work and roles for themselves in Babylon, and Daniel became indispensable to Nebuchadnezzar, working to interpret his troubled, rococo dreams. Even so, the Babylonians tried to make Daniel worship idols, and when he refused, they threw him into a fiery furnace, but he survived, unsinged, and became even more admired and powerful. So he must have been startled to find Belshazzar boozing from the sacred gold vessels that had been stolen from Jerusalem, and it must have been quite satisfying to tell him that the writing on the wall meant that Babylon would fall.

Why couldn't Belshazzar read God's graffiti himself,

though? I used to think it was because it was in Hebrew. The first time I saw Rembrandt's *Belshazzar's Feast* I felt exhilarated, *included*, by seeing Hebrew on the walls of the National Gallery, along with all those Christian saints and English kings. But in fact the writing in the painting is in Aramaic, which was Belshazzar's language. So why couldn't he read it? Was he illiterate? Or just too drunk? This bothered Rembrandt too, and he consulted a rabbi who said maybe the Aramaic was hard to read because it was written in columns instead of right to left. Rembrandt's Aramaic goes up and down.

If God wanted to give Belshazzar a message, why make it hard to read? Did He want the theatrics? The king panicking, his advisers flummoxed, the Jew coming in to save the day? The Old Testament God could, admittedly, be dramatic. The Talmudic rabbis worried about it too, and wondered if the writing *was* in Hebrew, but was in the wrong alphabet. In Jerusalem, Jews wrote in a script called paleo-Hebrew but in Babylon they adopted the square Aramaic letters which are still used for modern Hebrew today. So maybe, just maybe, the magical writing wasn't in Aramaic but in old Hebrew, and Daniel wasn't a codebreaker but a keeper of ancient secrets, someone who knew you forget alphabets at your peril, who knew a lost script might give you the keys to a kingdom. Anyway, Daniel was right. Babylon did fall. And Cyrus walked in, victorious, and scooped up a wodge of wet clay, shaped it into a cylinder and dictated his proclamation. It was baked dry in the hot sun, then ritually buried. Many Jews – around 40,000 – did take Cyrus up on his offer and went back to rebuild Jerusalem, inspired by Isaiah's call to 'Awake, awake, put on thy strength, O Zion'. These returning Jews, and their descendants, would see the Second Temple dedicated in 515 BCE, in time for Passover. They would see it made enormous, fabulous, numinous by the psychotic Jewish king Herod the Great. They would see Judah survive invasions and power play from vicious empires and brutal internal conflict, until the Romans finally conquered it in 70 CE. During the five-month siege of Jerusalem, the Romans crucified five hundred Jews a day. They destroyed the Temple, plundering its treasures, systematically murdered up to a million Jews, forced Jewish prisoners to fight each other (or wild animals) to death in their circuses, obliterated Jerusalem and built their own city in its place, and, after the Jews revolted again, in 135 CE, barred Jews from the city altogether.

However, not all the Jewish exiles had returned from Babylon when Cyrus made his offer. Many more stayed in Babylon. (And if the story of the Jewish festival of Purim is even half true, one of them, Esther, ended up marrying Cyrus's grandson, King Ahasuerus, and becoming Persia's queen.) What was amazing was that Cyrus gave Babylonian Jews the choice. To stay or to go. And he returned the gold vessels which had been stolen.

If artefacts are ever returned, they go to where they were excavated. So if the cylinder went anywhere it would be Iraq. Iraq doesn't want it though – Iran does. The last shah claimed the cylinder as the world's first bill of human rights. In 1971, he threw a party presenting himself as Cyrus's heir, and borrowed the cylinder to exhibit to his guests, a loan which terrified the Foreign Office who thought Prince Philip might go rogue and try to give it to Iran for good – particularly because the shah had just given him a miniature horse.

In 2010, the museum lent the cylinder to the National Museum of Iran, hoping it would inspire and comfort Iranians who were protesting against President Mahmoud Ahmadinejad. But when it arrived, Ahmadinejad spun the cylinder's story for his own political purposes, welcoming the artefact in a twisted ceremony where he presented an actor dressed as Cyrus with the scarf worn by his brutal paramilitary enforcers, the Basij. The Iranian opposition website Jaras raged that the cylinder had become 'a stranger in its own home'.

A museum in Baghdad

Here's a story about another ark. In May 2003, the Americans had been occupying Baghdad for a month, when Harold Rhode, who worked for the Pentagon and happened to be Jewish, got a tip-off that a rare seventh-century Talmud needed rescuing from the bombed-out basement of the HQ of the *mukhabarat*, Iraq's feared and hated secret police. He found the building flooded with putrid water and raw sewage, and waded in to see a wooden box floating towards him across the water. An ark. Or, actually, a *tiq*, a special wooden case for a Torah scroll, covered with purple velvet and decorated with a pattern of extravagantly blooming roses.

What other treasures might be in there? Rhode got help to start pumping out the water, pulling out what they could find, and drying the items in the sun. The American government sent a refrigerated truck so they wouldn't deteriorate. But what was it all?

It came to be called 'the Iraqi Jewish archive', but it wasn't an archive in the usual sense of a group of things curated and preserved with intention and care. Instead, it was a ragbag of stuff stolen by Saddam's secret police from Jews, and chucked into a basement. The *New York Times* wryly commented that 'very little intelligence was involved in this gathering of intelligence'. There was no seventh-century Talmud; there were school reports, class registers, chemistry textbooks and yearbooks; divorce agreements from Baghdad's rabbinical court; receipts from a Jewish sports centre; phonebooks; newspapers; Hebrew calendars; vaccination certificates; private letters. There was a much later Talmud, from 1793, and several damaged Torah scrolls. At best it was what scholar Jeffrey Spurr called 'stray but meaningful textual vestiges' of Iraq's Jewish community. And it was waterlogged and rotting. The Americans wanted to take it away, arguing that it couldn't be preserved in Baghdad where the Iraq Museum had just been looted (the museum Gertrude Bell had dreamed into being), and the Iraq National Library and Archive (INLA) had been burned *and* looted *twice*, acts of ransacking and vandalism which scholars compared to the cultural apocalypse perpetrated by the Mongols. And yes, the Coalition could have done more to protect the museum and library, and not shrugged it off with Donald Rumsfeld's infamous 'stuff happens'. And *yes*, all this sounded a lot like the conversation about the Samarra antiquities in 1917. But in 2003, Iraq had an antiquities law, and there was no question that the contents of that basement could be considered spoils of war. Not this time. So when they put the tattered, sodden, frozen, intimate remnants of my community on a plane, the Americans made a legal promise to return them to Iraq.

Two decades on, however, it was all still in the US, partly because Iraqi Jews didn't see why what was stolen from us should go back to the country that did the thieving. I read pages and pages of dense legal opinions about it, and impassioned journalism, and angry speech-making. Then I realised the Americans had digitised much of what they'd found so I went online to have a look myself.

I was overwhelmed by the mass of undigested material. The first file I opened was just pages and pages of class rosters for one of the Jewish schools. Everything was yellowed with age, torn, stained by water and by mould and by rust from paper clips, and often so damaged that the writing was illegible. Each file contained hundreds of documents, mostly in Arabic, seemingly in no particular order. Nevertheless, when I drafted in my mum, within minutes we found pictures of people we knew. We found an entrance exam for a Jewish secondary school which asked the children to write twenty lines in English on the subject of 'The Dates of Iraq' and to render in the passive voice sentences including 'People speak English all over the world', 'They have spilt a lot of ink on the floor' and 'They told me that a thief had stolen their camel'. And then we found my grandfather. There was a sheet of notepaper headed with his name, Dr Albert Hakim, printed in ornate English letters on one side and in Arabic on the other, and underneath, in faded blue ink, in his bold slanted writing, he certified someone 'free from illnesses'. A few minutes later we found another. It was incredibly moving to see his handwriting again. I yearned to have his notes, to treasure them. At the very least I wanted them to be kept somewhere I could visit, in the US perhaps, or, better still, in the small Iraqi Jewish museum in Tel Aviv, called the Babylonian Jewry Heritage Centre. This wouldn't happen, though, because Iraq wanted the 'archive' back.

There were some good reasons to return it all to Iraq. Saad Eskander, the visionary Kurdish ex-freedom fighter who ran the INLA between 2003 and 2015 and wrote a heartbreaking blog about it, said, 'It is vital that Iraqis know their history and that they be made aware that Jews were once part of this country.' The Americans made the same argument, more paternalistically, suggesting the archive could 'remind the Iraqi people, and especially younger Iraqis, that for centuries Jews and other minorities lived in Iraq in relative harmony with their Muslim compatriots'. I could imagine Eskander looking after the flotsam and jetsam of my vanished community, building a museum like the two Jewish museums in Morocco. However, there were still Jews in Morocco; those who left were allowed to keep their citizenship; and during the Second World War the Moroccan king protected the country's Jews from the Nazis. It was a very different story in Iraq. I was also concerned about what might happen if my grandfather's notes fell into unsympathetic hands. What if they were destroyed, or a weird, bad story was told about them? And why did Iraq need them anyway, when it could easily fill a museum with the contents of the homes Iraqi Jews had to leave behind (like my father's and my mother's), and when the Iraq Museum and the INLA already had thousands of Jewish objects, books and art? The more I thought about it, the more this idea of a museum about the Jews in Iraq, full of stolen goods and impossible for Iraqi Jews to visit, didn't feel like a place of learning or healing but more like the museum the Nazis were rumoured to be making with what they stole from the Jews: a Museum of an Extinct Race.

Some of the Torah fragments found in the basement were beyond repair, which meant that in Jewish tradition, they had to be buried. The ripped and damaged scrolls were lowered into a grave in an American cemetery in a place called, with bizarre resonance, West Babylon. I saw pictures of Iraqi Jewish exiles helping to shovel dirt into the grave. I was glad the shreds of Torah were buried in the States because they couldn't have been buried in Iraq, not properly. A Jewish funeral needs ten Jewish men and there were not ten Jews left in Iraq, let alone ten Jewish men.

Iraq 'n' Roll

Feeling sad about keeping, saving or remembering objects, I came across the idea of intangible cultural heritage. I lost hours to browsing UNESCO's Representative List of the Intangible Cultural Heritage of Humanity, exploring everything from Syrian shadow-play puppetry to camel racing in Oman, Estonian smoke saunas, sand drawing in Vanuatu, Armenian stone crosses and a procession carrying a relic of holy blood in Bruges. Turkish coffee was on there, and Belgian shrimp fishing and Korean wrestling and Bosnian grass-mowing competitions. It was a whole world of culture that was crucial, vital, teeming, alive – and, mostly, portable.

The first entry for Iraq was *maqam*, the classical music tradition where a singer improvises on a series of melodies, with a band of musicians on *daf* (tambourine), *santur* (dulcimer) or *qanun* (zither), *joza* (a spike fiddle, its body made from a coconut) and *dumbuk* (drum). It's intricate, ornate and beautiful, and from the 1920s to 1951 most musicians in Baghdad, especially *maqam* musicians, were Jewish. Some studied at Dar Mu'asat Al-'Amiyaan (the House of Consoling the Blind), a school founded in 1929 to teach blind children skills so they wouldn't end up begging on the streets. Set up by a Jewish businessman, the school was open to all children but it was mostly Jews who went, and blind Jewish musicians became famous. They played for Muslim women who felt comfortable unveiling in front of performers who couldn't see. They joined the Iraqi state radio band, which was led by two Jewish brothers, Daoud and Saleh al-Kuwaiti, who played oud and violin and composed hundreds of songs, more or less inventing modern Iraqi music. They wrote many of them for 'the voice of Baghdad'– the Jewish singer Salima Murad, known as Salima Pasha. Voluptuous and smoky-eyed, her eyebrows always arched in perfect bows, her lips always red, she sang songs like 'Galbak sakhar jalmud' (Your heart is stone), voice quivering, full of emotion, with her trademark catch in the throat. In 'Khadri-el-chay' (Brew the tea) she refused to make tea until her beloved came – if he didn't, she'd smash the teapot with an axe. (This was the kind of melodramatic inheritance I was already passing on, a vindication and relishing of Big Feelings.) She sang on the radio, in films and at Baghdad nightclubs, including one she ran with two other women. In Naqqāsh's novel *Tenants and Cobwebs*, a young man walks into the trap laid by Salima's eyes and starts writing terrible poetry. In *The Dove Flyer*, she appears as a 'golden-throated enchantress', 'haunting' and 'electric', in scarlet silk, with fiery eyes. She's 'lethal' to young men. Fans besiege her, sheikhs and politicians adore her, poets dedicate verses to her and suitors perish at her feet. When she improvises a song for the Jews who are leaving for Israel, about 'the paths that don't come back', she sings so ardently, her voice hushed and mournful, her eyes glistening, that 'Everyone's desire was in her voice. Everyone's love was offered up to her, and to a Baghdad that would be seen no more.' One man cries out, 'How are we Jews supposed to leave all this?' In real life, Murad converted to Islam to marry a heart-throb, the singer Nazem al-Ghazali. He was a patient of my grandfather's, and they used to come to my mother's house where she heard Murad sing, close up, with a voice that had a sort of echo that could never be recorded. She stayed in Baghdad. Her music is still popular, and online her picture often pops up next to one of Renée Dangoor, once a friend of my grandmother's, who was Iraq's first beauty queen, as if to prove Jews lived not just happily in Baghdad but also *glamorously*.

To fit the UNESCO definition, intangible cultural heritage has to be transmitted from generation to generation and constitute an important aspect of a community's identity. There is sometimes a rush to add heritage to the list for communities at risk, so after Russia invaded Ukraine, UNESCO marked Ukrainian borscht-cooking as 'in Need of Urgent Safeguarding', and two months into the brutal war between Hamas and Israel, UNESCO added the Palestinian *dabkeh* dance.

There is, though, controversy around whether the list can help vulnerable minorities; China has more entries on the list than any other country, mainly because it registers the cultural heritage of communities it censors and persecutes. It feels faintly obscene that while subjecting the Uyghur community to imprisonment, surveillance, forced sterilisation, forced labour and attempts at cultural erasure, China also registered the Uyghur musical tradition *muqam*, a relative of Iraqi *maqam*. It stuck in my throat, too, that the entry for Iraqi *maqam* did not mention the huge contribution of Jewish musicians (and especially of blind Jewish musicians) even though *maqam* was so dominated by Jews that one Iraqi prime minister apparently turned on the radio one day and found it silent. Demanding an explanation he was told it was the Jewish fast day, Yom Kippur, and there were no musicians available. There was more than one story, too, about Iraqis begging Jewish musicians not to leave the country. The ones who did leave found themselves written out of the story both in Israel and in Iraq.

In Israel, just as it was hard to speak Arabic, it was also difficult to play and hear Arabic music, apart from on the weekly radio show by the Israeli Broadcasting Authority's Arabic Orchestra (yes, there was one), and on recordings passed around and sold at Tel Aviv markets. The children of one Iraqi Jewish musician, Lulu Shamma, ashamed of the music she played, broke her drums. Yehezkel Kojaman, an ethnomusicologist so passionate about music that in prison in Iraq he made an oud out of a wooden tea box and a sieve, was shocked to find Daoud al-Kuwaiti, once the toast of Baghdad, selling kitchenware in a Tel Aviv market. And when Daoud's brother Saleh tuned in to Radio Iraq, he was crushed to hear his songs credited to other composers or described as *folk music*, as if no one had written them at all, because the Ba'athist government was expunging Jewish names from the records. In 1973, when he was vice president, Saddam Hussein was bothered enough about the continuing influence of Jewish musicians in Iraq to personally form a committee to 'review' the Iraqi musical tradition, purging or stealing credit for music by Jews.

I thought it would be easier to keep hold of a musical heritage, to carry culture that was portable, weightless, freely available. But Daoud and Saleh were so embittered by their experiences that they refused to let their children play music. The al-Kuwaiti brothers' songs are complex, swirling, serpentine, *long* – up to twenty minutes each – and desperately sad, full of lovers who were abandoned, heartsick, suicidal, insomniac. In one Daoud croons, 'My soul is weary / And sleeplessness has exhausted me.' In another, he keens, frantic, 'I don't have two hearts!' because he'd broken the only one he had and he knew the damage was permanent, he'd never get another. Even when I didn't understand the words, this music caught at my heart in ways other music didn't. But could I listen to it without thinking about Shamma's broken drums, or Hussein's committee?

Then I watched *Iraq 'n' Roll*. Just the title of this documentary gave me joy. It was about Daoud al-Kuwaiti's grandson, Dudu Tassa, who became a rock star even though his family felt that music had betrayed them, and about his journey back to his musical heritage. As I watched Tassa drinking black coffee, smoking and listening to scratchy recordings, sometimes humming along, sometimes reaching for his guitar, I felt a sort of soul shift. He didn't find it easy to reckon with his legacy, saying, 'Coming from a place of great fear, I didn't know what to do with all this,' and then, later, 'I don't feel like I'm fixing anything.' I could understand the pressure he felt to repair the damage of the wreckage, to knit back the broken hearts.

Tassa was part of a Mizrahi music boom, which also included the band Sidara which my mother's friend Linda Menuhin formed by gathering together old Iraqi Jewish musicians – an Iraqi Jewish Buena Vista Social Club. Tassa didn't just play his grandfather and great-uncle's songs; he reworked them, sampling the originals, speeding them up, adding intense beats and electric guitar and bringing in his mother to sing as she was never allowed to do. There was something electric about the way he was pulling the difficult past into now and towards a more hopeful future, going from being haunted by the past to making his ghosts his friends.

Ashteedek (Long live your hands)

I was keeping a list of Judeo-Iraqi Arabic words I knew, noting them down as I heard them or as they occurred to me, words that were familiar, on the tip of my tongue, or tantalisingly just beyond it. Words that had stuck. My own personal dictionary. My word hoard. So many of them were to do with food. When a meal was ready, I wanted to say *t'fadlu* (literally, be kind or be generous, but meaning, come and eat). I hoped, if my son liked the food, he'd say *ashteedek* (long live your hands), and I'd reply *awafi* (to your health). But this exchange – as familiar to me as breathing – was impossible for many reasons, not just linguistic. He would barely eat Iraqi Jewish food.

This flummoxed me. I'd thought it would be easy to pass on my culinary heritage at least. Uncomplicated. Delicious. Pleasurable. It did not occur to me he wouldn't like the food. Before I became a mother, I secretly judged friends who let their children subsist on white bread and pesto pasta. I assumed this was an English thing, and that any child of mine would be happy with spice and texture and a jumble of dishes. It served me right because my son was so picky he wouldn't even eat pesto. I had to dredge his spaghetti with cheese. Not even Parmesan: Cheddar. He did like a lot of foods I never ate as a child, like fish fingers and Marmite (not together), and although it was obviously important to eat English food, to honour that side of his heritage too, I couldn't help but feel a bit perplexed that he liked what I (still, and even having grown up here) thought of as peculiarly English oddities. I was happy if he ate anything (because it turned out, oh *God*, I wasn't just a mother but that sitcom cliché, a *Jewish* mother) but I did want him to love Iraqi food.

I wanted it for him because it was the food I reached for when I was sad or needed comfort. The food writer Bee Wilson, cooking her way out of the breakdown of her marriage, came to believe that a better word for comfort food was 'trauma food' because it's not just treats and stodge under the duvet (although it can be), but food that heals, sustains, consoles – and, of course, it also keeps you alive. When the pandemic started, and everyone else was panic-buying loo roll, I dashed out, masked and anxious, to get *silan* (date syrup), *amba* (mango pickle) and *mai kadakh* (orange flower water), and in the months to come, when I couldn't see my mother except on a screen, it was good to be able to taste home.

My son's preferred diet reminded me of a depressing, colourless time in my own life, when I didn't eat Iraqi Jewish food either. Not because I found something delicious I liked better, but out of embarrassment or shame; girls at school made fun of my packed lunches and like a coward I switched to white bread and cream cheese. I ate that every day, the same lunch, unvarying. When I think now of the lunches my mother lovingly made for me before I rejected them, how she went to the bakery specially to get soft, puffy pitta breads, and stuffed them with black eggs (they were actually brown, but that's what we called them) she cooked overnight sometimes around the *tbeet* chicken so they were infused with its flavours, how she added hummus, and slices of aubergine she fried to perfection, and *amba* obviously and salad, endless salad, fresh and crisp with the baby cucumbers you couldn't (then) get at the supermarket, I could weep. My chosen sandwiches were so boring in comparison, and almost entirely free of nutrition. Is this why I am only five foot three?

When I went to university, my mum bought me a rice cooker

(because what is life without rice?) and again, like an idiot, I let it gather dust, because what if I got mocked again? Away from my family and community, imposter syndrome kicked in. Who was I to cook Iraqi Jewish food? What if I got it wrong? I was bound to, because I was born here, not there. I wasn't *really* Iraqi. I was not like the first-generation Iraqi Jewish women I knew who were confident in their own skin, fabulous belly dancers, demons at *tawli* (backgammon), and seemingly able to cook any Iraqi Jewish food they wanted to without a recipe. I'd grown up here, experiencing everything second-hand and often not even in the right language. I felt like a tourist, and a tourist couldn't be a tour guide. When, once, cooking for a lot of friends, I hauled the rice cooker out of storage and used it, I felt like I was being a bit over the top about my identity, wearing it like a costume, teetering about in it like a child in my mother's high heels. It didn't fit. Or *I* didn't fit. Anywhere. Another student told me my gestures were too big, too exuberant – Iraqi Jews talk with our hands – and, embarrassed, wanting to be like my peers, I started trying to keep my hands down. Later I read *Lost in Translation* and shivered with recognition as the Polish Jewish writer Eva Hoffmann recalled that after she moved to Canada, a teacher told her to sit on her hands when she was talking. She learned to be more reserved, more restrained, but then found herself stuck in the uneasy in-between. 'My mother says I'm becoming "English",' she writes. 'This hurts me because I know she means I'm becoming cold.' If I didn't cook rice, speak my language or even talk with my hands, maybe I was doomed to white bread and cream cheese, or the dubious meals in the canteen. This angst and doubt went on for a boringly long time. A few months after I graduated, I moved in with a friend in London, and I felt less Iraqi Jewish than ever. There was, it turned out, a psychic cost to denying myself proper rice. I was disconnected from my community with its sometimes narrow expectations of what women should do, but I also missed being in the middle of it, and although I loved my new friends they sometimes felt alien to me, and I struggled to fit in. It felt strange that I didn't call their mothers *auntie*; that their grandmothers had never pinched my cheeks with surprising force; that some of them had furniture that went back more than one generation, and things their great-grandparents had loved, big things, heavy things, that wouldn't fit in suitcases; that they knew the names of trees and plants and flowers; that as soon as the sun started setting, even if it was three in the afternoon, they closed the curtains, which we never did because if you did someone would say *en'fa'as ras efadi* (the top of my heart is crushed). It was a chasm I couldn't bridge.

And then I started cooking Iraqi food and something shifted. I started unfurling, feeling more at home, more like me. In Judeo-Iraqi Arabic, the word *teyyeb* means both 'tasty' and 'alive', because food was life, and if you weren't savouring life, were you really living? When I was cooking, I didn't worry so much. My hands took over and they knew what to do. I made little meatballs called *ras asfour*, which literally means 'sparrow heads' because they are about that size, in a rich red beetroot stew. I made dense, cataclysmically cheesy omelettes called *ajjat b'jeben*, which means 'cheese storm', but I always thought were called *ajab jeben*, which means 'I love cheese'. (Some people call it *ajja* for short.) For quick snatched lunches I made *beidh b'laham*, egg burgers made with herbs and (my mother's secret ingredient) ketchup, or *m'farka*, eggs cooked with spinach and onions. On long lazy weekends I made *salona* (sweet and sour baked fish with cumin, turmeric, tomatoes and lemon and *silan*), or *ingriyi*, fried aubergine, layered with fried cubes of lamb or beef and sliced tomato, and simmered with turmeric, lemon juice and date syrup.

I rolled out dough flavoured with fennel and *mahlab*

(fenugreek) for *ka'akat*, bracelet-shaped bread which my mother jokingly calls Baghdadi bagels, which I dipped into thick Greek yogurt. Sometimes I even made *kubba*. I didn't know then that the name comes from the Arabic verb *kabbaba* (to form into a ball). But I knew how much I loved *kubba burghul*, beef or lamb mixed with pine nuts and sultanas, stuffed into a dough made from more minced meat and bulgur, first boiled *then* fried. Or *kubba pateta*, sometimes called *pateta chap*, my favourite, which is yet more spiced minced meat, mixed with parsley and encased in a dough made of (as the name suggests) mashed potatoes and egg, and fried till it's crispy. Or, if I really had a lot of time, I made *sambusek bel tawa*, crescents of dough, filled with chicken, chickpeas, turmeric and cumin, and deep-fried so the dough puffs up and goes golden.

I even had a go at *tbeet*, the mighty Iraqi Jewish dish. *Tbeet* literally means 'overnight', and it was one of the Jewish recipes (like Eastern European *cholent*, Spanish *hamin*, Moroccan *dfina*) that got around the prohibition on lighting a fire (or an oven) on Shabbat by cooking low and slow from just before sunset. For *tbeet*, you stuff a chicken with rice and giblets (the heart, gizzard and liver), spiced with cardamom, cinnamon, cloves and sometimes nutmeg, ginger and rose petals, cover the chicken in more rice and roast it with eggs all around it – ideally in a big copper cauldron over a slowly dying fire in a *kanoun*, a stove. You wake up to the smell of it cooking, take out the 'black' eggs, which taste of smoke, have them for breakfast and leave the chicken and rice cooking until lunch, heat and time working their magic, the flavours intensifying, the *hakaka*, the crust, getting thicker, crunchier and more delicious.

I cooked so *much* rice, buying basmati by the sack because who could manage with those mimsy bags from the supermarket? Let alone the minute packs of herbs. I made rice with a potato crust that looked like a crown. Rice decorated with sultanas soaked in hot water and crispy fried onions, blackened pine nuts, slivered almonds and pistachios, simmered and spiced chickpeas and vermicelli. Rice with broad beans and dill. And, most of all, *kechri*, the Iraqi Jewish comfort food: rice with red lentils, garlic, turmeric, cumin, tomato, melting onions, *so much* butter and melting slabs of halloumi, with yogurt spooned over the top.

I did not make many cakes. They're not a big Iraqi Jewish thing; our word for cakes, *kekayi*, was even borrowed from English. But I made *masafan*, chewy almond macaroons; my mother thought their name came from the English word *marzipan*, but other Iraqi Jews sometimes called them *hajibada*, and we wondered if the name had changed after the British mandate, if the language had shifted. (Some linguists believe that the word *marzipan* itself came from the Arabic word *mawthaban* meaning 'the king who sits', and if it is true, the word has come full circle.) I made *baklawa* (which we say with a *w* not a *v*) with almonds or pistachios or walnuts and cardamom, drenched in lemon juice, sugar and rose water; I made *makhboose* or *ba'aba b'tamur* (date pastries). I even, once, made *lowzina* (dense, jammy fruit sweets cut into diamond shapes; my favourite, *lowzina mel haiwah*, was made with quince, almonds and cardamom).

It was more than just the food. It was bringing people together. It was making a *lot*; my mother taught me to make so much that when everyone had finished eating, the table looked as full as if they hadn't started, a sprawling profusion of dishes, non-stop flavours. My brother and I often laughed when she took pictures of the food, as if it was as important to document it as the people, but now I see the work that went into it. I saw why you'd want to make a record of those blooming, teeming tables, that irrepressible creativity, that *joy*. In 2005, after Hurricane Katrina, I read an open letter from New Orleans poet Andrei Codrescu to the Americans preparing to host refugees from the flooded city. It began by promising the hosts that their food would get better. I found this so galvanising, so mischievous, so powerful; the way he cast refugees not as burdens but as joy-givers. Codrescu had left his first home, Romania, in 1965, along with many of the country's Jews, and now his new home was ravaged, but he still managed to wring pleasure out of the tragedy, and pride. Eight weeks after Katrina, so many people wrote in to the *New Orleans Times-Picayune* newspaper seeking recipes they'd lost in the hurricane that they started a column called 'Rebuilding New Orleans: Recipe by Recipe', which turned into a cookbook. It connected people who were trying to cook familiar foods for the people they loved, to make them feel safe in the wake of disaster. In the wake of my community's dispersal too, Iraqi Jewish businessman and philanthropist Naim Dangoor produced a newsletter which was posted out to Iraqi Jews across the world for years. Eccentric but vital, the *Scribe* made us feel like we'd never left Baghdad, as if instead of being spread across the world, with cousins in the US, Canada and Israel, we were popping in and out of each other's houses, swapping gossip and sharing recipes. My grandmother's friend, Alice Shashou, wrote a food column which later became a book freighted with longing. Reading her cookbook, like the New Orleans one, was not like reading other cookbooks; they were nourishing in an almost spiritual way. In 2022, as Ukrainian refugees started arriving in the UK, the Ukrainian food writer Olia Hercules posted a list of foods British hosts could stock up on to make them feel 'welcomed and comforted'. From the charity Migrateful, which trains and employs migrant chefs to teach cookery classes, I learned about 'contact theory', the idea that contact between different groups could reduce prejudice and conflict. I wanted to believe this could work, but I knew you could enjoy another culture's food as a purely economic transaction, and be just as racist as you were before you ate it.

And I worried that all this talk about food might get in the way of other, harder, more important conversations. I knew it was easier to eat or talk about Iraqi Jewish food than to really engage with our stories; that the food was literally easier to swallow than the trauma and political complexity. I worried that when I made or described the food, I was trying to make us more palatable. I worried about how the food was often exoticised or, the opposite, made more familiar; *kubba* described as dumplings. I'd done it myself, comparing *ka'akat* to bagels, or *ingriyi* to lasagne. It sometimes felt like the food had to be either impossibly complex and magical, or simplified to the point where it was robbed of its singularity.

Still, Hercules's list – which began with 'Fresh Dill (a lot of it)' – made me think about what would welcome and comfort Iraqi Jews. I always cooked lentils when I was sad, long before I learned that in many cultures they are cooked for mourners because their round shape echoes the cycle of death and renewal. Lentils were the 'pottage' Jacob cooked for his father, Isaac, to comfort him when he was grieving. When Esau came in hungry from hunting, demanded 'that red stuff' and scoffed the lot, he was being uncouth and selfish because he didn't need the comfort, not like his father did. He was also being an idiot because if the lentils were red they weren't yet cooked, still hard and raw, not softened down to yellow. That's why Jacob thought he wasn't worthy to be their father's heir and stole his birthright. Lentils are all over *The Book of Jewish Food* by Claudia Roden, who didn't plan to write a cookbook. She was studying art in London in 1956 when, in response to the Suez Crisis, Nasser declared Egyptian Jews enemies of the state, made mass arrests and expelled most of the community. Roden's family joined her and when they got together with other Jewish refugees, they shared recipes, she has said, 'with a kind of desperation'. When *The Book of Jewish Food* came out, I rushed to get it. I didn't just want the recipes – eight hundred of them, lovingly collected from ruined, scattered Jewish communities all over the world – I also wanted the stories. It made me laugh that the Ashkenazi section was tiny compared to the massive Sephardi one (and I knew I was annoying when I pointed this out to my Ashkenazi flatmate), and I loved how happy Roden sounded to discover that fish and chips were invented by Portuguese Jews. It was incredibly affirming to see recipes for dishes I'd only ever eaten at relatives' homes, or seen in Daisy Iny's out-of-print, dayglo-orange *The Best of Baghdad Cooking, with Treats from Teheran*, my copy of which was more scribble than text.

Most weeks I made lentil soup the way my mother made it, with an onion, a lemon, some cumin and turmeric and nothing else. My son, of course, wouldn't eat it. Even when I blitzed it because he didn't like 'bits'; even when I lost the lemon, and the onion; even when I sacrilegiously added cheese and called it 'Sunshine Soup'. Then my mother took up the challenge of giving him a love of Iraqi Jewish food, and when she told me she was making him *kubba shwandar*, I thought, *good luck with that!* For *kubba shwandar* you pound spices, meat and parsley, encase it in a shell of more pounded meat and ground rice and simmer it in a sweet and sour stock of beetroot, onions, water, lemon and sugar, which stains the *kubba* ruby red. There was no way my child who claimed he was 'allergic to sauce' would touch it. I brought a cheese sandwich, just in case. But when we sat down for lunch, he ate *twelve*. He declared it his new best food. He triumphantly wrote in his diary 'I ATE KUBBA' and drew a red *kubba*, in cross-section so you could see the meat inside.

Obviously this was terrible news. I wanted him to eat things I could sling together in five minutes, not laborious, time-consuming, multi-process dishes. It made no sense that he'd like *kubba shwandar* with its tang and its complexity and its sauce. But although this development clearly doomed me to hours of labour, I also felt – just slightly – thrilled. Inverting the family joke that I spoke Judeo-Iraqi Arabic like I had *kubba* in my mouth, my son actually *did* have *kubba* in his mouth. And he liked it.

Kubba shwandar

First, make the *kubba*. Mix 300g minced lamb (if you're me) or beef (if you're my mum) with a fistful of chopped parsley, a grated or finely chopped onion and season it and add a pinch of turmeric. Then make the dough by pounding 200g ground rice (you can buy it ready-ground, or use a processor) with another 100g of minced lamb or beef, and a little lemon juice, and season that. Dampen your hands with water and roll the dough into balls about the size of a walnut and put them on a tray. Then, one at a time (I did say this was labour-intensive), push your thumb into each ball of dough, put some of the filling in the indentation you've made, and wrap the dough around it. Put the ball on another tray, and keep going. You need a good friend to keep you company, or a really involving podcast, because otherwise, about three balls in, you lose the will to live. But after a while, it starts to become quite meditative, all the rolling and filling and wrapping, as the tray of dough empties and the tray of *kubba* fills. You can put them in the fridge now, covered, and make the sauce.

Which is easy. Peel and slice six or seven beetroots. Then chop an onion, fry it till it's translucent, add the beetroots, add enough water to cover, season it and squeeze in some lemon juice and sugar. Taste it. You can make it sourer with more lemon or sweeter with more sugar, just as you like. Some people use tamarind and date syrup, or pomegranate molasses, or even honey, but we have always used just lemon and sugar, and I always want more sour than sweet. Sweet and sour – *hamedh-helu* –is the Iraqi flavour and it's tempting to make a link between its complexity, its bitter-sweetness, and the country's complicated history, but my mother just says 'we eat things all mixed up'. Not everything has to be a metaphor.

Some people add a tin of tomatoes here, or just tomato paste. We don't. You might. It's up to you. You are joining in the story here. Add the beetroots, and then, carefully, so they don't break, the *kubba* balls. And simmer. For an hour or so. Until the *kubba* are cooked through and the beetroot is tender. If the beetroot is taking for ever, as beetroot sometimes does, you can (carefully!) lift out the *kubba* with a slotted spoon and save them on a plate while you keep going with the beetroot and then put the *kubba* back in. If everything is cooked but the sauce is watery, you can take out both beetroot and *kubba*, turn up the heat, reduce it and then put everything back in.

It's good with rice, and maybe a salad? Tabbouleh or *fattoush* if you can be bothered but sometimes I just chop up some cucumber and tomato and dress it with parsley, lemon and olive oil. After all I've made *kubba shwandar* and I don't owe anyone anything.

The Oxford School of Rare Jewish Languages

Wanting to make sure the language was safe on my ark, I started a Zoom course in Judeo-Iraqi Arabic. Of course, my teacher turned out to be someone my mum knew from Baghdad. On the screen, in our little boxes, we took turns saying why we were there. One woman said she it was because the language was 'almost disappearing'. Another said she'd heard her grandmother's stories in 'broken English', and wished she'd heard them 'whole'. The stories of these mostly third-generation Iraqi Jews made me lose heart. Learning a few words that I soon wouldn't be able to speak to anyone felt a scant, pathetic, hopeless attempt at repair in the face of this rupture. But then an Ashkenazi student chimed in; he had married an Iraqi Jew and wanted to surprise his in-laws by speaking to them in their own language, and to speak it to his children. I suddenly saw a language people could learn, a language we could pass on. I felt as though instead of passing on the pain of the rupture I could maybe pass on a way of reconnecting. And my language felt real, legitimate, worthy of study. Maybe.

My son burst in, asking, 'Are you learning ancient Egypt language?' He was very interested in hieroglyphs and codes. I tried to coax him out of the room, but he demanded, 'Ask the teacher how to say pirate in hieroglyphs!' He was also mad for pirates. It had not occurred to me to ask the word for *pirate* and I felt my curiosity expand. Now he was asking what they were saying. I told him we were saying good morning: *s'bakh el heir* (literally, 'morning of wellness'; the reply is 'morning of light'). He beamed at me. 'Sparkle Hair!' and I beamed back. But when I said to my mum, *Good morning, Sparkle Hair!*, she said 'We didn't use those words. Unless we were being very formal.' What did they say then? 'We just said *hello*.'

It was good to be learning – and it was frustrating. When I made notes, autocorrect changed *fedwa* (I would die for you) to *fudge*. Trying to make sentences, I faltered. When we learned the words for family, I realised why I'd always found it hard to know who anyone was talking about. We didn't just say *grandchild*, or even *grandson* or *granddaughter*. Instead there were separate words for *the son of my daughter*, *the daughter of my daughter*, *the son of my son* and *the daughter of my son*. We didn't just say *cousin* ; we had to specify whether it was *my mother's brother's son*, *my mother's sister's son* and so on. In the midst of this were words I recognised, the words for *lover*, masculine and feminine. How did I know these words? I imagined them coming up in long-ago gossip, once ripe and juicy, now stale and forgotten. I rolled the words on my tongue. *Urfiqi*. *Urfiqeti*. But I couldn't remember the story. I couldn't remember anything about it. The course ended and I wanted more. I craved the language and, even more, I craved connection.

When a friend told me about the Oxford School of Rare Jewish Languages, it didn't sound real. It sounded like something out of Borges! Or like it came from R. F. Kuang's historical fantasy novel *Babel*. Kuang conjures an alt-reality Victorian Oxford where gifted linguists from the colonies gather in the glittering heart of the British Empire to make magic by epic feats of translation. Realising they are being exploited, their work fuelling an empire which has got rich on subjugation and oppression, the linguists violently revolt. The book is jam-packed with etymologies and ancient and arcane languages, but there is nothing about the origins of the word *babel* (from the Hebrew *babhel*, which itself comes from the Akkadian *bab-ilu*, or Gate of God), and not one Jewish character.

Now I was part of a real-life school of rare Jewish languages, teaching everything from Judeo-Provençal to Judeo-Tat, which is spoken by the Mountain Jews of Dagestan who believe they are the descendants of the Ten Lost Tribes; their language probably sounds like Farsi because, way back in the seventh century, they journeyed to Dagestan from the other side of the Caucasus. You could learn *two* forms of Yiddish, Ladino, Judeo-Greek, Judeo-Italian, Kivruli, spoken by Jews in Georgia, and Judeo-Neo-Aramaic, spoken by Iraqi Jews in the Kurdish north. *And* Judeo-Iraqi Arabic – which the Oxford School called Baghdadi Judeo-Arabic – taught by the amazing Assaf Bar-Moshe. The school was set up in 2021, with the belief that Jewish languages are 'essential and incorporeal parts of Jewish history, creativity, culture and identity'. The school explained that, for all the research into languages' importance and fragility, there were few chances to actually learn them. This was the first school of its kind in the world, my chance to keep hold of my language, and I grabbed it with both hands.

It was disappointing that the classes weren't actually in Oxford, but while distinctly lacking in dreaming spires and revolting linguists, the Zoom course had its own exhilarating power. There were students in South Korea and Ukraine and another student who always seemed to be on a train; there was a student in Iraq where most of the others could not go. One student was a distant cousin, and we reconnected in real life, and dared to imagine we could one day have a conversation in our mother tongue. She showed me an *izar*, a sort of wrap robe which, long ago, Iraqi Jewish women wore over their clothes when they went out, sometimes with a veil. I'd never seen one and I ran my hands over it. It was gorgeous, made of heavy cream silk, richly embroidered with flowers and fruit, and fringed with fat tassels. We took it out of the box but neither of us could work out how to wear it.

Every week, I looked forward to that bright hour on Zoom. It felt hopeful to be learning a Jewish Arabic language with people from so many different places, religions and affiliations. Here we were. Together. It felt vulnerable to be stammering and making mistakes in a language I should have been able to think in and dream in and wield, but I was glad to have the space to be vulnerable with these strangers who were also being vulnerable with me. And every now and then, something clicked, and I got a surging feeling of *making sense* in this language. I felt whole in it. I felt very, very present. I often, also, felt quite baffled.

I learned that the Jews spoke Hebrew when they first came to Babylon, and as they became more familiar with the local language, Aramaic, they mixed the two, fashioning a language called Jewish Babylonian Aramaic. They borrowed words from the Persians when they came. And after the Arab conquest in the seventh century CE, the Jews switched to Arabic along with everyone else, but Judeo-Iraqi Arabic carried over much of the Aramaic grammar and words that other modern Arabic languages shed.

In an early class we learned the word 'thank you' – *ashkerak* – and all the Iraqis looked confused because we'd never heard it before. The British students looked a bit appalled both that we didn't know it and that it wasn't often used. I could see why. I remembered a long-ago ex of mine watching me at a supermarket checkout, counting my *pleases* and *thank yous* and telling me they were both in double figures. He was trying to prove I was ridiculous, and more English than I thought I was. And when it came to excessive, nervous politeness at least, he was right. I asked Bar-Moshe the word for *please*, and he used another unfamiliar word. I wrote it down and asked my mother how she'd say *please*. My polite and lovely mother hesitated. The word *please* was somehow not at the tip of her tongue. Then she said *bela zahma* – 'without hassle' or 'without burden' or 'no trouble'. It sort of meant *please.* You could say *bela zahma jeeb li chai* (literally, no hassle bring me tea). I tried the other word Bar-Moshe had given me – *rij'aan.* And she shrugged. She knew it but she didn't *use* it. When I asked other Iraqi Jews what they say for please, there was always a pause. One suggested *dahebak* (I love you); *dahebak jeeb li chai* (I love you, bring me tea) also works. But everyone felt a bit unsure about *rij'aan.* 'Maybe it's modern?' someone suggested.

Did I want to be modern? My instinctive response was no, I wanted to speak the real, old Judeo-Iraqi Arabic my parents spoke in Baghdad. But then I caught myself. If I was trapping the language in aspic, preserving it as a relic, it may as well sit in the archives, as a memory, not a living thing. And that's not what I wanted. I was wary of falling into the tropes used by many people writing about endangered languages, especially of a tendency to wallow in sadness. Of stories such as the one told in Mark Abley's book *Spoken Here*, about the eighteenth-century explorer Alexander von Humboldt being taken, by torchlight, in shadows, to meet the 'last speaker' of Atures in Venezuela, only to be introduced to a talking parrot. Atures had 'died out among humans' and only survived in this bird's repeating squawks. Of the story of the last two speakers of the Aboriginal language Mati Ke, who didn't speak it to each other because tribal taboos forbade them to communicate after puberty. Or the last two speakers of Ayapeneco in Mexico who didn't talk to each other either, and no one knew if it was because they held a long and terrible grudge or they weren't friends in the first place. Of the difficulties of linguists trying to help last speakers, as explored in books like K. David Harrison's *The Last Speakers: The Quest to Save the World's Most Endangered Languages*, where he described travelling epic distances to remote places not shown on maps, working by candlelight, struggling to understand last speakers who were 'too shy', 'missing teeth and spoke nearly incoherently' and, in one case, 'possibly inebriated, and might have had Tourette's syndrome'. Last speakers were often compared to Lonesome George, the Galapagos Islands tortoise who was the last of his kind, lived to more than a hundred, and died in captivity, far from home, failing to mate with tortoises from related species.

As I was actively trying to communicate in Judeo-Iraqi Arabic, twisting my tongue around the words again, texting my mum way too much (sorry, Mum!) to ask for phrases and meanings, these doomy, gloomy stories increasingly irritated me. Instead of functioning as calls to arms, they seemed to be fetishising grief. Analysing the way books and articles about endangered languages often included a 'countdown' of last speakers, linguistic anthropologist Shaylih Muehlmann concluded that anticipating extinction exerted a certain pull, of 'pleasure' or 'spectacle'. She pushed back against this, asking why a language was only interesting when nearly zero people spoke it, and not, say, when there were a hundred or a thousand and a chance it didn't have to die? An elder in Mexico's Cucapá community complained to Muehlmann, 'Outsiders are always coming in to count something,' whether it was speakers, birds or fish. Cucapá's speaker count was actually going up, because the government that once forced them to speak Spanish now only protected their rights if they spoke their own language. Some speakers found this so hypocritical that when the government asked if they spoke Cucapá, they replied with strings of Cucapá swear words.

Where once I was fatally mesmerised by stories of speakers counting down to zero, in this more optimistic mood I started collecting examples of the numbers going up, and even about languages resurrected long after their supposed last speakers had died. Fishwife Dolly Pentreath, thought to be the last speaker of the Cornish language Kernewek (which she used to curse people in long monologues they couldn't understand), died in 1777. But Kernewek was back thanks to the efforts of, as the BBC affectionately put it, 'academics and eccentrics'. Manx's apparent last speaker, fisherman Ned Maddrell, died at ninety-seven in 1974, leaving recordings of himself asking *Vel ny partanyn snaue, Joe?* ('Are the crabs crawling, Joe?'); in fact, when UNESCO tried to classify it as extinct in 2009, children at a primary school where lessons were almost all in Manx wrote in, asking, 'If our language is extinct then what language are we writing in?'

And then there were the most miraculous stories, of ancient languages, silent for millennia, utterly lost . . . until they were not. My twenty-first-century son liked writing his name in hieroglyphs, comprehensible only because the Rosetta Stone was deciphered. I marvelled also that I was able to read him Ludmila Zeman's three picture books, in English, of *The Epic of Gilgamesh* because for 4,000 years no one had even known the *Epic* existed and its language, Akkadian, had been lost. My son liked 'the bits where they battle'. I told him that for years archaeologists dug up thousands of shards of clay with writing on and no one knew what it meant. The shards were covered in one of the oldest forms of writing there ever was, called cuneiform, which means 'wedge-shaped', because to write it you used reeds to make wedge-shaped marks on clay. I told him no one could read it until a hero came along.

George Smith was a plucky, clever working-class engraver with hardly any formal education, who turned up at the British Museum around 1861 and started working on the shards they held, for free, whenever he could get away from his actual job. He jigsawed them together in a dark, stuffy room. There were endless wine bills, shopping lists, property deeds, but, amazingly, the first tablet Smith decoded was a fragment of an exquisite, long-lost epic, about a flood coming, and a man saving what he could on a boat. Later, Smith went to Iraq, having never excavated before or been to the Middle East, and almost instantly found the other half of the Flood Tablet. Later still, he died in Aleppo, a world away from his wife and six children.

I didn't tell my son that in Smith's account of his trip, he came over just as racist as his peers, disgusted by 'natives . . . cooking dirty-looking messes', repulsed by kebabs (!) which he described, revoltingly and long-windedly, as 'small portions of meat and intestines of kids strung on skewers like cat's meat'. He compared an Arab to an ape. He ridiculed an illiterate hotel owner who proudly showed off a guest book full of terrible reviews he couldn't read. It felt like poetic justice when Ottoman officials gave him a letter which he thought granted him safe passage, but which actually instructed port officials to seize his finds. They were able to trick him because while Smith had deciphered the region's most opaque and impossible language, Akkadian, he couldn't read a word of Arabic or Turkish.

Not such a hero then.

Anyway, the story of how Akkadian was deciphered didn't begin with Smith. It wasn't really a lone hero tale, but a much more collective, inclusive one. It started with the Behistun Rock in Persia, which, like the Rosetta Stone, had an inscription written in three languages, and was the key to deciphering Akkadian. But while the Rosetta was small and portable, the Behistun inscription was massive (120 feet tall and 125 feet wide), so it couldn't be hacked out of the rock and taken away to study. It was also carved impossibly high up a sheer limestone cliff. No one was mad enough to try to climb up to it until Sir Henry Creswicke Rawlinson came along. In 1833, he went to Persia to work for the East India Company, which had already conquered, subjugated and plundered the Indian subcontinent (ironically even taking the word *loot* from Hindustani) and was aiming to do the same again. Rawlinson was obsessed by Behistun. Every chance he got, he'd climb up and inch along a narrow, crumbling ledge, clinging on with one hand, transcribing with the other, sometimes even hauling up a ladder to balance precariously on the ledge so he could see the top sections. There was no doubting his courage and tenacity. I felt dizzy just thinking about it. But when he got to the most dangerous bit, he did what imperial British men always did: he recruited a local. Or two locals. In some accounts it was 'a wild Kurdish boy' who climbed up and pressed damp paper into the inscription, creating an impression which would harden into what was called a 'squeeze'. But sometimes it was two Kurdish boys or two Kurdish men (wildness unspecified). Rawlinson was willing to risk his life to read what ancient, dead Middle Eastern people had written, but he did not bother recording the name (or names) of the living Middle Eastern person (or people) who risked his life (or their lives) to help him.

Rawlinson then started trying to decipher the inscription, while also holding down various diplomatic jobs. It was *much* harder than deciphering the Rosetta Stone. Both inscriptions were trilingual, but one of Rosetta's languages was ancient Greek which any well-educated Victorian could read. *All three* of Behistun's languages were cuneiform, and one was Elamite, an isolate language with no links to any others, so no help at all. Unlike hieroglyphs, cuneiform was not pictorial, so you couldn't guess at the meanings. Rosetta's languages ran in horizontal lines, but cuneiform could be written left to right or right to left or top to bottom. Worst of all, cuneiform characters could have multiple meanings. And because cuneiform was invented in Mesopotamia by people who spoke Sumerian (another isolate language) and the writing system was then adopted by Akkadian, scribes often sprinkled in bits of Sumerian. For years Smith thought Gilgamesh was called Izdubar – the distance between the two names gives some sense of how challenging it was to read Akkadian. It was, honestly, amazing that Rawlinson hammered it into sense, but it's striking that he got more credit for it than other people who worked on it too, people who were outsiders like the Irish clergyman Edward Hincks or the Jewish Assyriologist Jules Julius Oppert, not well-connected diplomats like Rawlinson.

Reading about these ancient languages didn't give me much hope for mine being revived in an impossibly distant future but it did make me feel, suddenly and quite violently, that I didn't want to say, ever again, that I was speaking a *dying* language. Judeo-Iraqi Arabic wasn't Akkadian. *Dying* or *dead* felt like my language was decaying in my mouth, clogging up my throat with dust. I didn't like *vanishing* either, as if Judeo-Iraqi Arabic was scurrying off and I had to chase it. *Endangerment* and *extinction* felt like invitations only to despair or lament, instead of to act. And talk of death and extinction and silence made no sense when I could visit any number of people any day of the week and hear my noisy language alive and well, and when I was feeling it spark back to life in my mouth.

Anthropologist Mark Turin pointed me to Wesley Leonard, a linguist who speaks Myaamia, as part of the Miami Tribe of Oklahoma. I read an essay by Leonard in which he was so dedicated to 'eradicating the e-word' that he refused even to say it, just hinting it had something to do with dinosaurs. Nearly dormant in the 1960s, Myaamia was being spoken again, but every time Leonard changed the Wikipedia page for Myaamia someone changed it back. Another academic scoffed at him for trying to find a Myaamia word for *baking soda* because why on earth did he need a word for rising agents in a dead language? In fact Leonard and some students were baking cornbread, and they needed to talk about it – and languages only survive if you use them, if you bake in them. For Leonard, 'the paradox of speaking an extinct language is not imaginary' and I lived in this paradox too. Leonard's hope and humour and rage galvanised me. The adjective he suggested instead was 'sleeping'.

Sleeping languages could be kissed back to life – perhaps by a handsome princess, as happened to Wôpanâak. Jessie 'Little Doe' Baird grew up in a community in Cape Cod severed from its language. Wôpanâak had been dead for six generations – more than a century – when, in the early nineties, Baird, a social worker pregnant with her fifth child, dreamed of ghosts speaking a dead language. She thought they were telling her to ask her community if they wanted their language back. So she asked, and everyone said yes, but they said it wasn't possible because it had been too long, because Wôpanâak was an oral language without written records, and because the community was too traumatised. They had been the 'friendly Indians' who welcomed the Mayflower Pilgrims, feasted with them and taught them how to farm, and in return were killed in battle, or sent to Europe as slaves or to be exhibited, had their land stolen and their children forced into schools where their language was erased, and lost up to 90 per cent of the community to 'the Great Dying' caused by a European-spread pandemic. They were also pressured to convert to Christianity and give up their own beliefs, but ironically, this created the key Baird used to unlock Wôpanâak. A missionary called John Eliot was so determined to convert people that he translated the whole Bible into Wôpanâak in 1663. Then he got sidetracked, captivated more by the language than by saving souls, and he wrote an *Indian Grammar*, praising Wôpanâak's 'new ways of Grammar' and its 'elegancies'. His *Grammar* became Baird's Rosetta Stone. She worked with speakers of other Algonquin languages to work out how the words were pronounced. She started teaching Wôpanâak and coining new words for things like cars and bikes. Mae Alice, the baby Baird was pregnant with when she first dreamed of

Wôpanâak, became a native speaker. You could learn Wôpanâak at schools, and the language's website proclaimed 'We are still here', and showed pictures of people holding up signs saying 'Now I can pray in my language', 'My ancestors are pleased with me', 'I am the first person in my family to speak our language in 100 years' or (this one broke me) 'I want my grandchildren to speak our language'.

At times I felt less like a speaker than like the parrot, able to repeat silly phrases in Judeo-Iraqi Arabic but not to actually have a conversation. It was only when I read *Language City* by Ross Perlin, co-director of New York's amazing Endangered Language Alliance, that I found some space for people like me. He wrote that 'Languages may need keepers as well as speakers'. Maybe I could aim to be a keeper. Of course, some people were both, like Eli Timan who created the archive my mother found for me when I first started thinking about all of this. I went to see him to find out how he did it.

Timan was studying Aramaic when a friend told him he should make a dictionary in Judeo-Iraqi Arabic. He decided to interview people and work from the transcripts, but soon realised it would be incredibly difficult to make a dictionary, to isolate individual words from streams of speech. So he applied to SOAS and the British Academy and got a grant, instead, to create an archive of interviews, supported by linguist Peter Austin. He was talking to friends at first, but it was 'easy even with people I didn't know, because immediately they felt at ease'. In fact, some felt almost too relaxed and 'would suddenly go on to talk about personal stuff that you couldn't publish'. He recorded hundreds of hours of interviews, and it became much more than a linguistic exercise; as he interviewed people who remembered Iraq at different times, 'it became a history'. He hadn't taught his daughter to speak Judeo-Iraqi Arabic, but he realised that what he wanted to pass on most were the stories.

He felt the language couldn't live again, because, he said, 'Language is very dynamic. It's a live entity. So if you don't speak it in the environment it doesn't make sense, it doesn't live. That's why it's dying in Israel because the environment isn't like Iraq.'

So it wasn't just us but the language itself that was a fish out of water, displaced. My meagre ability to understand it relied on context. But so much context was lost when my family and friends left Iraq, and more was vanishing every day. And yet, books and word lists and course notes piled up on my desk. It looked like I was getting ready to go on holiday – but instead I was travelling home.

The first surprise was that I felt liberated by learning grammar. I *hated* grammar. I was very, very bad at it. When I learned languages at school I only really cared about vocab. I still deeply resented the sheer quantity of grammar in Judeo-Iraqi Arabic, seemingly more than standard Arabic, which was also no picnic. When I complained, my mother said, maddeningly, 'But there is no grammar in our language.' Because of course you never notice it when it's your mother tongue. I realised I'd felt frozen by the fear of getting things wrong, but learning the genders suddenly liberated me to say *ash lonek* (how are you?) to a woman and *ash lonak* to a man without worrying I was getting it wrong. My words started to release, as if a stopper had been holding them back. As for *ash lonek/ak*, it literally means 'what colour are you?' and *might* derive from a plague in Baghdad that changed the colour of people's skin, so that it was originally a way of asking: do you have the plague? (Most linguists think this pop etymology is not true.)

I learned that *enhajem beit* (destroy the house) was used as a compliment, as in *enhajam beita hay el jiji esh teybee* which literally meant 'your chicken's house is destroyed how tasty', but you could probably translate as something like 'this chicken is delicious!' or 'this chicken is apocalyptically tasty!' I learned that pronouns were grafted onto nouns; instead of a separate word for *my* or *our*, suffixes were added onto the things that were mine, were ours. Rachel Shabi wrote that this made it, like Hebrew and like other Arabic languages, 'a language of belonging'. I learned that we sometimes didn't bother with verbs. Asked how I was in Judeo-Iraqi Arabic, I could just say *ana mliha* (I good). Asked my name, I could just say *ana Samantha* (I Samantha). I learned that Judeo-Iraqi Arabic had a sort of phobia of having three consonants in a row, so breaks them up with 'helping vowels' which I secretly called 'unhelping vowels' because random vowels popping up between letters was quite confusing. We had no infinitive, split or otherwise. The alphabet was divided into sun and moon letters which dictated whether the definite article melted into them (the sun letters) or stayed separate (the moon). Most Arabic languages had roughly half sun and half moon letters, whereas Judeo-Iraqi Arabic had more sun than moon (I felt this should mean something profound, but I didn't know what). And one reason I constantly heard *qa qa qa* (and could *still* barely say it) was that Judeo-Iraqi Arabic, unlike other languages, added the sound *qa* or *qad* to mean something was happening in the present: *Ana qad ahki haki malna* (I am talking our language.) Or at least: *Ana rah ahki haki malna* (I will be talking our language).

Lilith

I went back to the British Museum because I wanted to see the magic bowls. No one knows why Babylonians started making magic bowls in the sixth century and stopped two hundred years later. For a long time, archaeologists thought they were just crockery. Even though they often had strange drawings on, and tiny writing spiralling from their centres, and were often found at the thresholds of houses. Which wasn't what you usually did with bowls, but who knew, it was so long ago. Museums all over the world hold magic bowls; there's a roaring trade in them on the black market; a flood of monographs, translations and transcriptions; a Virtual Magic Bowl Archive online; a novel by Maggie Anton, *Rav Hisda's Daughter*, about a Jewish sorceress who makes bowls; and an album called *The Bowls Project* by the radical musician Jewlia Eisenberg.

Archaeologists thought they were made by non-Jews, and by men, but now they think they were made by Jewish women. Iraqi Jewish women. While some of them were written in Syriac or in Mandaic (the language of the tiny, ancient Mandaean community, who worship in water, baptising themselves again and again in the Tigris), most of the bowls were inscribed with Jewish Babylonian Aramaic, the language that was the precursor to *my* language, the language the Babylonian Talmud was written in, that vast, sprawling, spiralling compendium of stories and laws, created by rabbis arguing with each other, in synagogues, on the page and across time. The Babylonian Talmud became the basis of all Jewish law, and a guide to life for Jews across the world; not just a rulebook but a rudder in rough seas; a mad, marvellous, meandering stream of Jewish consciousness. For a long time everyone thought men also wrote the magic bowls, which some called demon bowls, or incantation bowls, mainly because no one thought sixth-century Iraqi Jewish women could write. Recently the feminist scholar Dorit Kedar has found evidence that not only could they write but some were professional scribes, some wrote their own divorces, and some wrote and made the bowls – and the rabbis didn't like it. The Babylonian Talmud is full of rabbis shaming and marginalising magic women. They wanted a monopoly on magic. They wanted people in trouble to come to them, yet they kept asking for bowls to protect them from demons, and one demon in particular: the mighty, terrifying Lilith.

She was in the middle of the bowl I'd come to see, staring out with big eyes, wild, dishevelled hair, cartoon breasts, struggling to break the chains that bound her, all chaos, sex and danger, a fuck-you to the patriarchy. She looked like my own rage. She had my hair. She looked like she could burst the bowl, which was small, made of pale unglazed clay the colour of shortbread – unglazed earthenware is actually called *biscuitware* – with a crack down one side. In the museum's Iraq study room, I turned it to follow the spiral of tiny black writing and looked at the translation to see her called 'evil Lilith who leads astray the hearts of human beings . . . slaying boys and girls'. The words were a spell, a wish for Lilith to 'be subdued and sealed', and they just made her sound more powerful. She looked like she could eat the world.

I'd been a bit in love with Lilith since my childhood rabbi mentioned her, just once, saying she was Adam's first wife. His *bad* wife. Later I learned that Lilith came in because Genesis was too confusing. First God creates man and then it says

'He created him; male and female He created them' (what?). Then it says God makes a woman out of Adam's rib. Who were 'them', and if there was a 'them' which was 'male and female' then why did Adam need *another* woman made from his rib? When the rabbis tried to answer these questions, they sometimes got carried away, and told stories that were wilder, stranger and more freewheeling than what they'd started with. Some said Adam was intersex but others said he had a first wife, a wrong wife, which is why he needed to sacrifice a rib to make a second. They needed a name for this first wife and they used Lilith which means 'night creature', 'night monster', 'night hag' or 'screech owl' or 'witch'. They accused Lilith of causing miscarriages, killing babies, snatching babies, seducing and murdering adults, and marrying Satan.

All these stories swirled around for a long time until around 800 when Lilith snapped into focus in a much-contested text called *The Alphabet of Ben Sira*. In *The Alphabet*, Lilith is made out of clay at the same time as Adam. She refuses to have sex in the missionary position and gets turned into a demon who kills babies and causes wet dreams (one of these things is not like the other). *The Alphabet* sets it up as a comedy: 'God created a woman . . . and called her Lilith. They promptly began to argue.' She tells him they're equal but he won't let her go on top so she says God's name – His unsayable, holy Name – and suddenly she's *flying*. Actually flying. Airborne. Where before she could only walk. Did she know that saying it would give her wings? Or was it just an impulse? Was she surprised when her feet left the ground? Exhilarated? Terrified? Empowered even?

God sends angels to give Lilith an ultimatum; she can go back to Adam or a hundred of her children will die every day. 'Leave me alone!' she cries, magnificent in her malevolence.

'I was only created to sicken babies: if they are boys, from birth to day eight I will have power over them; if they are girls, from birth to day twenty.' The angels beg Lilith to reconsider, and she relents; if the babies wear amulets she will not take them. (I was rethinking the salt, and the evil eyes.)

Lilith raged on through generations of Jewish lore and stories, a demon to scare mothers. A curly-haired fiend. After Eve eats the apple, according to one Talmudic rabbi, 'She grows hair like Lilith.' My hair. It's curious that while a lot of Jewish women have curly hair, Lilith hair, many straighten it or, if they are married and Orthodox, cover it up, often with wigs. Curly wigs are hard to make so the wigs are often sleek and straight. All this taming and smoothing and flattening made me uncomfortable. Jewish women don't face the hair discrimination Black women do, but Jewish hair has still been problematised – the Nazis used it as a marker of racial impurity. There are reasons Lilith's hair feels like a revolt. When I first saw a reproduction of Dante Gabriel Rossetti's painting *Lady Lilith*, with her combing masses of hair – which he called *enchanted* in a sonnet he wrote on the painting's frame – I was exhilarated. I was drawn to feminist reclamations of Lilith, like Judith Plaskow's revisionist 1972 *midrash* 'The Coming of Lilith', where, having rejected Adam, God and the patriarchy, Lilith longs for a female friend; so she sneaks back into the garden and helps Eve quest for forbidden knowledge. I loved writing for the American Jewish feminist magazine *Lilith*, and I admired the Lilith Fund, a Texas charity supporting women needing abortions.

I also feared Lilith, especially when I became a mother. If I could have found a magic woman to make me a bowl to protect my child from Lilith, I would have done it in a heartbeat. I imagined going to the sorceress, making my request, and her making my bowl, maybe as described on one of the bowls: 'Upon a rock that is not split I shall sit, and I shall write upon a new bowl of clay.' I could almost see, reaching back through time, a woman who looked like me, walking and walking till she found the right rock, scooping up clay and shaping it, and turning it round and round as she wrote. Another bowl said it was written 'in the name of the menstruating woman', adding, *slightly* too viscerally, 'My hands in blood I dipped.' Some of the bowls used legal language, to divorce the demon from her victim; some were more obviously incantations. One was inscribed, 'Accursed. Overturned overturned overturned overturned overturned overturned overturned. Overturned be the earth and the heavens, overturned be the stars and the planets, overturned be markets and streets, overturned be the hour of all human kind, overturned be the curse of the mother and her daughter, of the daughter-in-law and her mother-in-law, of men and women who stand in the field and in the town and in the mountain and temple and synagogue.' Some bowls referred to rituals the magic women did, involving 'shaking bodies' (maybe trances?), whispering, hissing, making circles, drawing the shape of a house with a knife, binding adversaries and eating ritual cakes. After that the bowls were buried, upside down, and sometimes cemented in place with bitumen. 'I am pressing down this press,' says one bowl, 'and I am burying demons and devils . . . and I am inverting [this bowl] at the threshold of his house . . . and I am pressing down this press upon them.' Most people thought they were traps for demons. And when archaeologists excavated the bowls, they turned them right side up and the demons were released.

In the Iraq Study Room, I sat at a long wooden desk, surrounded by cabinets stuffed with tablets and fragments, and pulled on my blue latex gloves. In front of me was a tray of magic bowls, facing down. I didn't know whether I dared release the demons. On either side of me, scholars were painstakingly translating cuneiform, and I was gazing at the bowls, and stroking their smooth sides. I decided to be brave. Carefully, I spun the bowls and then I turned them one by one. If the demons weren't out, well, they were now.

Holding the bowls, I felt like I was in the kitchens with the women, trying to protect themselves and their families in a ravaged, uncertain world. The bowls were loud with stories of sickness and sadness, of petty rivalries and unrequited passions, of heartbreak and healing. The way they talked to the demons felt intimate; they didn't order them about but cajoled them, connected with them. And what if the women didn't commission bowls because they feared Lilith? What if they did it because they were scared they'd be blamed if bad things happened to their children, so they gave the blame to Lilith? And what if she took that weight? With generosity, with strength, to break the cycle of victim-blaming. It made me sad to think that if she did do this, she was then trapped, like a spider in a cup, her trap cemented down at the threshold. No wonder she tried to crack the bowl to get free. But then, as I held the bowls, willing them to reveal their secrets, I wondered: what if they weren't traps but *homes*? What if, instead of warding Lilith off, the sorceresses were making deals with her, saying: stop haunting this house, and live instead in a room of your own, a tiny, domed dwelling, a place of safety where you can rest from all your wandering. I imagined her for a moment, beside me in the museum, looking at the bowls to see if she liked the look of them, and nodding. *Yes*. This was an agreement we could make. This was something we could honour. And then I flipped the bowls back one by one, each small, safe home. This was what you were supposed to do with your demons, wasn't it? To name them and contain them, to give them somewhere safe to be so they weren't roaming everywhere, fingers in everything, eyes roving wildly, wreaking havoc. To befriend them, perhaps?

I was thinking, of course, about my demons too.

Sifting

Raqi (watermelon)

I was seven when my grandfather told me he was going to die soon and I would have to look after everyone. The whole family. My parents. My brother. My aunt and uncles. Cousins. Even my *grandmother*. Terrified of this epic responsibility, I burst into tears, and my mother heard and rushed into the room and said my grandfather had only said all this 'because of what happened in Iraq'. I never knew him as the dapper doctor in a suit and tie who treated celebrities and healed people who gave him gazelles and helped him leave Iraq. The grandfather I knew was deep in depression. They took him to doctors, who treated him with ECT. It didn't help. I mostly remember him miserable, chain-smoking in pyjamas.

Sometimes I still tried to look after people when it was not appropriate, when they didn't want it, when I should have been looking after myself. I was determined my son wouldn't be like this.

He wouldn't inherit my recurring nightmare of running through a desert, chased by secret policemen in moustaches. Or my anxiety about having my hair touched because it reminded me of torture. He would not spend his childhood Sundays alternating *The Sound of Music* with *Fiddler on the Roof*, getting the impression that whether you were a singing nun or a philosophical tailor you'd always end up forced to escape people who hated Jews. When we booked holidays, he would not check the flight path to make sure we weren't flying over Iraq, because what if the plane had to make an emergency landing and we were back there, at the mercy of the secret police again? He would not pick up the phone with 'what's wrong?' instead of 'hello'. As if every call was an SOS. He would eat watermelon.

Actually I thought I was doing OK with watermelon. I wanted my son to like it. I offered it to him with a smile, early on, and he loved it from first bite. By itself and also the Iraqi way, with halloumi slices dipped into hot water. I liked going to the Iranian grocer who spotted the tiny gold filigree *hamsa* I wore, with the turquoise stone in the palm and made sure I got the juiciest, reddest fruit. I liked lugging it home, its roundness curving against my stomach, saving the seeds (*habb*) to rinse, salt and roast, along with pumpkin seeds and sunflower seeds. The sound of *habb*-cracking is the sound of my childhood, and maybe it could become a sound of his. It felt like healing. Until the day a stranger used watermelon to other us.

My son was eighteen months old. Lounging in his pushchair, clutching a fat pink triangle of watermelon, his chin spattered with pink juice, singing 'The Wheels on the Bus'. You couldn't blame me for feeling smug about my parenting, as he stuffed his face with fruit. So I was taken aback when a woman stepped into our path to exclaim, 'Exotic!' She was blocking our way and she sounded *affronted*. I immediately felt guilty. Had I done something terrible without realising it? Had I wheeled the pushchair over her foot perhaps? In an even more outraged voice, she went on: 'Watermelon?! For a *baby*?!!'

I mean, there were worse things he could have been eating.

I blinked. I muttered that he liked it. Did I say it was cooling and hydrating? I may have done. She didn't move. I had to manoeuvre awkwardly around her to get past.

Six years on, I still hadn't got past. I was still imagining the conversation going differently, picturing myself sitting down with her, explaining that watermelon isn't exotic for me; it's familiar. That exotic is not a neutral word, and, yes, it can mean *excitingly strange* but usually it just means *foreign*, and *exo* is Greek for outside; it's a word that puts people (and fruit) outside the magic circle of citizens. It's also inaccurate. I got that watermelon at the supermarket. It might even have been British-grown. Tesco's watermelons have been known to come from Wisbech, Asda's from Kent. (The Garden of England!) Watermelons have in fact been grown in the UK since 1597. How long did it take for something to stop being exotic? If four centuries weren't enough for a fruit then what about a person – a person whose roots here only went back fifty years? I imagined her listening, taking everything on board. I imagined feeling seen, feeling that my son and I belonged.

Instead, her xenophobia tainted every watermelon we'd had since.

Then one hot afternoon in 2022, I took my son to the park. I mean I took him to the park almost every hot afternoon in 2022, and many cold afternoons and rainy mornings too, and one time we got there just after a thunderstorm and found our path blocked by a tree that had been hit by lightning and crashed and we marvelled at the scorch marks in its ruined trunk, and I had the urge to stroke its wrecked branches, to soothe it somehow. The park was our happy place, our safe place, every inch of it thick with memories. There was the big round swing I used to climb onto with my son still snuggled up against me in the sling; which, later, he'd laze on with a friend, giggling and blinking at the sun shining through the trees; and later still he'd ride standing up, propelling it impossibly high. The tiny slope he toddled up and called a mountain. The pirate ship he captained. The path he chalked rainbows over during the pandemic. The hedge he used as a hideout. The tree he crashed his scooter into and the tree he crashed his balance bike into. There would be more memories layered over these, of him at six amassing small stacks of treasures like old buttons, shiny silver washers and 'interesting stones', or at seven sitting on a log and trading

Pokémon cards with his friends. But in 2022 he was five, and we picked up a neighbour and a football and we were off. We knew we'd probably run into more friends in the park, or make some. He'd made so many friends there and so had I.

It was this park, known locally as 'the secret park', a little bit hidden, and very green, that had really made me feel part of a community, connected, rooted. The nesting urge I'd had while I was pregnant had transmuted into an urge to root. To stop being a seed adrift in the wind, to root myself so I could give my son roots too. To plant myself more securely in this place. The Jewish story was a story about being uprooted, again and again, but the Jewish Puerto Rican writer Aurora Levins Morales wrote that planting seeds and tending land could be 'an amulet against dispossession', and I wanted to try. To grow hope as well as trees.

I was a terrible gardener, though, and every attempt sent me into second-generation panic. Who was I to garden in England? It seemed the preserve of English women in floppy hats who could reel off Latin plant names and take cuttings from their grandparents' gardens and eat fruit from trees their ancestors planted. I felt excluded by seed catalogues that called 'non-native' plants *alien*, *invasive*, *fast-growing*, *destructive*, *unwanted*, and troubled by the difficult histories of plants, often taken from colonised land or brought here by botanists who forced enslaved people to collect them, and then renamed them, erasing the original indigenous names. I was disturbed to find a plant for sale (still!) called the Wandering Jew, named for the antisemitic myth about a figure who rejects Christ and is cursed to roam the earth for ever, with no home, no place to rest.

I was doing my best to keep my son safe from the bad stories, from the trauma. Yes, I sang him 'Edelweiss' at night, over and over in the dark, but I told myself it was just a show tune. It was only masquerading as an Austrian folk ballad sung by a man protesting the Nazi annexation of his homeland. Yes, I sometimes read him picture books like *Tia Fortuna's New Home*, where a Jewish Cuban grandmother remembers all the times she has packed up her mezuzah and her memories. Or *Raquela's Seder*, where a small girl in Inquisition Spain has a secret Pesach on a boat. Or *The Chocolate King* by Michael Leventhal, where a Jewish family is forced to leave Spain. He was captivated by the surreal, bold illustrations in Chris Naylor-Ballesteros's *The Suitcase* where a strange-looking animal arrives in a new place after a long and traumatic journey and faces suspicion and violence; he lingered over the picture of the mysterious refugee clinging to his suitcase in a rough sea. 'His home is so far away!' he said one day, eyes brimming.

None of it mattered in the park. Yes, I'd dressed him in clodhopping shoes, thick joggers, three layers on top, while his friends were in sandals and T-shirts. Even though in my twenties, once, my coat rack snapped off the wall, strained by the weight of all my coats, and my flatmate gathered up the scattered screws, contemplated the ugly gouge in the plaster, and said, 'You second-generation refugees! You're always buying coats and bags and shoes in case you have to walk across Europe.' He was right. I was always preparing for that journey. But as my son hit the park and ripped off his coat, I watched him joyously shedding layers, dressing for now not then, for his life, no one else's, living without weight.

And then I saw a swastika on the bench.

I froze. It was right beside me, a malignant spider. I was suddenly very aware that I was here with my Jewish son (he needed the adjective now, or maybe I did). I tried not to respond, to scare him, and put my backpack on top of the swastika, to cover it up before he saw it. He didn't know what a swastika was. Yet. For the first time I realised I couldn't shield him from this. For the first time, darkly, I thought he needed to know because it would armour him against what might come. He ran off with his friend but I couldn't breathe. My head was pounding *we're not safe here. We are hated. We have to leave.*

I called the council, spent half an hour on hold during which I also gave out snacks, refereed a football game, rescued a lost toy – and then the line went dead. When I called the police, I was directed to a website with a form that made no sense. On the council's website I filled in a different form. I tried to scour the swastika off with a wet wipe, then with hand sanitiser, but it wouldn't budge. I couldn't make it go away and in the morning we were due to go out of town and the swastika would just be sitting there, in the park, our park. In a last-ditch effort I posted about it on the local parents' Facebook group.

I'd been talking to a therapist who worked on generational trauma. She'd told me about hypervigilance, about how the second generation are always on high alert, waiting for danger, eyes swivelling for trouble, or, as a cousin once said, living 'like a piano was about to fall on our heads'. I did not live through what happened to my family, but I also had no choice about it weighing me down. It gave me nightmares, made me a people-pleaser trying to make up for the bad things that had happened (as if they could be made up for); a fixer trying to mend things that were irretrievably broken; an imposter, always code-switching and hiding and changing to fit in, wanting to be both Iraqi Jewish and not, but often feeling neither; a Lot's wife, helplessly looking back even though I'd been told not to, and being frozen in that looking, unable to move forward. The therapist told me to separate worries I could do something about from worries I couldn't. That I shouldn't try to carry the whole burden. But as we left London, I felt frustrated. I'd tried to shift the burden but no one else would take the weight. Not the police, not the council. I felt heavy, sad and disorientated. Maybe this was never a home or a community. Maybe I was never rooted and these were not real friends but just a loose affiliation of people who happened to have children around the same time and lived in the same postcode.

Then, scrambling up a Devon tor, I got a message from one of my son's friend's mums. She and two other parents had seen my Facebook post, taken sandpaper to the park and removed the swastika. I felt the burden literally lift off my shoulders. The next day another parent alerted a local councillor and the head of parks rang to apologise for not dealing with it sooner, sent a team in hi-vis jackets to check the swastika was really gone, and made a plan to act on offensive graffiti faster. It was a community after all. I felt held. I felt lighter.

Sifting

The therapist asked me to think about other baggage I could let go of. But I couldn't let go of the stories; it was my duty to tell them, to keep them alive, to fight erasure. I'd been brought up to hold on to them. As a child it sometimes felt like my community was clinging to our identity and culture like a life raft in a storm. It was stifling, and for a long time I did my best to get away, studying English literature, resisting the pressure to marry within my community, blocking out my fears. It was much later that I started wanting, *needing* the stories that told me where I came from so I knew where I was going. I started cooking the food, and found my own way back. After all this it seemed like a wrong turn to suddenly let go.

My therapist smiled. 'Yes, but maybe you can do a bit of sifting.' I suddenly imagined clouds of flour passing through a sieve. I imagined what it might be like to set down the weight or at least try to carry it lightly. Sifting *felt* appealing but I still didn't know if it was *right* or how to go about it.

There were some things I actively wanted to let go of. There was a recipe which involved stuffing raw cow intestines with meat and herbs and then sewing them up, before cooking them, and after I did the sewing once, I honestly didn't think I could do it again. There was the word *gawad*, which literally meant *pimp*, but which we used for cheeky boys, for rascals; my brother was regularly called *gawad* as a child, but no one has called my son that, and I hope no one will.

I *wished* I could let go of the genetic disease that disproportionately affects Iraqi Jews. When I was pregnant I was terrified

I would pass it on. I didn't know its name, just that my family used to say 'It turns your blood to water!' and that it was something to do with broad beans. It is either called favism, after the beans, or G6PD deficiency, after the enzyme you don't have enough of which helps red blood cells work properly. Without it, your red blood cells rapidly break down and you can get stomach pain, vomiting, pallor, jaundice and brown urine (thought not, actually, *blood turning to water*). Growing up we avoided broad beans, which was a downer given one of the *best* Iraqi recipes is rice with broad beans, dill and saffron. (Make it. Top it with a fried egg. You won't regret it.) When I was sixteen, a test for G6PD became available and the whole community signed up; on the way home from discovering no one in the family had it, we hit the Iranian grocer's for armfuls of fresh broad beans, and podded them before we'd got our coats off. I knew, though, that I could still be a carrier, so I avoided broad beans during my pregnancy. My son was tested at five days old, as part of his 'heel prick' test. He didn't have it. I took a breath.

I was delighted to discard sugaring, the form of hair removal favoured by Iraqi Jews. I only tried it once, in early puberty, when my mother decided it was time to do something about my hairy legs. There were no sugaring salons then, let alone any like the fancy Notting Hill establishment which calls sugaring 'the next hair-removal trend you are going to be obsessed with', and promises 'silky-smooth, glowing skin' and 'a technique that is quick with the minimum discomfort'. That salon also emphasises that the sugaring paste is applied at body temperature – which 'removes all risk of burning'. Maybe this is where we went wrong because I remember sugar so hot it made me yelp. I never tried it again.

What about my longing to go to Baghdad? Could I let go of that? Could I make peace with the fact I might never go? I always felt a vague, inchoate resistance to the structure of the hero's journey that underpins so many Hollywood films, and, of course, the very oldest stories, even the epic of Gilgamesh. The narrative arc of *home – adventure – return* didn't make space for the stories of refugees and migrants. Gilgamesh went back to Uruk but my parents were unlikely to go back to Iraq, and I probably wouldn't get to go there either.

My mother and I tried to go there virtually. On Google Earth, we started out on satellite view. It was so exciting, like flying above Baghdad on a magic carpet perhaps. She quickly found her suburb, Al Masbeh, and then – wow – she found her street. We hovered just above. That's it, she said. For sure. We tried Street View. We zoomed in, but she was suddenly lost and I couldn't help her. We zoomed out again, and she got her bearings. She found a roundabout she remembered, then traced her steps from the river. I watched with my heart in my mouth, wanting her to find home, but we couldn't get any closer. The magnification stopped way before we could see separate buildings. It got blurry and pixelated. Much of Baghdad was the same and online there was fierce speculation about why, and *many* conspiracy theories. For us, anyway, it was a dead end. Just another way we couldn't return.

Could I reframe it, though? Could there be something heroic about a journey that didn't end at home but where the hero(ine) summoned up the courage to live with the lack of resolution, with the absence, with the uncertainty? In principle this could be healing, but the idea felt horrible, like being permanently on the ark with the flood waters never going down, the sway and swell never giving way to dry land, never getting the chance to stop and plant and root and rest and live. Then it struck me that in the Flood story, neither Noah nor Utnapishtim before him, or Atrahasis before *them*, went back home. They landed somewhere else, and made new homes there. They planted in new places.

There are other heroes who don't return home either. Paddington Bear doesn't go back to Peru; he finds a new home in Windsor Gardens. Superman is rocketed to earth as a baby just before his planet, Krypton, explodes, and he doesn't get to go back home, but he does get to keep adventuring. (His story, incidentally, was written by two second-generation Jewish refugees, from Ukraine and Lithuania.) Wonder Woman chooses to leave the Amazons with the sexy captain who has crash-landed, and she also commits to the adventure. In the *Alien* films, Ripley never makes it back to her home planet but finds she's been in space so long that her daughter has died. In *Alien Resurrection*, she sees Earth, flying low above it, and, asked what happens now, she replies, hauntingly, 'I don't know. I'm a stranger here myself.' I liked the idea of never-ending stories, like the *Thousand and One Nights* where every story leads to another story. It is said that if you ever reach the end you will die, but as Marina Warner wryly says, 'the danger is not very serious', because the *Nights* are impossible to finish, not because of their length but because of the 'myriad variations and the efflorescence of the structure'. There is so much trauma in the *Thousand and One Nights*. The trauma of the women the sultan married, raped and murdered, night after night after night. The trauma of the other women who feared they'd be next. The trauma of the people who loved and lost the women. And also, although it's hard to get up much sympathy for him, the trauma of the sultan who was so wounded after his wife betrayed him that he didn't know how to help himself, and instead turned his pain into violence and rage. Scheherazade doesn't just tell him stories, a thousand and one of them, each with a cliffhanger so intriguing that he keeps her alive to hear the rest; she doesn't just save her own life and the lives of all the women he'd have raped and murdered if she hadn't stopped him; she also saves the sultan. She does it by telling stories in a way that forces the sultan to work through his trauma and find a way to deal with it, ways that don't involve rape and murder. When she starts with stories about bad women, the sultan nods along, happy that Scheherazade is confirming his view that women can't be trusted; but as she goes on to introduce, as Warner writes, 'maltreated wives, subjugated daughters, faithful female lovers, clever and courageous slave girls, courageous loving mothers, intelligent teachers, loyal sisters and devoted peris or fairies in an increasingly shining procession of women', he is forced to reconsider his misogyny. By the time she presents him with the three children she's implausibly had without him noticing, there is some hope that he has changed and will be a better husband and father. In Gabrielle Zevin's novel about writing games, *Tomorrow, and Tomorrow, and Tomorrow*, she spins Macbeth's despairing line into something more hopeful, asking, 'What is a game? It's tomorrow, and tomorrow, and tomorrow. It's the possibility of infinite rebirth, infinite redemption. The idea that if you keep playing, you could win. No loss is permanent . . .' *No loss is permanent*. This felt like something to hope for, the idea that if you just kept playing, you could keep loss at bay; if you gave up on an eventual return home, you could stay on the adventure. Maybe, after all, I could do this big bit of sifting. Maybe.

I was still unsure when, at Yom Kippur, the Jewish festival of atonement, I joined a Zoom service with Rachel Rose Reid, a performance poet who was ordained as a Hebrew priestess, or *kohenet*, by the radical and beautiful Kohenet Hebrew Priestess Institute, who reimagine ritual and women's roles in Jewish life. Reid startled me by saying Yom Kippur was a festival of letting go. I'd always thought it was gloomy and guilt-making, about atoning for wrongs, feeling bad about all the ways I'd fallen short over the year, while also feeling ravenous and thirsty with a kicking headache. But Reid smiled and said it could be joyful. That the service Kol Nidre literally meant 'all vows' and I'd been saying, all these years, in a mix of Hebrew and Aramaic, 'May we be absolved of them, may we be released from them, may they be null and void and of no effect. May they not be binding upon us.' On the Zoom, some of the others were talking about release. One person shared that they had eating disorders, so they'd sometimes enjoyed fasting because Yom Kippur was the one day of the year they weren't being told to eat; they wanted to release themselves from the obligation to fast and instead to focus on nourishment. Another released themselves from a promise to be with someone who was bad to them, another from duties they should never have taken on. I had not realised Judaism contained this brilliant mechanism for letting go. After I closed my laptop, I kept unknotting. I found the fast easier than I had ever found it. I had a slow day and a very gentle walk and sat under a tree with leaves like spun silver. I wanted to break the fast the way I would have broken it in Baghdad, with *hariri* (home-made almond milk with cardamom), but I ran out of steam and couldn't face all the soaking and blending and sieving, so I approximated that other Iraqi Jewish fast-breaker, *silan* and buffalo milk cream, with my best date syrup and a tub of mascarpone. I listened to Iraqi Jewish Broadway actress Sharone Sayegh sing Kol Nidre to an Iraqi tune and just felt it happen; sifting, releasing, clouds of flour rising and falling.

York

Even so, there was a worry I couldn't shift. A creeping unease that woke me in the night. The knowledge that I was bringing up my son in a country that once expelled every last one of its Jews. I was haunted by the work of academic Geraldine Heng who analysed the intensity and twisted creativity of medieval English antisemitism in her book *The Invention of Race in the European Middle Ages*, pointing out that England was the first country to expel its Jews (setting off a wave of other expulsions) and, before that, innovated other forms of antisemitism: the ghetto (medieval English Jews had to live separately from Christians); the blood libel (the notion that Jews torture and murder Christian children and use their blood to bake bread); and *possibly* the identifying badge, although, ironically for me, some people think Jews first had to mark themselves out with badges in Baghdad.

The worry took me to York, despite the old joke that 'Jews don't do York and pork' and rumours there was a *cherem* (rabbinical ban) on Jews living there or even staying overnight. In 1190, the city's Jews were ethnically cleansed. They were chased by an antisemitic mob, took refuge in a castle and, realising they wouldn't get out alive, committed mass suicide in a horrifying echo of what had happened to the Jewish rebels besieged by Romans in Masada. The survivors were butchered in the morning. The site, Clifford's Tower, is now run by English Heritage, who aim to remember and tell England's stories. I went to York to find out how they were telling this one.

I could see it wasn't easy for them. The castle sitting on top of the grassy mound in the middle of the city is not the castle the Jews hid in, but a newer one, which later became quite important to the history of the north, and which has England's only surviving medieval toilet. Still, I wished English Heritage's website didn't focus quite so much on the toilet. I also wished they hadn't once tried to insert a gift shop into the mound that ran with Jewish blood.

The trouble began in 1189 with the new king, Richard I, the Lionheart, who I knew from the Robin Hood stories. He was always away, being heroic, but the stories skated around the fact that he was on a Crusade, killing Muslims, and also Jews, or forcing them to convert, or selling them into slavery, or barricading them into synagogues and burning them alive. He started his reign with a bang, banning Jews from his coronation, and when some turned up anyway (with presents!), he had them stripped and flogged. This inspired Londoners to go on a rampage, robbing, beating and killing Jews – or forcing them to convert. The chronicler Richard of Devizes called this a 'holocaust'. The next day, the king summoned one of the Jews who'd converted, a moneylender called Benedict of York. Forbidden to own land or join trade guilds, Jews often turned to moneylending. They bankrolled medieval England and were resented for it – and this was still going on in the Facebook memes I saw blaming the Rothschilds for Covid, as if Jewish moneylenders were still responsible for everything bad in the world. Richard I asked Benedict if his conversion was sincere – as if he didn't know Benedict had been forced to choose between converting and being murdered, and as if he couldn't see that Benedict was visibly wounded. When Benedict admitted that he'd only converted to stay alive, the king laughed.

Benedict died on the way home to York. He was unable to protect his widow and children when, after copycat massacres of Jews in King's Lynn, Norwich, Stamford and Bury St Edmunds, an armed band looted their home, and burned them alive inside. York's Jews, terrified, asked for help and were allowed to put their money in the castle for safe keeping. But the rampage continued – because it wasn't all about the money. So this time the Jews fled to the castle, to keep themselves safe. The warden let them in and then lied to the city's governor saying the Jews had *taken* the castle. The governor ordered a siege, and when the Jews saw the siege engine they gave up hope.

A local monk and chronicler called William of Newburgh praised the people of York for 'sweeping away the whole race' of Jews, in what he called 'the just judgment of Christ', but he didn't like them murdering the Jews who asked for mercy. He was annoyed by the murderers 'refusing the grace of Christ to those who sought it'. I had to read this twice. Did he really think the traumatised survivors, surrounded by corpses, threatened with a siege, wanted Christ's grace? Apparently he did. He even promised that any Jews who had converted 'with no fiction' would be considered 'baptised with their own blood' and 'by no means defrauded' of this grace. He meant this to be comforting. It made me shiver. It felt like Jews were never – *are* never – allowed to just be Jews. Even in 2019, when the Church of England issued an amazing report apologising for the way Christian institutions in England created a 'fertile seed-bed for murderous antisemitism', the chief rabbi rightly criticised them for failing to mention what he called the 'real and persistent concern . . .that even now in the 21st century, Jews are seen by some as quarry to be pursued and converted'.

I was at university when it happened to me. The Christian students' union ran a mission, asking students to convert their friends. Over a fortnight, five or six friends appeared in my room with Bibles. They were nice, apologetic, embarrassed, under pressure. But I started feeling unwelcome and uneasy. And one evening, a proselytising student – not a friend – tried to start an argument about heaven, not letting me go until I stopped being polite and walked away. The past didn't feel very past then (and the union is still running its mission now, in 2024). And the past didn't feel very past when I missed the New Testament imagery in medieval poetry and my tutor asked where I was from. When I said my parents were from Baghdad, he joked, 'That's just down the road!' because the Knights Templar returning from the Crusades had named a Hertfordshire town after Baghdad. (An attempt to console themselves for never actually managing to conquer Baghdad?) I was discomfited to find that Baldock had a school, a restaurant and several sports teams named for the Crusaders with, of course, no mention of killing people. From *The Da Vinci Code* to the video game *Assassin's Creed*, Crusaders still carry an aura of glamour.

In York I found the grassy mound covered with daffodils. Thousands of them. From English Heritage's website I learned that they were a memorial, blooming around the anniversary of the massacre, each with six points which echoed the Star of David; but many people were confused by them, wondering if they were supposed to recall the yellow stars Nazis made Jews wear. On the mound itself there was no explanation. I wondered if, like other sites of atrocities, Clifford's Tower would attract 'dark tourism'. It was a stop on York's ghost walks where the guides said the tower's stones sometimes turned red because of the blood shed that night, but when I visited, no one seemed to be having a particularly emotional response. Of the 2,000 Tripadvisor reviews I slogged through, only thirty-one mentioned the Jews. Psychologist David Uzzell suggested Clifford's Tower couldn't elicit a 'hot interpretation' because it happened too long ago – it was *too past*. Maybe.

There was a plaque telling the story of the tragedy, which was surrounded by a well of white stones because Jews place stones on graves. I wanted to say a prayer, but two women were taking selfies, so I put my stone down awkwardly and retreated, feeling burned up inside and empty. I didn't understand why the plaque was off to one side of the mound, easy to miss, and had only been unveiled after a long campaign by Jewish activists. It felt like the story was being told in a way that was uneasy and half-hearted, and it was troubling. I'd read in *Everyday Hate* by Dave Rich, who is intimately aware of antisemitism in Britain through his work at the Community Security Trust, that 'the treatment of Jews in medieval England . . . is the subterranean bedrock upon which more recent anti-Jewish myths are layered, but it has largely been erased from our shared popular memory . . . This act of forgetting has left a vacuum in which modern antisemitism grows.' Neo-Nazis still met at Clifford's Tower, not to commemorate the massacre and suicide but to celebrate it. In 2022 they had even managed to hang a White Lives Matter banner off the tower.

Still in the vacuum, ten minutes later, I was taking a picture of another plaque, marking a Jewish cemetery now vanished under a supermarket car park, and two men came by, shaven-headed, with a nasty-looking dog, and told me I was 'fucking sad!' Repeating it. Angry. 'It used to be a cemetery,' I said. They laughed.

Still in the vacuum, I went to the site of a synagogue that, I was astonished to learn, opened its doors *after* 1190. This site also had a plaque – which mentioned pretty much everything that had been there apart from the synagogue. It even said Charlotte and Anne Brontë once spent the night at a coaching inn there. One night. But not the Jews who tried, for a whole century, to feel at home in a place they had been hated, hounded, murdered. I felt rattled to my bones. I wondered if the Jews who'd gathered here had hoped they would be safe once the frenzy was over, like my mother's family who stayed after most of the Jews left Iraq. They were wrong. In 1200 the government established an

Exchequer of the Jews, to spy on them, tax them and imprison them. Ten years later, the king imprisoned every Jew in the country, then released them but made them wear a 'badge of shame', and executed hundreds on trumped-up charges of coin-clipping – filing bits of silver off the edges of coins, melting them down and selling them. In 1231 Simon de Montfort expelled all the Jews of Leicester; in 1255 Jews were accused of murdering a nine-year-old boy in Lincoln and one was executed and ninety arrested; in 1264 de Montfort (again) massacred five hundred Jews in London. In 1275 the Statute of Jewry increased the size of the yellow badge, outlawed moneylending and made Jews live apart from Christians. In 1278, every single Jew in England was imprisoned (again!), and 293 Jews were executed in London. And then, in 1290, as another monk chronicler, John of Oxnead, put it, 'The Lord the king condemned all Jews of whatever sex or age living throughout England into perpetual exile without any hope of return.' These words struck home. I realised I had gone to York because I couldn't go to Baghdad, and that I was fatally attracted to stories of Jews facing more and more discrimination until they had to leave, going on perilous and uncertain journeys to places that could also turn just as hostile.

Would the Jews of York have had a better time in Baghdad? Yes, according to Jewish traveller Benjamin of Tudela. He visited the city around 1160 and was pleasantly surprised to find about 40,000 Jews living freely under a benevolent and just caliph, with twenty-eight synagogues connected to two thriving Talmudic academies (at Sura in the south, and at Pumbedita in what is now Fallujah), making it the ersatz capital of the Jewish world. It wasn't all rosy, however; Jews (and Christians too) had *dhimmi* status, officially considered inferior to Muslims and taxed for protection, which, as Lyn Julius writes in *Uprooted*, 'begs the question: protection from whom?' Some caliphs persecuted the Jews, and forced them to wear a yellow patch. They were not allowed to build homes higher than Muslim ones, to testify against Muslims, to marry Muslims, or to ride horses. Jews suffered along with everyone else when the Mongols took Baghdad in 1258, and when the Mongol ruler converted to Islam, he forced the Jews to choose between conversion or death. Despite all this, Jews continued to live in Baghdad for the centuries that they were expelled from England, and some European Jews found refuge in the Middle East. When Spain expelled its Jews in 1492, Sultan Bayezid II sent his navy to evacuate them safely to Ottoman lands. Perhaps some of the Jews from that blighted synagogue in York ended up in Baghdad.

In England, after the Jews were gone, their stories were suppressed. De Montfort has a university named after him, Richard I is the Lionheart of all the Robin Hood stories, but when it comes to the Jews of medieval England, there is so little left. The archives go silent, trails go dead, and all that is left are punitive laws, and records of debts, fines, imprisonments and executions. In York, after the massacre, the murderers went to the Minster to burn the records of their debts to Jews, to further erase them. I didn't learn about the expulsion at school. I did, however, read some of the literature about Jews that was written in the 366 years when there were no Jews in England, except the converts forced to eke out an existence at the House of Converts in London, or secret Jews, like Elizabeth I's doctor, Rodrigo Lopez (who was accused of trying to poison her), and, possibly, Emilia Lanier, the poet who may have been Shakespeare's Dark Lady. It was unnerving to realise that Chaucer wrote his blood libel fantasia *The Prioress's Tale*, and Marlowe and Shakespeare wrote *The Jew of Malta* and *The Merchant of Venice*, plays that aired antisemitic tropes, in an England where Jews had been forced to leave. It was almost as if, in the absence of Jews, English antisemitism was kept alive by literature. The Globe theatre's director of education Farah Karim-Cooper writes in *The Great White Bard: How to Love Shakespeare While Talking About Race* that stage representations of Jews from Shakespeare's day up until Jews returned to England were 'almost an entirely fantastical affair' given that no one in the theatre, from the actors (who, she speculates, may have worn prosthetic noses), to the audiences, would have knowingly met a Jew – and they might well have emerged from the theatre 'feeling more racial prejudice than when they walked in' – and in 2010, a Swedish study found that this was the case even for modern audiences watching *The Merchant of Venice*. I think (and hope) Shakespeare was trying to hold a mirror to our prejudices, rather than to confirm them, but in my heart I can't be sure.

The expulsion is now taught in (some) schools but the teaching materials I've seen claim that in 1656 it was reversed, and that Oliver Cromwell invited Jews to resettle in England. That's not entirely true. In fact, in 1655 Cromwell asked his government how the Church was supposed to convert Jews if there were no Jews to convert. It was all about conversion (*again*)! After that the government turned a blind eye, but the Jews who came here (or just came out of hiding) were harassed and threatened with expulsion and classed as aliens and discriminated against – until the nineteenth century.

Feeling weighed down by these sad old stories, and by the ways they were only being half told, or not told at all, one cold dark night in December I found something that gave me hope. It was a video on Facebook of the York Jewish community lighting Hanukkah candles on Clifford's Tower, the candles that are a wish for more light, that tell the story of a small band of Jews boldly resisting oppression, winning out against the coercive Greek Empire and being rewarded with a miracle. I hadn't known there was a Jewish community in York. One of its former rabbis assured me there never was a *cherem*, a ban, on

Jews living in the city. I also learned that the community's Torah scroll came from the former Czechoslovakia. It had been stolen by the Nazis, with thousands of others, which they may have been planning to exhibit in a Museum of an Extinct Race. After the war, so many Jewish communities were destroyed that the scrolls were unclaimed. In the 1960s the Czech government put them up for sale. A philanthropist bought over a thousand and started lending them to Jewish communities from Costa Rica to Barbados to New Zealand; it was very moving to realise that the York where Jews were back after such trauma, had adopted a scroll that carried its own story of salvage and rescue, its own hopes for resilience and repair.

Amba (mango pickle)

When it came to food, I avidly resisted the idea of sifting. I wanted to eat Iraqi Jewish food exactly like my parents had eaten it in Baghdad. When I was cooking I was fighting the sickening sensation of everything disappearing, but it was also about feeling I had something to prove, that I had to earn my sense of belonging. I became a stickler for authenticity. I railed against fusion food loudly and often. I knew this was classic second-generation angst, that I hated fusion food because I was scared I was a fusion *person*, neither one thing nor another; too English with my family, too Iraqi Jewish everywhere else. But knowing why I was doing something didn't make me able to stop. One reason I love *amba* is because it has such an uncompromising taste. I've never met a person who likes it who isn't Iraqi or Jewish or both.

The iconic Iraqi Jewish mango pickle (not chutney; I have had this argument many times) is its own thing, stubborn and steadfast. It can't be mixed or diluted or messed about with or fused. It's not sweet; it's sour and spicy, tangy, dayglo yellow and intense. It's the Iraqi Jewish umami, our ketchup, our soy sauce. It's good with *kubba*; or in a sharp chopped salad of cucumber, tomato and spring onions; with cheese; with falafel; transcendental with egg (scrambled, hard-boiled, or, oh my God, egg mayo). I can't think of a meal or especially a snack that wouldn't be improved by *amba*. It's a food that's defined our community, too. The Iraqi Jews who brought it to Israel were called 'stinky', but the pickle has become a national condiment, the key ingredient in what Israelis call *sabich* or just *Iraqi sandwich*: pitta stuffed with *amba*, fried aubergine and black eggs. There are legends about *sabich*, stories that it was first sold in a kiosk in Ramat Gan, the Iraqi Jewish suburb of Tel Aviv known as Ramat Baghdad, or Pyjama Town because Iraqi Jews were mocked for sitting out on their balconies in pyjamas (there is even a punk rock band called Iraqis in Pajamas). During the Gulf War in 1991, when Iraq's scud missiles disproportionately hit Ramat Gan, we joked they had been lured by the smell of *amba*.

Amba also has a backstory. A really good one. It was, *apparently*, invented by Siegfried Sassoon's great-grandfather. Did you know the poet was an Iraqi Jew? I didn't. When I fell for his poems, I thought he was a Merchant Ivory character, gorgeous, melancholy, tormented and deeply, indelibly *English*. He loved fox-hunting and steeplechasing. He called his autobiographical novel *Memoirs of a Fox-Hunting Man*. T. E. Lawrence once said if he ever needed to put an ideal Englishman on show in an international exhibition, he'd choose Siegfried Sassoon. That's how English he seemed to Lawrence *of Arabia*. He didn't seem to know that Siegfried's great-grandfather was born in Baghdad in 1793. One dark night, a fortune-teller grabbed David Sassoon on his way home from synagogue, and told him to go to India where he would become rich. Before he could decide whether to act on her advice, he was kidnapped by the despotic Ottoman ruler, Daud Pasha. As soon as he was free, he fled. In Bombay he started an international business empire – the Sassoons were called the Rothschilds of the East – had fourteen children and, *possibly*, found time to faff around with fenugreek. He fell in love with Indian mangoes and wanted to share them with his friends in Baghdad; realising they wouldn't survive the journey, he pickled them. If he did invent *amba*, Siegfried probably never tried it, because while David clung to his Iraqi Jewish identity, Siegfried never had a grip on his. Their story is not just the story of a pickle but a story about the decisions we make about holding on to culture or letting go of it, and the ways in which these decisions aren't made but just happen, because of history and chance and time.

In Bombay, David joined an established satellite community of Baghdadi Jews who still spoke Judeo-Iraqi Arabic and sent their children back to Baghdad to find partners. David carried on speaking it too, and it became his superpower; he found that it was useful to have a language he could use in his business that couldn't be understood by outsiders, and since he was working mainly with his sons, he kept it going, as a secret language that continued as the company spread across the world. One reason biographers have often written little about Siegfried's heritage is because they couldn't read the Sassoon archive. But when one of his distant relatives, Joseph Sassoon, who *can* read Judeo-Iraqi Arabic, wrote a recent family biography, he didn't mention that they may have invented *amba*. I find this, sorry, *AMBA*-lievable, because what a legacy it is, to have invented the pickle that is unique to our community.

Amba is the only legacy that's really left. Most of David's wealth was frittered away by his less business-minded descendants, who also lost touch with their culture and heritage. There is a striking picture of David's son, Sassoon David, always known as SD, soon after he moved to London, looking stiff and awkward in a suit, flanked by his father and brothers in flowing robes. They look Iraqi; SD looks like he could be in a Mayfair drawing room. In fact, he often *was* in Mayfair drawing rooms, or in his ivy-covered Jacobean house, set in acres of land in Surrey where he rode, hunted and fished on what had once been Hampton Court's hunting grounds. His wife anglicised her name from Farha to Flora. One brother made friends with the royal family; another got knighted and changed his name from Abdallah to Albert (but stuck an Iraqi palm tree and a Hebrew motto on his family crest); his sister became a newspaper editor, his nephew an MP. When the Jewish historian Cecil

Roth wrote a book about the Sassoons, he dedicated it to Hitler, because he had a mad, wild hope that Hitler would stop being so antisemitic once he saw how admirably a family of Jewish immigrants had integrated and contributed.

SD's son Alfred, the first Sassoon to be born in England, was so assimilated that he probably thought his family wouldn't mind when he married a non-Jew, Theresa Thorneycroft, a High Anglican from a family of sculptors and farmers. They did mind, though and Farha/Flora even declared her son dead to her. Without his family or community to anchor him, Alfred brought up his sons as Christians, in Kent. He named Siegfried after the works of Wagner, a composer who would become inextricably associated with antisemitism, and gave him a middle name, Loraine, after the clergyman who had helped Alfred and Theresa marry. In a church. Siegfried's start seemed as far away from his great-grandfather David Sassoon as it was possible to be. His life would take him even further from his heritage.

He was only four when his parents' marriage broke down. After that, he didn't see his father much. He remembered him, with a moustache and sad brown eyes, visiting rarely, bringing guava jelly and pomegranate. Was Alfred trying to give his sons the tastes of his own childhood? If he brought *amba*, Siegfried does not mention it. When he was eight years old, Siegfried was told his father was dying and taken to his deathbed where he met his grandmother, Farha, for the first time. He described her 'brown' face, said she talked fast in a 'foreign' voice and showed him a family tree, which one of his biographers thought he found 'flaunting' and 'vulgar' (maybe not realising that *vulgar* is one of those bad words people use about Jews). To me it felt heart-rending. Farha had not seen her son in ten years, and now he was dying she was meeting her grandsons, and might never see them again. Maybe she wanted to make them feel they were part of something, to give them roots. She printed their names at the bottom of the family tree, and it was the first time Siegfried saw his name in print; she gave the future poet a gift she could not know she was giving.

Siegfried was too upset to go to the funeral, and from his brother's descriptions of men 'in funny-looking hats . . . saying jabber-jabber-jabber' it felt 'queer and gruesome', 'a shock', 'strange' and 'outlandish' as if 'our father had been taken away from us by strangers'. He couldn't understand why his father hadn't been buried in the local churchyard with its yew trees and bells, but of course an Iraqi Jew couldn't rest easy in an English churchyard with yew trees and bells. Siegfried took to sniffing a bottle of rose perfume his father had given his mother, which he thought came from Persia, believing the faint scent was 'a sort of essence of my father's oriental extraction'. The closest he could get to his identity was to smell half-gone scent in a bottle that had once belonged to his father, who was estranged and now dead. He didn't even get the country right.

Later, he became disgusted with his father's family and wrote about their 'dirty trading, millions and millions of coins' and his 'jewelled, merchant Ancestors' stroking their beards and 'barter[ing] monstrous wealth'. It sounded like he was reflecting back the antisemitic things people had said to him. His story made me sad. His heritage had been sifted for him, or, rather, the baby had been thrown out with the bathwater. He was told his hands were 'over-illustrative'. Me too, Siegfried, me too. I always thought Sassoon was tortured and repressed because he was a pacifist during a war, and gay when it was impossible to be out, but now I wonder if he was always pushing his hands down because he couldn't be out as Iraqi Jewish either. His story feels like a cautionary tale about what losing culture can do to a person. Perhaps his life might have been different if he'd tasted *amba*, if he'd known who he was.

Writing his story sent me to the fridge, but as I grabbed the jar I realised something: I'd always thought of *amba* as authentically Iraqi Jewish. But if it was true, if it was invented (even by an Iraqi Jew) in Bombay, a mash-up of Indian mangoes and Iraqi Jewish pickling, then *amba* was never authentic. It was fusion food. *Amba* was not even an Arabic word, but the Marathi word for mango. This shocked me. I'd known *amba* was invented in Bombay, I'd even known that my community's favourite brand was an Indian company, MM Poonjiaji Spices, the green labels marked Ship Brand with a picture of a ship that looks like Sinbad the Sailor's, and underneath it, a warning in stern capitals, BEWARE OF IMITATIONS. Holding the jar in my hand, I finally joined the dots and realised this must mean it didn't, after all, conform to my stupidly strict criteria of authenticity. It was never authentic. Not when I had it as a child, not even when my dad had it as a child in Baghdad, bought from Abu Amba (literally, father of *amba*) who ran a street stall that would sell you *amba* oozing out of hot *samoon*, Iraqi bread shaped like a teardrop, with a puffy middle and a crunchy crust dusted with sesame seeds.

I felt quite depressed by this for a week or two and almost cancelled a phone call I'd set up with a company called Hoxton Beach who made their own (delicious) *amba*. When we did talk, though, I asked the owner if he knew the story of *amba*, and he said, 'It seems crucial that the British colonised India and were in Iraq too.' And suddenly, I found myself saying with outraged pride, 'We were eating it in Iraq before the British came!' I paused. I didn't say 'we' much. I often felt I couldn't call myself Iraqi since I hadn't been there; but faced with the suggestion that the British were crucial to the invention of *amba*, there it was. The 'we'. This made me realise something else: *amba* might have started as fusion food, but it had become authentic to my community, to me. What if Iraqi Jews loved *amba* so much *because* it was invented outside Iraq? Because the homesickness was always baked in? Maybe *amba* satisfied a hunger for meaning as well as for mango.

The food writer Soleil Ho describes foods like *banh mi* on sliced bread as not authentically Vietnamese but the best their grandmother could do in rural Illinois; and frames them as happy compromises, not tragic. Ho calls this 'assimilation food', which sidesteps the authenticity debate and instead explores how far you can 'stretch' loved, familiar dishes without losing their soul. I wanted to stop worrying about losing my soul too. To stretch. I watched the romcom *Always Be My Maybe*, where a woman makes joyful fusion food until a man tells her she's being inauthentic. She ends up making *kimchi jjigae* using his mother's recipe – not even her own mother's! I think I was supposed to think she had come back to her authentic self, but instead I felt the heroine ended the film smaller, tamer, meeker, less creative. And that wasn't what I wanted for myself. I didn't want to be a person slavishly following recipes, always scared I was getting them wrong. I wanted to be like the bold second-generation cooks, like Joanna Hu and Rosheen Kaul whose cookbook is called *Chinese-ish: Home cooking, not quite authentic, 100 % delicious*, or Priya Krishna, author of *Indian-ish: Recipes and Antics from a Modern American Family*, or Ravinder Bhogal who calls her recipes 'proudly inauthentic', or Michael Twitty whose book *Koshersoul: The Faith and Food Journey of an African American Jew* includes recipes for collard greens made with *schmaltz*, and brisket flavoured with Ethiopian *berbere*. I wondered if I could feel freer in my cooking (or even in my life?). The pressure to be authentic felt like one it might be joyful to let go of.

The Shoes of Tanboury

It was Purim so I made *hamantaschen*, the triangular pastries which are supposed to recall the three-cornered hat of the villain of the festival's story, Haman, who, according to the Book of Esther, tried to kill all the Jews of Persia. 'Was Haman a pirate?' asked my son, eating three without stopping and then, in a rather sticky voice, adding, 'They don't look like hats.' He was right. They didn't. In Israel they call them *oznei Haman* (Haman's ears) but they didn't look like ears either. I discovered that more than one Jewish scholar thought the pastries were supposed to be vaginas, associated *not* with the villain but with the heroine, Esther, the Jewish beauty queen who became a real queen and saved her people from destruction, and who was inextricably linked with the Babylonian goddess Ishtar, who Jewish women called 'the queen of heaven' and honoured by baking cakes. The cakes were 'marked with her image', but it didn't say which bit of her. It didn't say it had to be her face. I was laughing at unwittingly making my son jam tarts in the shape of a Babylonian goddess's vagina, when I found that *hamantaschen* was more likely to be derived from the German word for *pockets*.

Authenticity anxiety struck again, and I felt deflated as I picked up my son and took him to the park with a Tupperware full of the German biscuits I'd totally lost my taste for. And then I heard peals of laughter coming from inside a massive hollowed-out log. My son appeared at one end and his friend appeared at the other, each clutching a *hamantasch*, and I let go of my argument and my worries. Even if I'd been a bit messy about it, I'd given him something Siegfried Sassoon never had: confidence and pleasure in his identity. After all, Purim is not a festival of earnestly straining to get things right, but a carnivalesque shebang where you're supposed to dress up and get so drunk you forget the difference between good and evil. In Iraq, it used to be the biggest festival of the Jewish year, celebrated with parties where everybody played the card game *dosa* for money, and ate *sambusek bel tawa*, deep-fried chickpea pastries, like samosas or empanadas. They are also triangular – their name comes from the Persian word *sanbosag* (beautiful triangle) – and amazing with a glass of crisp white wine or any kind of gin. I imagined Esther in the palace, gorgeous and powerful, necking a dirty martini and dispatching a plateful of these while she schemed to save her family and friends.

Sambusek bel tawa

First, soak your chickpeas. About 500g of them, overnight, in lots of water, in a covered bowl. This is not a quick recipe. In the morning, drain them and simmer them, on the stove, with about twice the amount of water you have chickpeas, for about an hour. Save some water for the dough, mash the chickpeas and put them aside.

Now make the dough. Mix 360g of plain white flour and 60g of wholemeal flour, with a teaspoon of salt, half a sachet of dried yeast, a tablespoon of olive oil and 350 ml of the chickpea cooking water until it's pliable. (If it's stiff, add more chickpea water, a tablespoon at a time, until you're happy.) Knead it until it's smooth and not so sticky. Cover it with a damp tea towel and let it rise until it's doubled in size. It takes half an hour in my mum's kitchen, but mine is colder and I usually wait at least an hour. While you're waiting, chop four onions and fry them in olive oil until they're soft and dark, then mix them with the chickpeas, and add a tablespoon of curry powder and two teaspoons of ground cumin and season.

When the dough's risen, roll it out until it's very thin and use a glass or a cookie cutter to cut into 10 cm circles. Put a tablespoon of the chickpeas onto each and fold the dough over and crimp to seal with damp fingers. Put them on a greased baking tray until you've used up all the dough. If you're not ready to fry you can put them in the fridge. You can even freeze them on baking sheets and then pack them into boxes.

People say you can bake sambusek *but I tried once and they came out so dry and flaky that I wept. Instead, pour quite a lot of vegetable oil (two or three centimetres) into a deep frying pan and heat until it's hot. Add a few* sambusek *at a time (if you've frozen them, you can add them straight from the freezer). Leave lots of space. They will puff up. When they're crisp and golden take them out with a slotted spoon, and put them on kitchen paper to soak up any extra oil.*

While I was frying, I got the urge to make *zangoola*. They are sometimes called *zalabia* but I think that's more Persian, and they're a lot like Indian *jalebi*. Daisy Iny calls them the 'oldest Baghdad confection'; Nigella Lawson calls them, rather brilliantly, 'fried dough squiggles'; I felt such joy when she started including Iraqi Jewish recipes in her books, recipes from her (then) mother-in-law Daisy Saatchi. It felt like our food had arrived, like it existed, like this was a world in which people who weren't Iraqi or Jewish might make *zangoola* one day and lemon drizzle cake the next. The absolute pleasure of being *seen*.

I usually make *zangoola* for Hanukkah but in Iraq they were made for Purim too.

Zangoola

Sprinkle a sachet of dried yeast over 230 ml of warm water and leave it for ten minutes. Then mix in 120g of plain flour and a pinch of salt, and beat till the mixture's smooth as cream. Leave it again, for half an hour. Make the syrup by dissolving 600g of sugar in 320 ml of water, adding a splash of lemon juice and cooking for another two minutes, and then adding rose water or orange flower water, stirring briefly, then taking it off the heat. I like orange flower water. Linda Dangoor, who put *zangoola* in her book *Flavours of Babylon*, likes rose water. Nigella likes both.

Get a big frying pan and heat about an inch of vegetable oil. Then you need to pipe spirals of dough into it. You can do this messily with a teaspoon, or you can use a piping bag, or a squeezy ketchup bottle with an opening about the size of a lentil. You can make rosettes or pretzels but squiggles are fine. More than fine. Fry them and flip them till both sides are golden, then take out each one with a fork, dip them in the syrup and put them on a wire rack to dry. They will be crunchy, sticky, sweet and scented.

Purim is also the festival of dressing up. As a child, I was Esther every year in a dress my mother made and trimmed with gold braid. It is the festival of theatre, too. As a theatremaker I have always been quite bad at improvisation, but I wanted to be more confident with my culture, to make magic with it. So when I got the opportunity to help Lilac Yosiphon make a show, I couldn't resist. She is also Iraqi Jewish, the granddaughter of the mighty Shimon Ballas, and she wanted to adapt his children's book, *The Shoes of Tanboury*. It is about a poor, glum man in Baghdad who everyone mocks for his clod-hopping, worn-out shoes. He secretly saves up to buy new ones but can't get rid of the old ones. Every time he throws them away, they come back and cause trouble. He even gets thrown into a dungeon! But then, miraculously, the caliph himself intervenes to get him released. The ending recalls Gilgamesh relishing his city at the end of the epic. Tanboury, too, walks around Baghdad as if he has never seen his city before, blinking in the bright sunshine. He decides to keep his shoes, because they got him into trouble but they also got him out again, so maybe, despite everything, they are lucky.

When I took my son to a work-in-progress performance, he was entranced. Lilac invited the children to make-believe they were at a Baghdad *souq*, teaching them to haggle and pretend to walk away to get a better price. They loved it. 'I'm walking away!' sang my son, peering back to see the effect he was having. I felt anxious and silly though. Was this a travesty of my culture? Was I turning my heritage into a joke? Was I the worst actor in the room? (YES.) Suddenly, my Turkish Jewish friend Philip and his children were bargaining with us and I just felt so happy, haggling at the *souq* with my boy. I didn't care that it wasn't real or authentic, that I still couldn't go to Iraq, that we'd probably never go to a *souq* and we were doing it in English, at the Royal Festival Hall, and it was ridiculous . . . even so: we were imagining ourselves there, my son and I. We were working together to suspend our disbelief, using sheer desire to power our magic carpet across the skies.

We were also *remembering* our culture. We weren't ignoring or forgetting it. We were getting it wrong but we were trying, having fun. I thought about this during a public conversation I had with queer Jewish writer-performer Rachel Mars, as part of her installation *Forge*. Rachel, whose grandparents made it to Britain at the eleventh hour in August 1939, had taken over a gallery space and spent a week forging a replica of a gate that was stolen from Dachau concentration camp in 2014, probably by neo-Nazis. It was eventually found in a lock-up in Norway and put in a museum for safe keeping, so people who make the painful trip to Dachau now see a replica, not the real thing. Rachel and I talked about memorials, who they helped (if anyone), what value they might have (or not), and she told an old Jewish joke: 'A synagogue gets a new rabbi and the congregation immediately start arguing, because they can't remember if their tradition is to stand or to sit for one of the prayers. Eventually they go back to ask their old rabbi, and he tells them the tradition is not to stand *or* to sit; the tradition is the argument.'

The tradition is the argument. If we were arguing, we were remembering. We weren't like Siegfried Sassoon who couldn't remember because he didn't know in the first place. We weren't like I used to be, earnestly straining for authenticity. And we weren't like Noah, who didn't argue with God, just silently obeyed. Argument is at the very heart of being Jewish; the Talmud is mostly a record of rabbis' arguments, and of later rabbis arguing with those arguments, those ghosts, scribbling in the margins, leaving arguments for people of the future to argue with, arguing across time. If we are arguing, we care.

Babel

Our different languages started with an argument too, if you believe the story of the Tower of Babel. In that story we were all cooperating, working together to build a tower to the sky, when God stomped on us and scrambled up our languages. Then we started arguing and we never got our tower after all. It is an Iraqi story (another one); it is about language; and it feels personal, bewildering, disorientating. Its first line makes my heart squeeze: 'Everyone on earth had the same language and the same words.' I yearned for this world, where we could all talk to each other and always know what we meant, always understand and be understood, a world where no one was lost in translation.

It makes sense that the invented universal language is called Esperanto, meaning 'one who hopes', and it is no surprise to find that the man who invented Esperanto was Jewish, and had always lived between languages. Born in 1859, Ludwik Lejzer Zamenhof grew up in Bialystok which was part of Russia and is now part of Poland – a transition that happened with great violence and trauma. He grew up with Jews, Russians, Poles and Germans all at odds and he diagnosed the cause as 'the misery caused by language division'. He thought 'the diversity of language' was not a positive, but the reason for 'the separation of the human family into groups of enemies', so that his home town suffered pogroms where 'savages with axes and iron stakes have flung themselves, like the fiercest beasts, against the quiet town-dwellers, whose sole crime was that they spoke another language and practiced another people's religion'.

By the age of ten he'd written a play called *The Tower of Babel, or the Bialystok Tragedy in Five Acts*. By nineteen, he'd started creating a common language for humanity. When his father made him stop and study medicine, he spent his spare time modernising Yiddish to make it work as a common Jewish language, but then he decided he wanted to unite *everyone*, not just Jews. He poured everything he had into Esperanto, his language of hope, an antidote to the violence and hate, and to the terror, described by Derrida, induced by the gap between words and things, a gap we all fall into sometimes, stumbling to communicate. All the tower-builders wanted was not to 'be scattered all over the world'. It was scattering they feared, and after it happened, they couldn't build their city any more. They were expelled from real, true communication. Maybe we needed Esperanto to knit us back together, so we could build our tower.

Despite this longing for universal clear communication, something about it dragged at my heart. If we all spoke one language, we'd lose complexity and nuance and difference. We'd lose the pleasures of untranslatable words. We'd lose the world Zamenhof grew up in, which was violent and divided, sure, but also dazzlingly polyglot. Zamenhof spoke Yiddish, Russian and possibly Polish at home, learned German, French and Hebrew from his father, studied Latin, Greek and Aramaic at school, and later picked up quite a lot of Lithuanian, Italian, Spanish and, finally, English (it's quite satisfying, and quite unusual, to see English come at the end of a long list like that). He was clearly a genius linguist, but also: this was how the world was. Many Iraqi Jews of my grandparents' generation spoke standard Iraqi Arabic out, Judeo-Iraqi Arabic with friends and family, read *fusha*, spoke French because of Jewish schools being run by a French organisation, English because of the British mandate, Turkish because of the Ottomans, a bit of Hebrew for synagogue and maybe some Persian if they had friends across the border. If I couldn't pass on my language to my son, could I pass on the idea of a joyous, jumbled, multilingual life instead? Could I encourage him to escape the dour narrowness of monolingualism, to have the confidence to try to speak to other people in their own languages, and the humility to not always expect to understand or be understood?

As ever, he was already ahead of me. He told a boy who joined his class from Korea, 'My grandmother came here and had to learn English, just like you.' He was thrilled that he might be able to help his friend learn English, and decided he wanted to learn Korean too. And *lesh la?* (why not?). His Greek friend taught him the Greek for *onion* and for *grandmother* (after all, what else do you need?). At an exhibition, he was asked to listen to two birds chirping and imagine what they were saying. Gripping his pencil, he wrote in the speech bubble coming out of the first bird's beak 'Hi my friend' and made the second bird reply 'I love you'. A perfect bit of dialogue. Maybe I didn't need to worry that he didn't know Judeo-Iraqi Arabic if he had everything else languages give you: an open heart, a desire to understand, a passion to communicate – and love.

Maybe I could tell him that when Babel fell, we didn't just get confusion, we also got *translation*. I could tell him translation is crossing bridges over roaring seas. Working hard to make spaces where we can talk to each other. Creative and nimble and lithe. Powered by – impossible without – empathy. And we are all doing it, all the time. Even when speaking the same language, we can't be sure we're hearing what the other person means. Where there is more than one language, the act of empathy requires more care, more attention, more effort. Translators often talk about putting on someone else's shoes. They may pinch or gape, may be too heavy or too light, may be worn out or magic or, like Tanboury's, both. It's noticing all those things as you walk in them that give translation its specificity and power. Without translation, George Steiner said, 'we would inhabit parishes bordering on silence'. After Babel, those scattered, shattered people taught themselves how to break that silence, and in doing so they invented a new form of magic.

'Making Babel work' is how Ross Perlin sums up the mission of the Endangered Language Alliance in New York, where he is co-director; the ELA celebrates and protects language diversity, instead of seeing it as confusion and divine punishment. Perlin calls the Babel story 'baseless and pernicious' and points out that there were different languages before anyone tried to build a tower; Genesis 10 lists the names of Noah's descendants *ish lilshono* (every one after his tongue, or each with his language). This instance of Genesis contradicting itself maybe offers a chance to tell the story a different way.

I couldn't translate much but I could translate a little for my son. I told him that in Judeo-Iraqi Arabic, the word for toilet was *adeb* which literally meant 'politeness'. He thought this was hilarious. I didn't tell him *adebsez* (no politeness) was an insult. I told him when people said *b'frahak* it meant 'to your happiness' but really it means 'to your wedding' or, as I translated it as a child, MAYYOUGETMARRIEDSOONANDTO-SOMEONESUITABLE. When he was making a lot of noise I suddenly said *tash machy!* (my head is exploding!). It just came out. He looked surprised. I felt surprised. I told him what it meant and we laughed. I translated, and even though my vocabulary was pitifully small and my grammar was all over the shop, it really did feel like magic.

Nabug

Maybe translation magic didn't just apply to words. Maybe you could also do it with rice pudding.

Watermelon Woman would probably have said there was nothing Iraqi about English food. I used to believe the two cultures were complete opposites, that medieval Brits only used spices to mask the smell of rotten meat; that there was no olive oil before Elizabeth David, and no sumac before Yotam Ottolenghi; that, as per the internet meme, 'Britain invaded half the world for spices and it didn't like any of them'; that there was a lot of truth in the gleeful *Goodness Gracious Me* sketch about an Indian family going 'for an English', challenging each other to eat the blandest food on the menu. If spice and watermelons were exotic, then British food had to be tasteless and boring. Then I learned that ancient Britons imported olive oil *before* the Romans invaded, that Dark Age labourers grew their own coriander, that there were vineyards in the Domesday Book. Food historian Kate Colquhoun has written that medieval food in England was closest to Moroccan food now, a riot of ginger, cinnamon, cloves, mace, raisins, prunes, figs, dates and almonds; I would eat at that table. And actually my ancestors *could* have done, because many of the spice traders supplying the ingredients for those meals were Jews, who could move more freely through the Spice Routes than either Muslims (who couldn't travel in Christian countries) or Christians (who couldn't travel in the East). Jewish traders travelled mind-blowing distances, overland in Europe, across the Mediterranean, on camel caravan from Morocco to Baghdad, along the Tigris to Basra, across the sea to India, and then on to China, breaking their journeys at Jewish communities around the world. As early as the twelfth century, a cookbook the Baghdad pharmacologist Ibn Jazla had written a century before was translated into Latin and the recipes shared across Europe. The Tudors liked food to be spicy and surprising, hence the pigs sewn to capons to pretend they were cockatrices; the peacocks roasted, cooled, stitched back into their feathers, and served with fire bursting from their beaks, to conjure up another mythical beast, the phoenix; the blackbird pies, frog-meat blancmanges, and cheesecakes made with almond milk and rose water. They grew such fields and fields of yellow crocuses in Essex that a whole town was renamed Saffron Walden.

So why did Elizabeth David say British food was boring? Why did she rage (magnificently) that 'The grotesque prudishness and archness with which garlic is treated in this country has led to the superstition that rubbing the bowl with it before putting the salad in gives sufficient flavour. It rather depends whether you are going to eat the bowl or the salad'? Jonathan Nunn, omnivorous editor of the food newsletter *Vittles*, told me that when the Industrial Revolution displaced people from their farms and their families to factories in cities, they couldn't forage any more or grow their own food or learn recipes from their mothers. Into this cooking gap, Victorians started obsessively copying French food. Badly. (Although even then, some adventurous English eaters were cooking from the curry chapter in Eliza Acton's 1845 book *Modern Cookery for Private Families*, or trying her recipe for 'the King of Oude's Omelet'.) Elizabeth David, born in 1913, lived through the worst time for British food. She grew up on boiled meat, plain vegetables and tapioca, but when she lambasted this boring diet, she never mentioned that her family's cook was contending with rationing. I knew about rationing in the Second World War, but had no idea that food was rationed in the First as well. David was unlucky enough to live through both. She did escape Britain during the Second World War but was appalled to return to a land of vile flour-and-water soups and bread-and-gristle rissoles. She assumed no one else cared that the food was disgusting, but this doesn't square with Barbara Pym's starving spinsters hoarding olive oil to conjure up minimal but perfect gourmet meals of salad, cheese, bread and greengages, or Enid Blyton's *Faraway Tree* books, written between 1939 and 1951, so crammed with children gorging on invented treats like Pop Cakes and Toffee Shocks and Google Buns, that I had to stop reading them to my son at bedtime because he started demanding biscuits in bed. The mad wartime recipes for chocolate truffles made of cocoa powder, margarine and mashed potatoes, or cheese-and-tomato 'mock crab' don't sound appealing but they do suggest that many people confronted rationing with a certain desperate creativity.

While David was ranting about garlic in the 1950s, so many people were eating Chinese food in Britain (the first Chinese restaurants opened in London in the 1880s) that in 1958 chop suey went on the menu at Butlins. Meanwhile Bangladeshi men who had come over during the war, working in the engine rooms of British steamships, took over bombed-out fish and chip shops and added rice and curry to the menus. Britain was well on the way to its curry house boom. For Middle Eastern food, the game-changer was Claudia Roden's exhilarating debut, *A Book of Middle Eastern Food*, published in 1968 (the year Ottolenghi was born), wonderful in itself but also extraordinary because it prompted David to change her mind, and to completely rewrite the story she'd told about English food.

In a book I wish was better known, *Spices, Salt and Aromatics in the English Kitchen*, David says English cookery was 'extremely spice-conscious' for 2,000 years. She re-spins her own food journey, recalling that as an aspiring actor in London she learned to cook from an eccentric 1925 book called *The Gentle Art of Cookery* by Olga Hartley and Hilda Leyel, which went big on 'Arabian nights' recipes, including one almost parodically Middle Eastern concoction of eggs cooked for twelve hours in Turkish coffee and olive oil. On the eve of war, David hooked up with a married East End Jewish pacifist and actor, and sailed away with him on a rickety boat. From her other books I'd always assumed she'd spent the war in Italy or France, but in fact she was mostly in Cairo and Alexandria. Reading *Spices, Salt and Aromatics* felt like a wall coming down, and a light shining on a web of connections between Middle Eastern and British food. David even pointed out that Middle Eastern ingredients were at the heart of some of the most quintessentially English foods, like Christmas pudding, mince pies, brown sauce . . . and rice pudding.

My grandfather loved *muhallebi* (rice pudding), but no one could remember how he liked it, warm or cold, scented with *mai warad* (rose water) or with *mai kadakh* (orange flower water), swirled with date syrup or with honey. I went hunting for recipes anyway. The word for rice in Iraq is different from the word used in the rest of the Arabic-speaking world. They call it *ruz*. We call it *timman*. There is a story that during the First World War, the British imported a brand of basmati from India called Ten Men, and that Iraqi porters carrying sacks of it morphed the name from Ten Men to *timman*. It isn't true, though; the word *timman* appeared in a cookbook written in Baghdad in the tenth century, by Ibn Sayyar al-Warraq, and called *Kitab al-Tabikh* (Book of Cooking). Although al-Warraq's book promised 'Salubrious Foods and Delectable Dishes, Extracted from Medical Books and Told by Proficient Cooks and the Wise' and was also sometimes called *The Book of Winning a Lover's Heart and Sparing Him the Need for a Doctor*, not all of his five recipes for rice pudding immediately appealed. One involved noodles. Another centred on chicken. This is the one I thought my grandfather might have liked:

> Wash the rice at night and put it in a new piece of cloth. In the following morning, crush the rice into fine powder like flour. For each 10 ratls of milk, use 1½ ratls of rice flour. Put warm milk in a pot and bring it to a boil. Sprinkle the rice flour on the milk the way you do with flour, stirring all the time. Let the pot cook on medium heat until rice is cooked. Pour on it walnut oil or fresh clarified butter. If pudding comes out thick, add more milk as needed. When it is finished cooking, sprinkle it with sugar. If you prefer the pudding white, keep it as it is. If you prefer it yellow, add some saffron.

Rice pudding did not take long to make its way over here. There was a savoury Ryse of Flesh recipe in the earliest English cookbook, published in 1390, and in a 1430 English cookbook there was a recipe for, simply, Rys, that goes like this:

> Take a porcyoun of Rys, & pyke hem clene, & sethe hem well, & late hem kele; then take gode Mylke of Almaundys & do ther-to, & sethe & stere hem wyl; & do ther-to Sugre an hony, & serue forth.

It was nearly the same. It gave me hope that while I couldn't make my son his great-grandfather's rice pudding, I could tell him a story in which English and Iraqi food were not in opposition, in which watermelons weren't exotic and nor were we, a story about a conversation that has been going on a long, long time, and that he could be proud of and part of.

Yet some things could not be translated and some foods seemed out of reach of the exchange of flavours. Like the *nabug*. In Iraq, there were *nabug* trees in everyone's gardens. The small, yellow fruit were like dates or chocolate, said my grandmother. I longed to try one. But my family said they'd never seen them in the UK, and when I asked at Iraqi shops, they smiled at my pronunciation and shook their heads. No *nabug* here. To search online, I needed a translation. What *was* a *nabug*? After much frenzied detective work and WhatsApping pictures to my family, we decided it was probably the Christ's Thorn Jujube (the *Ziziphus spina-christi*), which got its name because it was supposed to have produced the thorns for Christ's crown. The Bedouins called it *sidr*. The ancient Egyptians called it *nabs*, ate the fruit and pounded the leaves into powder, which they mixed with water to make shampoo. The Greek botanist Theophrastus suggested pouring wine over *nabugs*, to make them sweeter. In Islam the *nabug* was a blessed tree. It was a thermophile; it liked it hot (I thought I might be a thermophile). It didn't mind drought or salty soil but it *could not survive* freezing. My neighbour, a Welsh landscape gardener who can grow anything, told me he didn't think a *nabug* could survive even a mild London winter, but I still wanted to try. If I could only get a seed. Surely this would be possible. I dreamed of feeling less alien, more rooted, under the shade of my *nabug* tree in London. But here, the internet failed me! I read about similar fruits growing in Saudi Arabia, in Egypt, in Greece. I found seeds for sale in the UAE but they wouldn't send them here. I scoured gardening catalogues without success. I asked Iraqi friends. Even the Iraqi Seed Collective, who share their library of Iraqi seeds with growers and seed savers, couldn't help. The *nabug* started to seem like a mythical fruit, something I'd never taste, let alone grow.

And then I got a message from an Iraqi Muslim friend, Laith. Born here and, like me, longing for Baghdad, he'd managed to visit for the first time. And, unbelievably, he'd brought me *nabug*. It was so kind of him to even remember. I couldn't believe he'd brought me fruit. When he sent me a picture, I nearly cried.

We arranged to meet the next day, because some were ripe already and soon they would spoil. It was pouring in Hoxton, and I was shivering in my jumper as Laith gave me a punnet of small fruit, explaining it was not the season for them, and they should be bigger. I didn't care. They were still *nabug*. In Hoxton. I felt a bit at sea. I didn't even know which ones were ripe. He told me the brown ones were ready to eat.

At my mother's, I got them out of the bag and she lit up. 'It's *nabug*!' As I took off the cling film a sharp, sweet scent hit me, a totally unfamiliar smell. 'I haven't had this fruit for fifty years,' she told my son. 'Do you want to try one?' He said no, he wanted a Haribo instead, but we each ate one, my mum and I. They were crisp and sweet and slightly fibrous. Like a cross between an apricot and a date. We divided the punnet, giving fruit to other relatives who had been craving them.

I took some home, and after savouring them, I planted the stones. My gardener neighbour told me to keep them warm so I put the plant pots in a purple plastic tub I usually used for storing dishcloths and placed it under the kitchen radiator. It made me laugh to look at it. I'd made a miniature Iraq. A small hot space. I ignored my ineptitude as a gardener and allowed myself to hope. I tried to draw on the energy of my gardening forebears. I thought about how Noah was often jeered at because he came straight off the ark and planted a vineyard, so he could get drunk, but you absolutely *would*, wouldn't you, after all that? And maybe the wine wasn't the point. Maybe what he wanted was to plunge his hands into the soil, to root himself deep in this new place he had washed up in. Maybe he was chasing permanence, stability, as he pushed his seeds into the earth. I thought about Nebuchadnezzar making the Hanging Gardens of Babylon for his wife Amytis because she missed her homeland in what is now Iran. The garden's 'hanging' tiers were supposed to look like mountains, while complex watering systems made it look green, like a forest. It's strange to think that while the Jews Nebuchadnezzar had forcibly deported to Babylon were weeping with homesickness, so was his queen. It almost made me feel a bit sorry for Nebuchadnezzar. I certainly liked him more for making his wife a garden to cure her homesickness.

I'd planted a quince tree in the shared garden of where I'd lived before, and there was a fig tree, an olive tree and a tiny pomegranate tree in our garden now. I dared to imagine a *nabug* tree beside them, a garden to cure my homesickness – for a place I'd never been.

There and then

Still not sure about sifting the stories, I asked the therapist, 'Is the goal to pass them on without the emotional charge?' She said, 'You tell me.' I thought again about how telling the stories made me feel like they were actually happening to me, like I was reliving them. That was what I didn't want to pass on, the unwanted flashbacks, the feeling of the past intruding into the present, the inability to draw a line between *there and then* and *here and now*.

At Passover, I was taught, we were supposed to feel like *we* were there in Egypt, like *we* survived. What a recipe for generational trauma! After all, I was not a slave in ancient Egypt. (I also was not in prison in Baghdad.) But that is how generational trauma works. Psychiatrist Rachel Yehuda thought that when the prophet Ezekiel said 'The fathers ate sour grapes, and the children's teeth were set on edge', he understood, long before anyone else, that trauma is passed down the generations, in our bodies, our bones, our teeth; that children carry their parents' burdens. This made me feel rebellious. I didn't want to *only* be my parents' daughter, defined entirely by them, still less by what they went through. I didn't want to feel as though their lives were vivid and in colour while mine was in black and white, vicarious, second-hand, in their shadow. I wanted, like Nora Ephron said, to be the heroine of my life. And I wanted my son to be the hero of his.

Yehuda came to her theories about generational trauma when, researching PTSD at the start of her career, she found herself comparing the Holocaust survivors she had known growing up in Cleveland to the Vietnam veterans she was working with. Her team went to Cleveland where they found that the survivors had the same low levels of the stress hormone cortisol as the veterans, and had also been suffering nightmares, flashbacks and other PTSD symptoms for years. When they started a clinic for survivors, their children started coming in with the same low cortisol, the same nightmares and flashbacks. Yehuda realised that trauma could *change your genes* and be passed down. This made me feel quite bleak, because it meant that trauma had been sitting in my genes all my life, and my son's as well.

However, Yehuda also said we weren't prisoners of our genes; that if our genes could be changed by trauma, they could also be changed by therapy, friendship, love. By channelling trauma into social justice. By being cared for, and by caring. This felt incredibly empowering. I thought about how my family wanted to be together so much, how we checked in on each other, how much we talked, cramming a lot into every conversation, and how my son, like me, loved parties and got called a chatterbox. Maybe I'd passed something useful on already.

Yehuda suggested that the Jewish calendar offers regular opportunities to remember trauma, but in a time-limited way that stops it seeping into the rest of your life. I thought about the same rituals done every year. How you got to Passover and it hadn't changed, but you had. One year, someone wasn't well. Another year, there was a new baby. One year my brother was singing the song for the youngest person at the table, and then it was my son and now he has two younger cousins who will one day sing it in turn. But we were still at the table, together.

Passover encourages you to question the story, to retell it, even to argue about it, and this was what I really wanted to pass on: the *work*. I couldn't decide for my son how he'd feel about our family's stories. I couldn't even decide if he'd want to know where he came from, or if he'd pull away. If he did, though, I could at least try to give him the tools to grapple with the mess and trauma himself and find his own way through.

At a very dark time in 2023 I had the realisation that I might be able to pass on a heritage of healing as well. It was after Hamas's attack on Israel, and the beginning of Israel's war on Gaza. The world was more polarised than ever before, and the Iraqi Jewish story was being denied and erased with more ferocity than usual because it didn't fit into the narrative that all Israelis were white European settler-colonisers. Even food was a battleground. A row blew up online about falafel, with fierce accusations that it was stolen from Egyptians and Palestinians. When the *New Yorker*'s food critic Helen Rosner pointed out that Jews in both those countries might have contributed to the invention of falafel, someone scoffed in reply that even the *word* falafel is Arabic and I felt the wind pushed out of me. The assumption was that no Arabic word could be Jewish, no Jew could speak Arabic, that there were no Jewish Arabic languages. When Rosner responded 'Boy do I have news for you about a language spoken by Middle Eastern Jews', I felt tearful at the recognition of our existence. I imagined my grandmothers' grandmothers, and back and back, cooking in Iraq for 2,000 years and being told they never dreamed up a single recipe, changed an ingredient, contributed anything, but were just parasites.

I joined a Zoom session with therapists and facilitators Alex Eisenberg, Daniel Eisenberg and Lea Misan, who wanted to help Jewish people release the weight of history and trauma, so we could 'show up better for the present'. They named their group Angels of History after Walter Benjamin's description of an angel who wants to linger with the wreckage of the past but keeps getting pushed forward by progress. They asked us to close our eyes, put our feet on the ground and imagine we were rooted. I did it with bad grace. Working in theatre, I'd done a million exercises like this in rehearsal rooms. I was not expecting it to mean anything. I could still hear my son's audiobook of *Winnie-the-Pooh* coming from his room, Alan Bennett doing the voices. My desk was covered with bills and forms to fill in for school and a list with nothing yet ticked off, and Eeyore was being given a burst balloon for a birthday present and I couldn't focus. I shut my eyes and was not expecting to find anything in the dark, but when they asked us to imagine an ancestor who could help us, my father's grandfather came into my head. I was surprised. He died before I was born. My dad didn't know him either, but he was named after him. That was all I knew until, some years ago, my father called with what seemed a very random question: 'Do you want to come to Jerusalem to see my grandfather's Torah scroll get married?' It turned out Hakham Ezra Murad, who was born in Baghdad in 1864, was not just a rabbi but a *sofer*, a scribe. He wrote Torah scrolls and other religious documents, dipping in a *mikveh* every morning before starting to write, on vellum from a kosher animal, using, probably, a reed from the Tigris and ink made of gall nuts and gum arabic. My dad was calling because two of the Torah scrolls his grandfather wrote had made it to Israel and were being 'married' to a synagogue. I was so intrigued I got on a plane.

In Jerusalem, we found a synagogue full of long-lost cousins. When Hakham Ezra died in 1936, his children prayed for sons to name after him, and my father was one of five Ezras. They told us Hakham Ezra's brother had got the scrolls out of Iraq in 1950, when Jews were barely allowed to take anything, by tucking one scroll under each arm and telling officials at the airport that they were holy, that bad things would happen if they got damaged, and they let him through. The scrolls later survived other perils, including a warehouse fire, and now they were going to have a new home.

They arrived like brides, carried by dancing men. There

was even a *chuppah*, a wedding canopy. As it was an Orthodox synagogue, I watched with the women from a gallery, behind a *mechitza*, a partition made of criss-crossed wood. The women told me one of the scrolls was dedicated to Hakham Ezra's sister, Chahla, who was divorced, which must have taken a lot in nineteenth-century Baghdad. She made dresses, helped people in need and fought for women's rights, and when Hakham Ezra's first wife died, she brought up his five children, including my grandmother, Gergia. Later, a rabbi spread out the scrolls for us to see the clear script which everybody said was perfect, just like print. Hakham Ezra had to follow 4,000 rules to write the scrolls, shaping and spacing each letter exactly right, and garlanding some with little crowns. A big part of his work was repairing scrolls – restitching split seams, using the dried-out sinew of a kosher animal as a needle; sanding down the wooden rollers; scratching out words that had cracked or flaked or smudged because the scrolls were held and hugged and danced with and read and used and loved; restoring the little crowns. He repaired scrolls that had been written hundreds of years before, and already repaired by earlier *sofers*, and he wrote his own scrolls in the hope that other *sofers*, who had not even been born yet, would care for them and repair them in the future. Maybe that was something I could learn from, and my son could too; to be part of a chain of caring and repairing from past to future. Maybe that's why Hakham Ezra came to me then. A good ancestor steering me towards being a good ancestor myself, one day, maybe. I couldn't honour him in the traditional ways. I couldn't put a stone on his grave; it was inaccessible to me, in Iraq. I didn't know if it was tended, or even if it was still there. In 2020, a report by the Jewish Cultural Heritage Initiative gave 89 per cent of Iraq's Jewish sites – including the cemeteries – the lowest possible preservation rating of 'no return', which felt rather heavy-handed for a metaphor – except it wasn't. It meant, the researchers said, that many of the places where my family had lived and loved were 'beyond repair'. Once a year, there was a global mass Kaddish (prayer for the dead) for Jews buried in cemeteries that could not be visited in Arab lands. I said it for all my ancestors and especially for him.

Samir Naqqāsh said that, while everyone found him such a problem, 'I am simply continuing to write in my own language.' I felt helpless in the face of the war. But maybe there was a value in 'simply continuing' to tell the story of what happened to my family in Iraq, in my own words, if not my own language, a value in remembering Hakham Ezra; because if ever there was a time to insist on the possibilities of being an Arabic-speaking Jew, this was it.

Recipes for outwitting death

There is an old joke that you can boil all Jewish festivals down to the formula 'They tried to kill us. We survived. Let's eat.' There is a breeziness to the way, at Passover, we go from telling the story of being slaves in Egypt to stuffing our faces. Sometimes I don't find the joke funny, but feel its weight, the way it goes straight from 'They tried to kill us' to 'We survived' with no mention of *how*, no tools or knowledge we can carry forward for future danger; just the ridiculous rush to eat?

We don't eat just anything, though; we eat the same food the survivors ate when they got to the other side of the Red Sea. Once the Jews knew they were safe, they ate their *matzah*. Just like us. I bet they complained about it just like we do, but it was a sign they'd survived, a relief and a luxury to be able to sit and criticise your own picnic. Maybe this is what we pass on: not just the eating but eating *together*. The *let's* part. Coming together to eat isn't just how we celebrate surviving; it has also, more than once, been *how we survived*. By sticking together, moaning about our *matzah*, telling the story, and then – crucially – joking about it. We aren't passing on generational trauma but generational *healing*. We light candles too. A wish for more light. And on the last day of Pesach, Iraqi Jews hit each other (gently!) with green branches saying *santak khathra* (have a green year). It is a wish for everything that greenness means; new growth, new roots, new trees, new fruit, new hope.

My son is mainly interested in the *charoset*, the treacly fruit-and-nut paste which is supposed to symbolise the mortar the Jews in Egypt used to stick bricks together when they were building for the pharaohs. While Ashkenazis make *charoset* out of apples and nuts, Iraqi *charoset* is denser, stickier, and actually looks like something you could build a pyramid with.

Of course, I know Jews didn't build the pyramids. Herodotus was wrong. Hollywood was wrong. It wasn't accurate – and it was *really* not polite – to go to Egypt like Israeli prime minister Menahem Begin once did, and claim 'We built the pyramids'. Jews didn't build the pyramids because Jews didn't exist when the pyramids were built. But Jews probably did build a city or two. And you can't build a city with apples. Make Iraqi *charoset* and tell me I am wrong.

Charoset

First acquire your *silan* (date syrup). It has to be from Iraq, ideally the one emblazoned with BASRA DATE SYRUP in red capitals over a picture of a date palm groaning with ripe fruit. It is 100 per cent date. It's velvety black and unctuous as caramel. More. You need walnuts too. Whole ones because if you get them ready-chopped, it's not going to be as jaggedy, and you miss out on the nut dust, which binds it all together. Take 150g of the nuts, chop them roughly, and mix them into 150g of the syrup. If you like, bash up a cardamom pod and add the smashed seeds. That's it. The *charoset* will be super-thick, crunchy, sticky, sturdy, and only just spreadable. If it doesn't look like it could cement together a pyramid, add more walnuts. Have it on toast. Swirl it through yogurt. Spoon it over porridge. Grill some peaches or nectarines and smear it on top. Eat it straight out of the jar.

This isn't just the *charoset* I grew up with; it is the *charoset* my mother grew up with, and my grandmothers, and *their* grandmothers, back in Baghdad. When I make it, time and space collapse. I am pounding cardamom, maybe in the courtyard of my house, maybe under a *nabug* tree. Trauma can trigger terrifying and disorientating flashbacks that pluck you out of the safety of *here and now* into the horror of *there and then*. But as I stir the stiff paste, I flash back to pleasure. To sweetness. To a time and place where I belonged. Where I made sense. Licking date syrup off the spoon, I can almost imagine I was eating it the way my parents ate it in Baghdad, for breakfast, with bread and *qemar*, water buffalo cream. The women who sold the cream would come into the city with huge round trays of it on their heads. It was so thick they would cut you a slice with a hairpin.

While Jews did not build the pyramids, in 2018 Iraqi Jewish artist Michael Rakowitz built a *lamassu* (an ancient Iraqi winged bull) out of date syrup *tins*. 10,500 of them. When I went to see it in Trafalgar Square, my son still small enough to nestle into me in a sling, I felt pure joy. It was enormous, a life-sized reconstruction of the one carved by Assyrian sculptors from a single slab of limestone 2,700 years ago. Standing 4.5 metres tall, weighing up to 30 tonnes, it was a mash-up of creatures, with a bull's body, an eagle's wings and a man's ferocious face. It was menacing, yes, but with its ringlets, big beard and half-smile, it was also wise. It looked like it could protect you, and for 2,700 years it did, guarding the city of Nineveh. When Rassam (of course) and his mentor Austen Henry Layard found it, they shipped two other *lamassu* to the British Museum, but they left this one at its post, protecting Nineveh against demons and invaders. Until Isis came along in 2015 and destroyed it. They videoed a black-clad militant taking a pneumatic drill to the *lamassu*'s eyes. In Arabic, eyes are not just eyes. *Ayouni* (my eyes) is what you say if you really love someone. That militant knew what he was doing when he gouged the eyes out first. How cruel he was being. How contemptuous.

Rakowitz's *lamassu* is only one of the Iraqi artefacts he has 'reappeared'; he started 'reappearing' looted and destroyed Iraqi artefacts in 2006, not to replace or replicate them, but to make them 'come back as ghosts', 'to keep the wound alive, and show the urgency, the impossibility, of making these things again'. He made his *lamassu* out of date syrup tins because his grandfather, who had to leave Iraq after the Farhud, once imported date syrup to the States. Later, to get past sanctions, Iraqi date syrup was labelled as a product of Lebanon, or Saudi Arabia, or even Sweden. Sweden! And now war, drought, pollution and climate change have ravaged Iraq's date palms.

The *lamassu* was stunning. The tins! Gorgeously coloured, folded, layered, crimped, sliced, they gleamed in the sun like scales. Along one flank was a repeating pattern of a picture of a luscious date. Across his beard, a word, over and over, like an incantation: *date date date*. And on his headdress: *Karbala Karbala Karbala*. It was marvellous (in both senses). It was witty: a heroic beast made of trash. The *lamassu* at the British Museum looked small, somehow, stuck indoors. Rakowitz's *lamassu* looked like it was supposed to look: looming, majestic, tall as the sky. The ancient *lamassu* were magic because people believed in them and imbued them with spirit. This *lamassu* was magic for me too; as I walked around it, I felt grief wash over me, but I also felt inspired to do something about it. To make something from it, like Rakowitz. Not to try to replace what was lost, without feeling, without love, like the sad, deracinated replica of the 1,800-year-old Arch of Palmyra (also destroyed by Isis) made recently using digital technology and robot carvers and exhibited without context, without story. In contrast, Rakowitz's *lamassu* was an invitation to gather the fragments and ruins and shards and to craft them into something joyous. It was an act of resistance. It was healing, yes, but its strangeness meant you didn't just forget the trauma either. Rakowitz said it was supposed to be a ghost that haunted us but also offered light. And it did feel like both spectre and protector.

Not wanting to let all that date syrup go to waste, Rakowitz published a cookbook of recipes to use it with. From *A House With a Date Palm Will Never Starve*, I learned that some Iraqis place a date in the mouths of their newborn babies, so their first taste of life is sweet. I wish I'd known to do this for my son, but if I didn't do it then, I could do it now. If I couldn't teach him Judeo-Iraqi Arabic, I could make magic in my kitchen. I could reappear the food our family ate in Baghdad. And thanks to my mother, among his favourite things to eat were the date-stuffed pastries called *makhboose*.

When his school asked him to bring in a food that represented his heritage, I admit I groaned when he asked for them – they were so much work to make! – but I was also secretly proud. He knew *makhboose* were special. When we read the picture book *Shoham's Bangle*, he immediately spotted the drawing of *makhboose*. Growing up I never saw my community represented and never ate *makhboose* outside my family and friends' homes. I was dubious that my ninja-loving son would go for the only other picture book about Iraqi Jews: Sigal Samuel's *Osnat and Her Dove*, about the world's first female rabbi, but when it arrived he pored over Vali Mintzi's gorgeous drawings of Hebrew letters dancing and transforming into birds and beasts, and lingered over the picture of medieval, moonlit Mosul, asking if that was where his grandparents grew up. I was so glad to have these books. Representation is important. A 2018 survey of more than 9,000 children's books in the UK found that only 4 per cent of them included a character – not just a protagonist, but *any* character – who was Black, Asian or minority ethnic. I signed my son up with the charity PJ Library, which distributes books on Jewish themes to children, and bought books from Green Bean Books, set up by writer Michael Leventhal to publish more books with Jewish characters. I wanted my son to have lots of characters to identify with, a full panoply of heroes and heroines to be curious about, and I wanted other children to read these stories too, to be surprised by them.

I still struggled to find him any films or TV with Iraqi or Jewish characters, let alone Iraqi Jewish characters. When we watched the 1992 *Aladdin* a warning popped up on the screen about its 'negative depictions and/or mistreatment of people or cultures'. It continued, 'These stereotypes were wrong then and are wrong now. Rather than remove this content, we want to acknowledge its harmful impact, learn from it and spark conversation to create a more inclusive future together.' I soon saw why. The film was not set in Baghdad, like the story, but in a made-up place a lot *like* Baghdad called Agrabah – because while the film was being made, the US were bombing the actual Baghdad. The opening song described Agrabah's people as 'barbaric', blaming it on the heat (the days of the aubergines?) but apparently the *original* lyrics – changed after protest – had said the people were barbaric because they'd cut off your ear if they didn't like your face. Aladdin and Princess Jasmine were fairer and softer-voiced than the baddies who had darker skin and thicker accents. The American-Arab Discrimination Committee objected to this at the time, as did the Lebanese-American author Jack Shaheen, author of *Reel Bad Arabs*.

I was too worried to revisit the swashbuckling 1924 *Thief of Baghdad* which I loved as a child. I knew Douglas Fairbanks didn't look or sound remotely Iraqi – and nor did his son who starred in another favourite, the 1947 *Sinbad the Sailor* – but these films gave me something, a feeling of connection. Maybe it was because, growing up in the 1980s, there were no other representations of Baghdad. Certainly, the films are Orientalist. But I've been called Orientalist for telling people that I – an Iraqi Jew – used to sit on our old Persian carpet and wish it would fly. A (white British) friend laughed when I said my dad called me *binti* (my daughter), because in Britain *bint* is a derogatory word;

British soldiers heard it in Egypt and made it misogynist. For me it's a term of affection, not abuse – and also for the British Palestinian author N. S. Nuseibeh who wanted to call her book of essays 'Bint' but her publishers insisted that she change it to *Namesake*. Maybe Disney has the right idea, about trying to start a conversation instead of just removing the film.

But for now it was time to bake. *Makhboose* actually means *baked*; the word comes from *khubz* (bread) which, in *The Epic of Gilgamesh* was what made the wild man, Enkidu, human. Bread and sex. It might not have been bread per se; it might have been anything baked, including *makhboose*, which some people also call *baba bit-tamar* (balls with dates), although they can also be made, in bulging half-moons, with walnuts pounded with sugar, cardamom and rose water, or with cheese. There is so much baking in *The Epic of Gilgamesh* that you can get a cuneiform rolling pin that will imprint your dough with a few lines of the text. (I have not succumbed to the temptation of this rolling pin. Yet.) Baking reappears near the end of the story when Enkidu is dead and Gilgamesh is so terrified of death that he journeys to the end of the world to meet Utnapishtim, the Babylonian Noah, to ask for the secret of immortality. Utnapishtim challenges Gilgamesh to stay awake for seven days and nights, but he immediately falls asleep, and Utnapishtim's wife (unnamed!) bakes a loaf of bread every day, so when Gilgamesh wakes and sees them lined up in order of staleness and mouldiness he has to accept change and loss, and go home. In a way he does outwit death, because he learns to stop fearing it, to relish his city, to take pleasure in life, a pleasure that doesn't come from raping women and fighting men. And maybe *all* bread outwits death. Or yeast does, anyway. It can survive indefinitely. In 2019, physicist and Xbox inventor Seamus Blackley worked with an archaeologist and a microbiologist to jab a syringe into ancient Egyptian pots and extract the 4,500-year-old yeast hibernating deep inside. When he fed the yeast *it woke up*. Like Sleeping Beauty. I couldn't help but be excited by the bread he baked with it, a hieroglyph scored on top. Like the languages that were revived after generations, and alive again in people's mouths, here was bread, back from the dead. Maybe nothing ever really disappears. Scientists are working, now, to bring back the woolly mammoth.

But you don't have to go that far to outwit death. You just have to pass on a recipe.

Makhboose

First, make the dough. Put 360g of self-raising flour in a bowl with 120 ml of light olive oil and a pinch of salt. Start adding water, slowly – up to 120 ml but you may not need that much – and mix it with a spatula till it comes together. Then knead it to a smooth dough. You can use a machine, but, if you don't have to, don't. It won't take long and it will feel fantastic. It will feel like you are shoving away your anger. It will feel like you are pummelling something into life.

My mum and Claudia Roden say if you want to know when the dough is ready, touch your earlobe, then touch the dough; it should feel the same. Of course they're right.

Put the dough in a bowl, wrap it in a damp towel and leave it to prove in a warm room for an hour or so. If you're in a hurry (or if the need for *makhboose* is very great) you can set your oven to 40°C and prove it in there in five minutes.

Time to make the filling. Tip 150g of pitted dates onto a chopping board and chop them up. Then squidge them together with your hands into a soft paste. If they're not soft enough, you can cook them down a little in a pan with a dab of butter and a splash of orange flower water. Let it cool. You might want to make yourself a cup of tea in a *stikan* (a tea glass) with a faded gold rim. Wash the *stikan*; you'll need it once the dough has risen.

Take out the dough. Punch it down. Preheat your oven to 180°C.

Now you have choices. You can roll out the dough, about half a centimetre thick, and cut out little circles. I use the *stikan* for this but a cookie cutter is also good. In *Shoham's Bangle* the heroine cuts out the circles with her grandmother's gold bangle. You can stamp, stamp, stamp, then squash the leftover dough into a ball and roll out again, until you've used up all your dough. Roll about a teaspoonful of date mix into a ball, put it in the middle of the circle of dough, lift up the sides of the dough around it, and pull them together around the filling to seal.

Or, you can do without a rolling pin or any kind of cutter at all. Instead, pinch off bits of the dough and roll them into balls the size of ping-pong balls. Hold a ball in one hand, and push your thumb into it to make an indentation. Fill it with a teaspoonful of date paste, close it up around the dates, and press to seal. When I do this now, I look down and see my hands are becoming my mother's hands (minus the manicure) and this steadies me.

Whichever choice you've made, now press each *makhboose* down to flatten it into a small, fat disc and pierce the top with a fork. Beat an egg with some water and brush the tops with egg wash. Scatter them with sesame seeds. Bake them in the oven till they're golden: about ten minutes. Keep checking. Don't let them bake too long and get dry. Tip them out onto a wire rack to cool. Don't do what I always want to do and bite into one straight off; you'll burn your mouth on molten dates. Put them on a wire rack and cover them with a tea towel so they don't dry out.

Even the smell of the *makhboose* makes me feel calmer. Connected. I have made *makhboose* through many difficult times, and maybe my son will do it too, for himself and for the people he loves.

The next morning, at six, he was up and shouting *mataboose*! It's what he called them before he could pronounce the word properly and now all my family say *mataboose*. Is this how language dies or how it evolves? He grabbed one, bit into it, and grinned, and we belonged, him and me. There was nothing to translate. I felt connected back to something ancient and forward to a future I will never see. Watching him eat *makhboose* messily, with joy, I felt I'd brought *there and then* into *here and now* not as trauma or anxiety but as a mnemonic to help us remember happiness. A gift from our affectionate ghosts. A magic spell. And not just that: he might have been mispronouncing Judeo-Iraqi Arabic but at least he was speaking it.

Epilogue

Evil Eye Guy

My *nabug* did not grow. Despite my patient, anxious tending, not a single shoot pushed its way out of the soil. I was still terrible at backgammon. I was turning up loyally every week for my language class, but was very far from speaking Judeo-Iraqi Arabic, let alone thinking in it or dreaming in it.

And yet . . .

One night my son and I were running back through the rain from Lego club and he said, furious it was so cold, 'Let's move to Iraq now so it will be hot.'

Another day, at a pizza restaurant, someone at the next table started playing Arabic music and my son jumped up on his chair and started dancing, making his cousins laugh and laugh. My mum said *jannu el jeej* (the chickens have gone mad). We didn't know if it was a real or proper Judeo-Iraqi Arabic phrase, but anyway, it was now.

Although I was careful not to mention the evil eye, and only very, very rarely stuffed salt in his pockets, and even then without telling him, he found his way to it anyway. At three, he stashed my big blue evil eye in his plastic pirate treasure chest with his 'gold' doubloons and other dubious treasures scavenged from the park. At five, he made a comic book about a hero called Evil Eye Guy (Siri, tell me your son is Iraqi Jewish without telling me your son is Iraqi Jewish). I was uneasy at first but I realised I had to let him find his own way through – and to have fun with it. Evil Eye Guy didn't seem a product of fear. Instead, the scribbled blue eye on stick legs, with a baby for a sidekick, boldly defeated a range of baddies.

One evening, he asked what I was writing about, and when I said our language was going extinct, he said, 'Like dinosaurs? In real life?' and his eyes widened. Then he said, 'But that can't be your book. Because I'm the hero' (he was very invested in the idea he was the hero) 'and if I'm the hero I have to save it at the end.' I was about to explain the ways in which Judeo-Iraqi Arabic could not be saved, but it suddenly occurred to me that 'real life' doesn't have an ending. It just goes on and on. So that's what I told him. That he hadn't saved it *yet*. That he might still save it one day. And after all, why not? He had an instinct for it, somehow, that went beyond anything I could tell him. It was his as well as mine.

In the summer, he went to forest school and came back muddy, tired, carrying sticks he'd whittled and a sprig of tiny yellow flowers he crushed in his hands and held up to my nose saying, 'Smell this! It's pineapple tea!' It really did smell sweet and fruity, and we looked it up and found it was called *pineapple weed* and you could make tea from it. My son grinned. 'Of course you can!' He was so confident. So *at home*. Teaching me the names of plants. I thought I'd burst with pride. We started seeing pineapple weed everywhere, suddenly, its clusters of yellow blooms. I learned it wasn't native. It came from Asia. It was a migrant, a successful migrant, a sociable migrant that thrived in well-trodden places; it loved a path or a verge. I thought I could learn a lot from pineapple weed, not least that for all my worries about trying to root, I'd already put out a root: my son.

I started thinking about the Polish Jewish writer Isaac Deutscher, who said, 'Trees have roots. Jews have legs.' This used to freak me out, with its implication that if I had legs, I'd have to walk, I could be made to walk. I realised I had never properly sifted or set down all the weight because I *preferred* 'travelling heavy', as the Cuban American Jewish writer Ruth

Behar put it, so heavy I couldn't be moved. I wanted roots so I'd be harder to *uproot*. But now I wondered if legs might stop me feeling so stuck. Maybe I'd be able to move more easily through the world. Maybe I'd be able to connect to the power of people in my family who started their lives from scratch. Maybe I'd be able to feel at home anywhere, a nomad or a cosmopolitan, transforming my feeling of uprootedness into a surge of curiosity and questioning. Maybe if I had legs, I could dance. Even belly-dance.

The words 'belly-dancing' made me feel a bit embarrassed – conjuring up harems and stripteases and tacky, skimpy costumes, jewelled navels and jiggling flesh. I asked my son what he thought belly-dancing was, and he said, 'Is it lying on your tummy and kicking your arms and legs like a turtle?' Which I preferred to the *OED* definition: 'an erotic oriental dance performed by women, involving abdominal contortions'.

When the women in my community lit up the floor at a wedding, it was pure joy. Sexy, certainly, but powerful too. They were doing it for themselves. You didn't have to be young to belly-dance, and you certainly didn't have to be thin. You didn't have to wear heels; you wanted your feet on the ground. And when I heard the music I did want to move and take up space. It made me feel more liquid, made my hips sway and my arms curve up, as if I could trace the curls and twists of Arabic calligraphy in the air, if not on paper. It bothered me that I couldn't dance any more than I could write Arabic. I felt I should be able to do it innately. I knew this was ridiculous.

I should give myself permission to do it badly – and also to learn. As I'd been trying to write a story back to where I come from so I can tell it forward to my son, I kept feeling blocked by the sense I should know it already. But there was no shame in learning. I connected with Jackie Barzvi, an American belly dancer with Iraqi Jewish heritage who set up a Mizrahi dance archive. I watched the videos she'd collected of dancers performing to Iraqi Jewish music, and I just started dancing along. In my kitchen, while I was making rice, my laptop propped up on the counter, shoes kicked off, knees soft, not locked. I stopped holding my stomach in. The warm fug of the kitchen was perfect; you had to be warm to dance like this; you wanted, Barzvi said, 'a loose big feeling'. On her teaching video, she reminded me to smile: 'There's nothing creepier than a serious shimmy.' She was right too. As I shimmied to the cupboard to grab the pine kernels, what I felt most of all was *present*. Not *there and then* but *here and now*.

Notes

4 **the language you speak from earliest childhood:** UNESCO, 'What is mother tongue, mother tongue education and multilingual education?', www.unesco.org, 20 February 2024.

4 **speaks of a 'milk language':** Sadiqa de Meijer, 'The poetic pleasures and pains we can only express in Dutch', *Literary Hub*, 25 June 2019.

5 **UNESCO's World Atlas of Languages**, https://en.wal.unesco.org/languages/judeo-iraqi-arabic.

6 **was made in 1945:** Max Weinreich, 'Der YIVO un di problemen fun undzer tsayt', *YIVO Bleter*, Vol. 25, 1, 1945.

8 **a dictionary with a love story:** Lyn Julius, 'Blessings and Curses of Judeo-Arabic', *Jerusalem Post*, 19 October 2015.

8 **an archive, held at SOAS**: the Eli Timan Archive (formerly hosted by SOAS), https://www.youtube.com/@elitiman1.

10 **two of the last seven speakers of Manoki died:** Simeon Tegel, 'Covid is threatening the world's rarest indigenous languages', *VICE*, 8 April 2021.

10 **Yahgan lost its last speaker:** Peter Trudgill, 'To the ends of the earth: The world's most extreme languages are on the brink of extinction as their last remaining speakers die out', *New European*, 9 February 2023.

10 **less likely to commit suicide:** Darcy Hallett and Michael J. Chandler, 'Aboriginal language knowledge and youth suicide', *Cognitive Development*, Vol. 22, Issue 3, 2007, 392–9.

11 **I ordered a textbook:** Assaf Bar-Moshe, *The Arabic Dialect of the Jews of Baghdad: Phonology, Morphology and Texts*, Harrassowitz, 2019.

12 **one of Iraq's last five Jews had died:** 'Sitt Marcelle dies, leaving four Jews in Iraq', Point of No Return blog, 13 September 2020.

12 **another had died, a doctor:** Sandy Rashty, 'Only three Jews are left in Iraq: Dhafar Fouad Eliyahu, a leading orthopaedic doctor, died on Sunday aged 61', *Jewish Chronicle*, 18 March 2021.

17 **they drank like it was New Year's!:** Sophus Helle, *Gilgamesh: A new translation of the ancient epic*, Yale University Press, 2021.

18 **analysis of New York Jews talking:** Deborah Tannen, 'New York Jewish Conversational Style', *International Journal of the Sociology of Language*, 30, 1981, 133–49.

20 **the languages are *gelet*:** Haim Blanc, *Communal Dialects in Baghdad*, distributed for the Center for Middle Eastern Studies of Harvard University by Harvard University Press, 1964.

22 **The lullabies she found:** Sara Manasseh, 'A Song to heal Your Wounds: Traditional Lullabies of the Jews of Iraq', *Musica Judaica*, Vol. 12, 5754, 1991–2, 1–29.

25 **restored to them in the wintertime:** Benjamin of Tuleda, *The Itinerary of Benjamin of Tudela: Travels in the Middle Ages*, Joseph Simon, 1993.

25 **going off the rails:** Violette Shamash et al., *Memories of Eden: A Journey through Jewish Baghdad*, Forum, 2008.

26 **he started collecting them:** Joseph Berger, 'He Rescued 1.5 million Yiddish Books. Now He Will Have Time to Read Some', *New York Times*, 27 February 2024.

26 **nobody comes around:** K. David Harrison, *The Last Speakers: The Quest to Save the World's Most Endangered Languages*, National Geographic Society, 2010.

30 **and for archives:** including: Sephardi Voices UK (https://www.sephardivoices.org.uk/Interviewee/-aida-hakim) and People of the Book (https://people-book.org/video-library/%D9%90aida-hakim-iraq/).

31 **aroused no interest:** quoted in Abbas Shiblak, *Iraqi Jews: A History of Mass Exodus*, Saqi, 2005.

31 **Zionism is an Ashkenazi thing:** Avi Shlaim, *Three Worlds: Memoirs of an Arab Jew*, Oneworld Publications, 2023.

31 **all are Iraqis:** quoted in Marina Benjamin, *Last Days in Babylon: The Story of the Jews of Baghdad*, Bloomsbury, 2007.

32 **tea and cakes and ices!:** Gertrude Bell, letter to her father, 20 July 1921, Gertrude Bell Archive, University of Newcastle.

32 **love letters to Iraq and to Arabic:** Reuven Snir, 'If I forget thee, O Baghdad: The demise of Arab-Jewish identity and culture', *Asian and African Studies*, 30, 1, 2021, 173–88.

32 **polemic against honour killing:** Nancy E. Berg, *Exile from Exile: Israeli writers from Iraq*, SUNY Press, 1996.

32 **for a British purpose:** Elie Kedourie, *The Chatham House Version and Other Middle Eastern Studies*, Weidenfeld & Nicolson, London, 1970.

33 **language, race or religion:** declaration of the kingdom of Iraq made on 30 May 1932.

34 **the idea of the Holocaust:** Peter Beaumont, 'Anger at Netanyahu claim Palestinian grand mufti inspired Holocaust', *Guardian*, 21 October 2015.

34 **protection of British power:** quoted in *Documents on German Foreign Policy, 1918–1945*, Series D, Vol. XIII, 1964.

35 **amateur dramatics:** Freya Stark, *Dust in the Lion's Paw: Autobiography 1939–1946*, Century Publishing, 1985.

35 **the shooting began:** Somerset de Chair, *The Golden Carpet*, Faber, 1945.

35 **their gold bangles:** Shamash et al.

36 **their carcasses hanging:** Samīr Naqqāsh, trans. Sadok Heskel Masliyah, *Tenants and Cobwebs*, Syracuse University Press, 2018.

36 **like a sheep:** Naïm Kattan, trans. Sheila Fischman, *Farewell, Babylon: Coming of Age in Jewish Baghdad*, Souvenir, 2007.

36 **looted, then burned:** Edwin Black, 'The expulsion that backfired: when Iraq kicked out its Jews', *Times of Israel*, 31 May 2015.

37 **would have suffered!:** de Chair.

37 **laden with spoil:** Stark.

37 **throughout the night:** quoted in Elie Kedourie, *Arabic Political Memoirs*, Frank Cass, 1974.

37 **injections of poison were administered:** Carole Basri, 'First came the Farhud: The 2-stage ethnic cleansing of Iraqi Jewry', *Times of Israel*, 2 June 2021.

37 **to which they could truly belong:** Benjamin, 2007.

37 **mud and sand:** Kattan.

38 **girls who had been raped:** Eli Amir, trans. Yael Lotan, *The Dove Flyer*, Halban, 2010.

38 **shame and horror:** quoted in Kedourie.

38 **made pathetic attempts:** quoted in Shamash.

38 **to give evidence:** quoted in Kedourie.

39 **twelve centuries before you:** Naqqāsh.

40 **with no exact parallel elsewhere:** Ian Black, *Enemies and Neighbours, Arabs and Jews in Palestine and Israel, 1917–2017*, Allen Lane, 2017.

41 **the Zionist movement:** Ari Alexander, 'The Jews of Baghdad and Zionism: 1920–1948', PhD, University of Oxford, 2004.

41 **Zionism's 'Jewish victims':** Ella Shohat, 'Sephardim in Israel: Zionism from the standpoint of its Jewish victims', *Social Text*, No. 19/20, Autumn 1988.

41 **a foreign import:** Avi Shlaim, *Three Worlds: Memoirs of an Arab Jew*, Oneworld Publications, 2023.

42 **don't know how to hear them:** Noreen Masud, *A Flat Place*, Hamish Hamilton, 2023.

42 **butchered as sheep!:** quoted in Orit Bashkin, *New Babylonians: A History of Jews in Modern Iraq*, Stanford University Press, 2012.

44 **the future of Iraqi culture:** Kattan.

45 **called Iraqi Jews 'hostages':** quoted in Nissim Rejwan, *The Jews of Iraq: 3000 Years of History and Culture*, Weidenfeld & Nicolson, 1985.

45 **the Iraqi Dreyfus:** Adi Schwartz 'The Adas Affair', *Tablet*, 9 December 2022.

46 **in time of tension:** quoted in Abbas Shiblak, *Iraqi Jews: A History of Mass Exodus*, Saqi, 2005.

46 **penniless displaced persons:** quoted in Shiblak.

47 **claimed he could prove it:** Shlaim.

48 **betrayal, manipulation and doctrinaire opportunism:** Shiblak.

49 **DDT powder enveloped [him]:** quoted in Nancy E. Berg, *More and More Equal: The Literary Works of Sami Michael*, Lexington Books, 2004.

50 ***Shoham's Bangle*:** Sarah Sassoon and Noa Kelner, *Shoham's Bangle*, Kar-Ben Publishing, 2023.

50 **greasy, undercooked herring:** Esther Meir-Glitzenstein, 'Longing for the Aromas of Baghdad: Food, Emigration, and Transformation in the lives of Iraqi Jews in Israel in the 1950s', in Anat Helman, *Jews and Their Foodways*, Oxford University Press, 2015.

52 **not a hallucination:** Ofer Aderet, 'Hundreds of Yemenite Children Were Abducted in State's Early Years, Says Israeli Cabinet Minister', *Haaretz*, 31 July 2016.

52 **budget of the Panthers:** Ben Reiff, 'Who is reaping the fruits of the Israeli Black Panthers' struggle?', *972 Magazine*, 26 July 2024.

52 **rehabilitating an oppressed identity:** Carroll Silow, 'How Israel's Black Panthers radicalised its Mizrahi Jews, and changed the country', *Jewish Telegraphic Agency*, 17 March 2024.

54 **inevitable and naturally occurring:** Aidan Pine and Mark Turin, 'Language Revitalisation', *Oxford Research Encyclopaedia of Linguistics*, 2017.

54 **spiritual subjugation:** Ngugi wa Thiong'o, *Decolonising the Mind: The Politics of Language in African Literature*, Currey, 1986.

54 **coined the word *linguicide*:** quoted in Mark Turin, 'Voices of vanishing worlds: endangered languages, orality, and cognition', *Análise Social*, 2012.

55 **the ban was reversed:** Mark Liberman, 'Turkey Legalizes the Letters Q, W, and X. Yay Alphabet!', *Slate*, 24 October 2013.

55 **insisted they spoke only in English:** Julia Hartley Brewer, 'Met Pays Damages for Raid on Actors', *Guardian*, 3 February 2000.

57 **displacement of Jews from Arab lands:** Ella Shohat, *Taboo Memories, Diasporic Voices*, Duke University Press, 2006.

57 **words and phrases from Arabic:** Alexander Jabbari, 'Yiddish and Arabic share an uncommon commonality', *New Lines Magazine*, 13 August 2021.

58 **force her grandmother to speak Hebrew:** *Forget Baghdad*, directed by Samir, https://www.imdb.com/title/tt0329094/.

58 **turning in his grave:** Seraj Assi, 'Opinion: Eliezer Ben-Yehuda Is Turning in His Grave Over Israel's Humiliation of Arabic', *Haaretz*, 15 May 2017.

59 **one that gets corrected:** Sara Shilo, *The Falafel King is Dead*, Portobello Books, 2010.

59 **avenging itself for being rejected:** *Forget Baghdad*.

60 **to spy for them:** Maya Sela, 'Author Sami Michael: Mossad tried to recruit me in 1950s', *Haaretz*, 1 July 2011.

60 **compares rabbis to prostitutes**: Sami Michael, trans. Dalia Bilu, *Victoria*, Macmillan, 1995.

60 **write in my own language:** *Forget Baghdad*.

61 **Comfortable . . . and 'deaf':** Almog Behar, 'My Arabic is Mute', https://www.poetryinternational.com/en/poets-poems/poems/poem/103-30010_MY-ARABIC-IS-MUTE.

62 **by the war and the pandemic:** Arwa Ibrahim, 'Baghdad's coppersmith souk: a fading cultural treasure', *Al Jazeera*, 7 August 2018.

63 **an island in the Tigris:** Nicolai Ouroussoff, 'When Iraq looked west', *Los Angeles Times*, 14 December 2003.

65 **The result was *Republic of Fear*:** Lawrence Wechsler, 'Architects Amid the Ruins', *New Yorker*, 29 December 1991.

66 **to wipe Israel off the map:** quoted in Lawrence Joffe, 'Abdul-Rahman Aref', *Guardian*, 4 September 2007.

66 **in the hearts of the occupiers:** Ofer Aderet, '"They Called Me a Traitor. I'm in Good Company": The Political Journey of Amos Oz', *Haaretz*, 30 December 2018.

67 **remain in jeopardy:** Jewish Telegraphic Agency, 'World Jewish Congress Makes New Plea for Jews in Arab Lands', *Jewish Telegraphic Agency Daily News Bulletin*, 1 August 1967.

67 **reverse the trauma of defeat:** Kanan Makiya, *Republic of Fear: The Politics of Modern Iraq*, University of California Press, 1998

67 **one spy for every adult Jew:** Benjamin, 2007.

67 **then starts 'unlearning Arabic':** Mona Yahia, *When the Grey Beetles Took over Baghdad*, Peter Halban, 2000.

68 **people went 'berserk':** Makiya.

69 **poor 'actors' of the scene:** Max Sawdayee, *All Waiting to be Hanged*, Tel Aviv Levanda Press, 1974.

69 **see them go unpunished:** Sawdayee.

69 **how the traitors are hanged!:** Sawdayee.

70 **they are not allowed to:** Irving Spiegel, 'A Victim's Brother, Here, Laments for Iraqi Jews', *New York Times*, 28 January 1969.

70 **savagely medieval** and **barbaric** and **unable to show clemency:** quoted in a letter from the permanent representative of Israel to the United Nations to the president of the Security Council, 6 February 1969.

73 **lives in fear and suffers** Jewish Telegraphic Agency, 'Amnesty International Confirms That Jews Are in Prison in Iraq; Gives JTA Names', *Jewish Telegraphic Agency Daily News Bulletin*, 16 April 1971.

74 **do not experience time as linear:** Maria M. Tumarkin, *Traumascapes*, Melbourne University Press, 2005.

75 **a dish like this:** Ruth Hoffman and Helen Hoffman, *We Married an Englishman. Written and Illustrated by R. & H. Hoffman*, Robert Hale, 1939.

75 **violent alchemy:** Nabih Bulos, 'It's the national dish that brought down a dictator. And it's delicious', *Los Angeles Times*, 3 March 2020.

76 **brought down Saddam Hussein:** Tony Raap, 'Appetite for fish proved fatal for Saddam Hussein, Iraq veteran says', *Pennsylvania Tribune-Review*, 22 April 2015.

77 **used to be their home:** Carol Isaacs, *The Wolf of Baghdad: Memoir of a Lost Homeland*, Myriad Editions, 2020.

77 **there had once been mezuzahs:** Benjamin, 2007.

77 **it seemed little to remember a people by:** Leon McCarron, *Wounded Tigris: A River Journey Through the Cradle of Civilisation*, Corsair, 2023.

77 **harrowing end:** Ephraim Nissan, 'Names for the Fishes of the River Tigris in Baghdadi Judeo-Arabic and in Zakho Jewish Neo-Aramaic', *La Linguistique*, Vol. 55, Fasc. 1, Les judéo-langues, 2019, 97–128.

78 **just like pork:** Ari Greenspan and Ari Z. Zivotofsky, 'Holy Shibuta: A fishy tale for Rosh Hashana', *Jerusalem* Post, 17 September 2007.

78 **a fatwa on eating *shibout*:** Steven Lee Myers, 'In Iraq, Reigniting a Flame for Roasting Carp', *New York Times*, 4 August 2009.

79 **INSTEAD OF THE CALIPH!:** René Goscinny and Jean Tabary, *Iznogoud the Infamous*, Cinebook, 2011.

79 **ark was a giant *guffa*:** Irving L. Finkel, *The Ark before Noah: Decoding the Story of the Flood*, Hodder & Stoughton, 2014.

80 **basket of reeds:** Nawal Nasrallah, '*Khirret* (cattail/ typha pollen), Gift of the marshes in southern Iraq, and the joyous festival of Baghdadi Jews', In My Iraqi Kitchen blog, 8 March 2013.

80 ***The Drift***: Eloise Moody, *The Drift*, https://unravelled.org.uk/projects/wetlands/eloise-moody/.

81 **started making arrests:** Jane Arraf, 'Talk of Iraq Recognising Israel Prompts Threats of Arrests or Death', *New York Times*, 29 September 2021.

81 **any association with Israel:** Raya Jalabi, 'Iraq bans citizens from interactions with Israel', *Financial Times*, 12 June 2022.

82 **the rupture was the story:** Saidiya Hartman, *Lose Your Mother: A Journey along the Atlantic Slave Route*, Serpent's Tail, 2021.

88 **left behind her heart:** Natal'ya, Vorozhbit, 'I grabbed two rings, took my mother, daughter and the cat': the playwright who fled Kyiv, *Guardian*, 30 March 2022.

91 **We are what we keep:** Terry Cook, '"We Are What We Keep; We Keep What We Are": Archival Appraisal Past, Present and Future', *Journal of the Society of Archivists*, 15 December 2011, 173–89.

92 **depressed and obsessive-compulsive:** Barbara J. Zebb and Michael C. Moore, 'Superstitiousness and perceived anxiety control as predictors of psychological distress', *Journal of Anxiety Disorders*, Vol. 17, Issue 1, 2003, 115–30.

93 **Jews and fellow seekers:** Ritualwell, https://ritualwell.org/.

94 **hospital with lead poisoning:** Kay Lazer, 'Boston Children's Hospital lead-poisoning mystery prompts federal warning about folk remedies', *Boston Globe*, 2 August 2012.

95 **dust and sand and sun:** Cynthia Graber, 'Peeper Health Keeper', *Scientific American*, 22 January 2010.

95 **dark, smoky, velvety black:** Maha Hussaini, 'How a Palestinian woman keeps the ancient craft of kohl alive', *Middle East Eye*, 13 April 2020.

97 **Iraqi kohl stick (the pot was lost):** https://www.britishmuseum.org/collection/object/W_OA-12436.

97 **witnesses and documents of human history:** British Museum Story at https://www.britishmuseum.org/about-us/british-museum-story.

97 **the magic of museums:** Rachel Morris and Isabel Greenberg, *The Museum Makers: A Journey Backwards, from Old Boxes of Dark Family Secrets to a Golden Era of Museums*, September Publishing, 2020.

98 **context about his murky past:** David Olusoga, 'It is not Hans Sloane who has been erased from history, but his slaves', *Guardian*, 30 August 2020.

99 **bursting into song and dance:** Hormuzd Rassam and Robert W. Rogers, *Asshur and the Land of Nimrod: Being an Account of the Discoveries Made in the Ancient Ruins of Nineveh, Asshur, Sepharvaim, Calah, Babylon, Borsippa, Cuthah, and Van, Including a Narrative of Different Journeys in Mesopotamia, Assyria, Asia Minor, and Koordistan*, Gregg, 1971.

100 **leaving the BM only 'rubbish':** quoted in David Damrosch, *The Buried Book: The Loss and Rediscovery of the Great Epic of Gilgamesh*, H. Holt, 2007.

101 **'suck' us** and **military occupation:** quoted in Magnus Thorkell Bernhardsson, *Reclaiming a Plundered Past: Archaeology and Nation Building in Modern Iraq*, University of Texas Press, 2005.

102 **cruelty to antiquities:** Juliette Desplat, 'The Other Battle of Samarra', National Archives blog, 18 August 2017.

102 **eating out her heart for Iraq:** Vita Sackville-West, *Passenger to Teheran*, Cockbird Press, 1990.

103 **sand was romantic:** Agatha Christie, *Come, Tell Me How You Live*, Collins, 1946.

103 **artefacts he wasn't entitled to:** Juliette Desplat, 'Decolonising Archaeology in Iraq?', National Archives blog, 27 June 2017.

103 **burning moment of 'The Division':** Christie.

103 **some kind of apology:** Desplat, 27 June 2017.

103 **Museum exists** and **archaeological junk:** quoted in Bernhardsson.

107 **shall ye have peace:** Jeremiah 29: 1–12, King James Bible.

108 **put on thy strength, O Zion:** Isaiah 52, King James Bible.

109 **given him a miniature horse:** Martin Bailey, 'How Britain tried to use the Cyrus Cylinder for political gain', *Art Newspaper*, 1 September 2004.

110 **a stranger in its own home:** Ian Black and Saeed Kamali Deghan, 'Iran lays claim to British Museum's Cyrus Cylinder', *Guardian*, 15 September 2010.

111 **found the building flooded:** Jerry Gordon, 'The Future of the Babylonian Jewish Archives: Interview with Dr. Harold Rhode', *New English Review*, June 2014.

111 **the Iraqi Jewish archive:** http://iraqijewisharchives.org/.

111 **this gathering of intelligence:** Edward Rothstein, 'The Remnants of a Culture's Heart and Soul', *New York Times*, 10 November 2013.

112 **stray but meaningful textual vestiges:** Jeff Spurr, 'Contested Patrimony: The Fate of the Iraqi Jewish Archive', presented at symposium: HOMEWARD BOUND: Returning Displaced Books and Manuscripts co-sponsored by SAFE (Saving Antiquities For Everyone) and the Antiquarian Booksellers Association of America, 2008.

112 **apocalypse perpetrated by the Mongols:** Eleanor Robson, 'Iraq's museums: what really happened', *Guardian*, 18 June 2003.

112 **stuff happens:** quoted in Sean Loughlin, 'Rumsfeld on looting in Iraq: "Stuff happens" ', CNN, 12 April 2003.

113 **free from illnesses:** https://ijarchive.org/s/iraqi-jewish-archive/item/16324.

113 **Jews were once part of this country:** Bruce P. Montgomery, 'Rescue or Return: The Fate of the Iraqi Jewish Archive', *International Journal of Cultural Property*, 20, 2013, 175–200.

113 **country's Jews from the Nazis:** Anne Cohen, 'Honouring the Moroccan king who saved Jews', *The Forward*, 22 December 2015.

114 **shovel dirt into the grave:** https://ijarchive.org/s/iraqi-jewish-archive/page/burial.

115 **were Jewish:** Esther R. Warkov, 'The Urban Arabic Repertoire of Jewish Professional Musicians in Iraq and Israel: Instrumental Improvisation and Culture Change', PhD, Hebrew University, 1987.

115 **blind Jewish musicians became famous:** Jonah Nelson and Esther Warkov, 'How a blind Jewish boy from Baghdad became a great musician', *The Forward*, 10 August 2022.

116 **the voice of Baghdad:** Eness Elias, 'Iraq Still Honors This Jewish Star Known as the "Voice of Baghdad" ', *Haaretz*, 20 November 2018.

116 **writing terrible poetry:** Naqqāsh.

116 **How are we Jews supposed to leave all this?:** Amir.

116 **Iraq's first beauty queen:** Jewish Women's Archive, 'Renée Dangoor Crowned Miss Baghdad', https://jwa.org/thisweek/dec/31/1946/renee-dangoor-crowned-miss-baghdad.

117 **in Need of Urgent Safeguarding:** Julian Lucas, 'UNESCO's Quest to Save the World's Intangible Heritage', *New Yorker*, 2 March 2024.

117 **the Palestinian *dabkeh* dance:** Amira Noshokaty, 'Palestinian Dabkeh stomps the ground of UNESCO', Ahram Online, 6 December 2023.

117 **communities it censors and persecutes:** Dale Berning Sawa, ' "This is our voice": The Uyghur traditions being erased by China's cultural crackdown', *Guardian*, 10 December 2021.

118 **selling kitchenware in a Tel Aviv market:** Rachel Aspden, 'A lost world', *New Statesman*, 17 July 2008.

119 **I don't feel like I'm fixing anything:** *Iraq 'n' Roll*, directed by Gili Gaon, https://www.ruthfilms.com/iraq-n-roll.html.

119 **Iraqi Jewish Buena Vista Social Club:** Linda Abdul Aziz Menuhin, 'From the Ghetto to the Mainstream', *Tel Aviv Review of Books*, Autumn 2020.

119 **as she was never allowed to do:** Robin Denselow, 'Dudu Tassa: An Iraqi Revival', *Songlines*, 31 January 2019.

121 **comfort food was 'trauma food':** Bee Wilson, 'When my husband left me, I headed for the kitchen – here's how comfort food can save the soul', *Guardian*, 21 May 2022.

122 **she means I'm becoming cold:** Eva Hoffman, *Lost in Translation: A Life in a New Language*, Vintage Digital, 2011.

126 **Rebuilding New Orleans, Recipe by Recipe:** Nicole K. Nieto, 'Recipes of Recovery and Rebuilding: The Role of Cookbooks in Post-Katrina New Orleans', PhD, Ohio State University, 2015.

126 **which turned into a cookbook:** Marcelle Bienvenu and Judy Walker (eds), *Cooking Up a Storm: Recipes Lost and Found from The Times-Picayune of New Orleans*, Chronicle Books, 2008.

126 **like we'd never left Baghdad:** *The Scribe* archive, http://www.thescribe.info/.

126 **a book freighted with longing:** Alice Shashou, *Alice's International Cuisine: Favourite Recipes*, Summerfield Press, 1993.

126 **could reduce prejudice and conflict:** https://www.migrateful.org/our-impact/.

127 **with a kind of desperation:** Mayukh Sen, 'Claudia Roden tells her immigrant story', *Food 52*, 9 March 2017.

135 **who didn't talk to each other either:** Jo Tuckman, 'Language at risk of dying out – the last two speakers aren't talking', *Guardian*, 13 April 2011.

136 **might have had Tourette's syndrome:** Harrison.

136 **pleasure or spectacle:** Shaylih Muehlmann, 'Von Humboldt's parrot and the countdown of last speakers in the Colorado Delta', *Language and Communication*, 1 May 2011.

137 **academics and eccentrics:** Richard Collett, 'Why Cornwall is resurrecting its indigenous language', BBC website, 24 April 2023.

137 **what language are we writing in?:** Sarah Whitehead, 'How the Manx Language Came Back from the Dead', *Guardian*, 2 April 2015.

138 **strung on skewers like cat's meat:** George Smith, *Assyrian Discoveries*, Scribner, Armstrong & Co., 1875.

140 **eradicating the e-word:** Wesley Y. Leonard, 'Eradicating the e-Word: Musings on Myaamia Language Reclamation', *World Literature Today*, 11 November 2019.

141 **extinct language is not imaginary:** Wesley Y. Leonard, 'When is an "extinct language" not extinct?: Miami, a formerly sleeping language', in K. A. King (ed.), *Sustaining Linguistic Diversity: endangered and minority languages and language varieties*, Georgetown University Press, 2008.

141 **grammar and its 'elegancies':** Steffi Dippold, 'The Wampanoag Word: John Eliot's "Indian Grammar", the Vernacular Rebellion, and the Elegancies of Native Speech', *Early American Literature*, Vol. 48, No. 3, 2013, 543–75.

142 **to speak our language:** https://www.wlrp.org/home.

142 **keepers as well as speakers:** Ross Perlin, *Language City*, Atlantic Books, 2024.

146 **some wrote and made the bowls:** Dorit Kedar, 'Who Wrote the Incantation Bowls?', PhD Dissertation, Freie Universität Berlin, 2018.

146 **bowl I'd come to see:** https://www.britishmuseum.org/collection/object/W_1974-1209-2.

147 **They promptly began to argue:** *The Alphabet of Ben Sira*, on the Jewish Women's Archive, https://jwa.org/node/23210.

148 **quest for forbidden knowledge:** Judith Plaskow, 'The Coming of Lilith', in Dianne Ashton and Ellen M. Umansky, *Four Centuries of Jewish Women's Spirituality: A Sourcebook*, Beacon Press, 1992.

149 **a new bowl of clay:** J. B. Segal, *Catalogue of the Aramaic and Mandaic Incantation Bowls in the British Museum*, British Museum Press, 2000.

158 **an amulet against dispossession:** Aurora Levins Morales, 'Nadie la tiene: Land, Ecology and Nationalism', *Medicine Stories: Essays for Radicals*, Duke University Press, 2019.

165 **efflorescence of the structure:** Marina Warner, *Stranger Magic: Charmed States & the Arabian Nights*, Chatto & Windus, 2011.

166 **No loss is permanent:** Gabrielle Zevin, *Tomorrow and Tomorrow and Tomorrow*, Chatto & Windus, 2022.

169 **ran with Jewish blood:** Josh Halliday, 'Plans for Clifford's Tower visitor centre scrapped after outcry', *Guardian*, 7 June 2018.

169 **called this a 'holocaust':** Richard of Devizes, trans. J. A. Giles, *The chronicle of Richard of Devizes concerning the deeds of Richard the First, King of England*, James Bohn, 1941.

170 **the just judgment of Christ:** William of Newburgh, *The History of English Affairs*, Aris, 1986.

170 **seed-bed for murderous antisemitism:** Faith and Order Commission, *God's Unfailing Word: Theological and Practical Perspectives on Christian-Jewish Relations*, Church House Publishing, 2019.

170 **quarry to be pursued and converted:** Harriet Sherwood, 'Church of England says Christians must repent for past antisemitism', *Guardian*, 21 November 2019.

171 **hot interpretation:** D. L. Uzzell, 'The hot interpretation of war and conflict', in D. L. Uzzell (ed.), *Heritage Interpretation*, Vol. 1, Belhaven, 1989.

172 **in which modern antisemitism grows:** Dave Rich, *Everyday Hate: How Antisemitism Is Built into Our World – and How You Can Change It*, Biteback Publishing, 2023.

172 **banner off the tower:** Haydn Lewis, 'White Lives Matter banner hung from Clifford's Tower, York', *York Press*, 9 August 2022.

173 **capital of the Jewish world:** Benjamin, 1993.

173 **protection from whom?:** Lyn Julius, *Uprooted: How 3,000 Years of Jewish Civilisation in the Arab World Vanished Overnight*, Valentine Mitchell, 2018.

175 **almost an entirely fantastical affair:** Farah Karim-Cooper, *The Great White Bard: How to Love Shakespeare While Talking About Race*, Viking, 2023.

177 **were called 'stinky':** Joel Hart, 'Amba: A Tale of Four Cities: The cultural production of mango pickle', *Vittles*, 28 February 2022.

179 **told the family story:** Joseph Sassoon, *The Global Merchants: The Enterprise and Extravagance of the Sassoon Dynasty*, Penguin Books, 2021.

180 **he dedicated it to Hitler:** Cecil Roth, *The Sassoon Dynasty*, Robert Hale Ltd, 1941.

180 **'flaunting' and 'vulgar':** Jean Moorcroft Wilson, *Siegfried Sassoon: The Making of a War Poet: A Biography 1886 – 1918*, Gerald Duckworth & Co. Ltd, 1998.

181 **my father's oriental extraction:** Siegfried Sassoon, *Memoirs of a Fox-Hunting Man*, Faber & Faber, 2017.

181 **monstrous wealth:** Siegfried Sassoon, 'Ancestors', in *Collected Poems*, Faber & Faber, 2002.

183 **this 'assimilation food':** Soleil Ho, 'Let's Call It Assimilation Food', *Taste*, 26 June 2017.

184 **which bit of her:** Arielle Kaplan, 'Yes, There's a Reason Hamantaschen Look Like Vaginas', *Hey Alma*, 5 March 2020.

186 **oldest Baghdad confection:** Daisy Iny, *The Best of Baghdad Cooking, with Treats from Teheran*, Saturday Review Press/EP Dutton & Co. Inc., 1976.

186 **fried dough squiggles:** Nigella Lawson, *Feast: Food That Celebrates Life*, Chatto & Windus, 2004.

187 **likes rose water:** Linda Dangoor, *Flavours of Babylon: A Family Cookbook*, Waterpoint, 2011.

187 ***The Shoes of Tanboury*:** Shimon Ballas, *The Shoes of Tanboury*, Hebrew Publishing Company, 1970.

190 **the misery caused by language division:** Ludwik Lejzer Zamenhof, in a letter to Nikolai Borovko, *c.*1895.

190 **another people's religion:** quoted in Esther Schor, *Bridge of Words*, Metropolitan Books, 2015.

193 **parishes bordering on silence:** George Steiner, *After Babel: Aspects of Language and Translation*, Oxford University Press, 1975.

193 **Making Babel work:** Perlin.

194 **Moroccan food now:** Kate Colquhoun, *Taste: The Story of Britain through Its Cooking*, Bloomsbury, 2007.

195 **the bowl or the salad:** Elizabeth David, *Summer Cooking*, Penguin, 2011.

195 **the King of Oude's Omelet:** Eliza Acton, *Modern Cookery for Private Families*, Quadrille, 2011.

196 **extremely spice-conscious:** Elizabeth David, *Spices, Salt and Aromatics in the English Kitchen*, Penguin Books, 1970.

197 **Cooks and the Wise:** Nasrallah Nawal, *Annals of the Caliphs' Kitchens: Ibn Sayyār al-Warrāq's Tenth-Century Baghdadi Cookbook*, Brill, 2010.

198 **& serue forth:** Thomas Austin, *Two Fifteenth-Century Cookery-Books: Harleian MS 279 (ab1430), & Harleian MS 4016 (ab1450), with extracts from Ashmole MS 1439, Laud MS 553 and Douce MS 55*, Oxford University Press, 1964.

202 **their parents' burdens:** Rachel Yehuda on the On Being podcast, https://onbeing.org/programs/rachel-yehuda-how-trauma-and-resilience-cross-generations-nov2017/.

206 **rating of 'no return':** Robert Philpot, 'Iraq's Jewish sites almost all ruined beyond repair, new heritage report finds', *Times of Israel*, 5 June 2020.

207 **in my own language:** *Forget Baghdad.*

209 **We built the pyramids:** Katarina Kratovac, 'Egypt says Jewish slaves didn't build pyramids', *Christian Science Monitor*, 11 January 2010.

212 **a 2018 survey:** Alison Flood, 'Only 1% of children's books have BAME main characters – UK study', *Guardian*, 17 July 2018.

213 **mistreatment of people or cultures:** Disney Stories Matter, https://storiesmatter.thewaltdisneycompany.com/.

214 **change it to *Namesake*:** N. S. Nuseibeh, *Namesake: Reflections on a Warrior Woman*, Canongate Books, 2024.

215 ***it woke up*:** Jenny G. Zhang, 'A Conversation With the Team That Made Bread With Ancient Egyptian Yeast', *Eater*, 8 August 2019.

220 **Jews have legs:** Martyn Hudson, 'Revisiting Isaac Deutscher', *Fathom Journal*, Winter 2014.

Other Sources

Interviews and Films

To hear interviews with Iraqi Jews: go to the Eli Timan archive, https://www.youtube.com/@elitiman1; Sephardi Voices UK, https://www.sephardivoices.org.uk/; People of the Book, https://people-book.org/category/video-library/jews-of-the-middle-east/; Mother Tongue, https://www.lashon.org/en/taxonomy/term/62); The Mizrahi Story, instagram.com/themizrahistory/; and Noor-W-Nar, https://www.youtube.com/@NoorWNar). Or watch the films: *The Dove Flyer* (based on Eli Amir's bestselling novel), directed by Nissim Dayan; *Baghdad Twist*, directed by Joe Balass; *Forget Baghdad*, directed by Samir: *Iraq 'n' Roll*, directed by Gili Gaon: and *Remember Baghdad*, directed by Fiona Murphy.

Further Reading

Preface: *Eeyam al babenjan* (Days of the aubergines)

Farrell, Stephen, 'Baghdad Jews Have Become a Fearful Few', *New York Times*, 1 June 2008.

Isaac, Mardean, 'Is the Lost Language of Iraqi Jews Really Lost?', *Tablet*, 1 June 2018.

Losing

Ekel qalbi (He ate my heart) or An incomplete list of Judeo-Iraqi Arabic idioms about the heart

Mitchell, Stephen, *Gilgamesh: A new English version*, Profile Books, 2004.

Schmidt, Michael, *Gilgamesh: The Life of a Poem*, Princeton University Press, 2021.

Farhud (The breakdown of order)

Barr, James, *A Line in the Sand*, Simon & Schuster, 2011.

Basri, Carole, 'The Jewish Refugees from Arab Countries: An Examination of Legal Rights – A Cast Study of the Human Rights Violations of Iraqi Jews', *Fordham International Law Journal* 26, No. 3, March 2003.

Fromkin, David, *A Peace to End All Peace: Creating the Modern Middle East 1914–1922*, Penguin Books, 1991.

Haim, Sylvia (ed.), *Arab Nationalism: An Anthology*, University of California Press, 1962.

Isaac, Mardean, 'Samir Naqqāsh: Master of the Double Exile', *Tablet*, 15 May 2019.

Kedourie, Elie, *Democracy and Arab Political Culture*, Washington Institute for Near East Policy, 1992.

Mahfouz, Sabrina, *These Bodies of Water*, Tinder Press, 2022.

Mazzig, Hen, *The Wrong Kind of Jew: A Mizrahi Manifesto*, Wicked Son, 2022.

Rejwan, Nissim. *The Last Jews in Baghdad: Remembering a Lost Homeland*, University of Texas Press, 2004.

Said, Edward, *Orientalism*, Penguin Books, 2003.

Tripp, Charles, *A History of Iraq*, Cambridge University Press, 2007.

Why my father left

Shohat, Ella, '"Sant al-Tasqit": Seventy years since the departure of Iraqi Jews', *Jadaliyya*, 14 January 2021.

Mizrahi

Abergel, Reuven, '"Our ideology is our pain": Notes of an Israeli Black Panther', *972 Magazine*, 26 June 2020.

Alcalay, Ammiel, *Keys to the Garden: New Israeli Writing*, City Lights Books, 1996.

Gavriely-Huri, Dalia, 'Why Have Transit Camps for Mizrahi Jews Been Written Out of Israeli History?', *Haaretz*, 18 April 2015.

Rossetto, Piera, 'Space of Transit, Place of Memory: Ma'abarah and Literary Landscapes of Arab Jews', *Quest: Issues in Contemporary Jewish History*, Issue 4, November 2012.

Shabi, Rachel, *Not the Enemy: Israel's Jews from Arab Lands*, Yale University Press, 2009.

Summers, Charlie, 'Charlie Biton, Black Panther founder who fought for Mizrahi equality, dies at 76', *Times of Israel*, 25 February 2024.

Tene, Ofra, '"The New Immigrant Must Not Only Learn, He Must Also Forget": The Making of Eretz Israeli Ashkenazi Cuisine', in Anat Helman, *Jews and Their Foodways*, Oxford University Press, 2015.

Tsabari, Ayelet, 'It's time Israel Believed the Victims in the Yemenite Babies Affair', *Forward*, 11 July 2016.

My Arabic is mute

Ballas, Shimon, *Outcast*, City Lights, 2007.

Banipal: Magazine of Modern Arab Literature, 72, Special Feature: Iraqi Jewish Writers, Banipal Books, 2021.

Behar, Almog, 'Ana Min Al Yahoud – I'm one of the Jews', *Haaretz*, 28 April 2005.

Buzago, Meir, 'A Little Arabic Within our Hebrew', *Jewish Review of Books*, Spring 2023.

Glinert, Lewis, *The Story of Hebrew*, Princeton University Press, 2017.

Golden, Zach, 'How Yiddish became a "foreign language" in Israel despite being spoken there since the 1400s', *Forward*, 11 September 2023.

Harshav, Benjamin, *Language in Time of Revolution*, University of California Press, 1993.

Hoffmann, Adina, and Cole, Peter, *Sacred Trash: The Lost and Found world of the Cairo Genizah*, Bravo Ltd, 2016.

Shohat, Ella, 'The Invention of Judeo-Arabic: Nation, Partition and the Linguistic Imaginary', *Interventions*, 19(2), 153–200.

Why my mother didn't leave

Jewish Telegraphic Agency, 'Eshkol Outraged, Denounces Hangings, and Denies Iraqi Jews Were Israeli Spies', *Jewish Telegraphic Agency Daily News Bulletin*, 28 January 1969.

Wisniewski, Katherine, 'Baghdad Could have Been a Mega-City by Frank Lloyd Wright', *Curbed*, 5 March 2015.

Masgouf, or All the foods I'll never eat

Halahmy, Miriam, *The Boy from Baghdad*, Green Bean Books, 2023.

Kresh, Miriam, 'Khirret, A Vanishing Iraqi Sweet made from Cattails', Green Prophet website, 14 August 2019.

Marozzi, Justin, *Baghdad: City of Peace, City of Blood*, Penguin Books, 2014.

Schwartzstein, Peter, 'The Slow Destruction of Much-Loved Masgouf, An Iraqi National Dish', NPR, 6 November 2017.

Keeping

How to pack an ark

Huberman, Michelle, 'Mabrouk! We're having a henna in Regent's Park!', *Jerusalem Post*, 19 August 2012.

In the British Museum

Abdul-Ahad, Ghaith, *A Stranger in Your Own City: Travels in the Middle East's Long War*, Hutchinson Heinemann, 2023.

Christie, Agatha, *Murder in Mesopotamia*, HarperCollins, 2001.

Delbourgo, James, *Collecting the World: The Life and Curiosity of Hans Sloane*, Allen Lane, 2017.

Desplat, Juliette, 'Archaeology and the Second World War in Iraq', National Archives blog, 1 March 2019.

Goode, James F., *Negotiating for the Past: Archaeology, Nationalism, and Diplomacy in the Middle East, 1919–1941*, University of Texas Press, 2007.

Goodhart, George, 'Unburying an Archaeologist: the Forgotten Story of Hormuzd Rassam', Uncomfortable Oxford website, 6 November 2022.

Hicks, Dan, *The Brutish Museums: The Benin Bronzes, Colonial Violence and Cultural Restitution*, Pluto Press, 2020.

Howell, Georgina, *Queen of the Desert: The Extraordinary Life of Gertrude Bell*, Pan Books, 2015.

Wallach, Janet, *Desert Queen: The Extraordinary Life of Gertrude Bell, Adventurer, Adviser to Kings, Ally of Lawrence of Arabia*, Anchor Books, 2005.

Other other other

Baghoolizadeh, Beeta, 'Reconstructing a Persian Past: Contemporary Uses and Misuses of the Cyrus Cylinder in Iranian Nationalist Discourse', *Ajam Media Collective*, 6 June 2013.

Curtis, John, and Finkel, Irving L., *The Cyrus Cylinder and Ancient Persia: A New Beginning for the Middle East*, British Museum, 2013.

Economist staff, 'Diplomatic whirl: A show that tests the limits of cultural politics', *Economist*, 23 March 2013.

Schulz, Matthias, 'Falling for Ancient Propaganda: UN Treasure Honors Persian Despot', *Der Spiegel*, 15 July 2008.

A museum in Baghdad

Basri, Carole, and Levin, Sarah, 'Iraqi Jewish archives need to be returned to Iraqi Jews – opinion', *Jerusalem Post*, 4 September 2022.

Jeffries, Stuart, 'Books, tears and blood: Saad Eskander, director of Baghdad's national library', *Guardian*, 9 June 2008.

Ledger, Dana, 'Remembrance of Things Past: The Iraqi Jewish Archive and the Legacy of the IR', *George Washington International Law Review*, 37, 3, 2005.

Leff, Lisa, 'Iraqi Jewish Treasures Displayed in D.C. Before Being Shipped Back to . . . Iraq', *Tablet*, 7 October 2013.

Schuster, Angela M., and Polk, Milbry (eds), *The Looting of the Iraq Museum, Baghdad: The Lost Legacy of Ancient Mesopotamia*, Harry N. Abrams, 2005.

Iraq 'n' Roll

Kojaman, Yeheskel, *The Maqam Music Tradition in Iraq*, Y. Kojaman, 2001.

Zeed, Adnan Abu, 'Iraqi musicians fight to revive ancient art of maqam', *Al Monitor*, 17 April 2018.

Zubaida, Sami, 'Entertainers in Baghdad, 1900–1950', in Eugene L. Rogan, *Outside in: On the Margins of the Modern Middle East*, I.B. Tauris, 2001.

Ashteedek (Long live your hands)

Roden, Claudia, *The Book of Jewish Food: An Odyssey from Samarkand and Vilna to the Present Day*, Viking, 1997.

Trachtenberg, Jeffrey, 'New Orleans State of Mind', *Wall Street Journal*, 18 February 2006.

The Oxford School of Rare Jewish Languages

Abley, Mark, *Spoken Here: Travels among Threatened Languages*, Heinemann, 2003.

Bar-Moshe, Assaf, *Baghdadi Judeo-Arabic: An Introductory Text*, UCL Press, 2024.

Hutton, Alice, '"The gooey overlay of sweetness over genocide": the myth of the "first Thanksgiving"', *Guardian*, 25 November 2021.

Kuang, R. F., *Babel: Or the Necessity of Violence: An Arcane History of the Oxford Translators' Revolution*, Harper Voyager, 2022.

Leonard, Wesley Y., 'Refusing "Endangered Languages" Narratives', *Daedalus*, Journal of the American Academy of Arts & Sciences, 152(3), 2023, 69–83.

Stille, Alexander, 'Speak, Cultural Memory: A Dead-Language Debate', *New York Times*, 30 September 2000.

Lilith

Anton, Maggie, *Rav Hisda's Daughter, Book 1: Apprentice: A Novel of Love, the Talmud and Sorcery*, Plume, 2012.

Frankfurter, David, 'Scorpion/Demon: On the Origin of the Mesopotamian Apotropaic Bowl', *Journal of Near Eastern Studies*, 74, 2015, 9–18.

Levene, Dan, 'Curse or Blessing? What's in the magic bowl', Ian Karten Lecture 2022, Parkes Institute Pamphlet, Southampton, 2002.

Rivlin, Lilly, 'Lilith', *Ms Magazine*, December 1972.

Rosen, Jonathan, *The Talmud and the Internet: A Journey Between Worlds*, Picador, 2001.

Secunda, Shai, 'Common Clay', *Jewish Review of Books*, Winter 2015.

Sifting

Raqi (watermelon)

Behar, Ruth (writer), and Holzwarth, Devon (illustrator), *Tia Fortuna's New Home: A Jewish Cuban Journey*, Alfred A. Knopf, 2022.

Leventhal, Michael (writer), and Catalán, Laura (illustrator), *The Chocolate King*, Green Bean Books, 2021.

Naylor-Ballesteros, Chris, *The Suitcase*, Nosy Crow, 2019.

Ratinon, Claire, *Unearthed: On race and roots, and how the soil taught me I belong*, Chatto & Windus, 2022.

Roman, Rachel, 'Uprooting the Wandering Jew: The grassroots movement to rename a plant', *Tablet*, 9 June 2022.

Stein, Joel Edward (writer), and Ugolotti, Sara (illustrator), *Raquela's Seder*, Kar-Ben Publishing, 2022.

Sifting

Horta, Paulo Lemos, and Seale, Yasmine, *The Annotated Arabian Nights: Tales from 1001 Nights*, Liveright Publishing Corporation, 2021.

Lyons, Malcolm C., and Lyons, Ursula, *Tales from 1,001 Nights: Aladdin, Ali Baba and Other Favourite Tales*, Penguin Classics, 2010.

York

Glaser, Eliane, 'Oliver Cromwell and the Jews: a correction', *Guardian*, 9 December 2005.

Green, Dominic, *The Double Life of Doctor Lopez: Spies, Shakespeare and the Plot to Poison Elizabeth I*, Century, 2003.

Heng, Geraldine, *The Invention of Race in the European Middle Ages*, Cambridge University Press, 2018.

Horowitz, David, 'Coming back to the castle: The improbable return of the Jews of York', *Times of Israel*, 8 November 2019.

Jacobs, Martin, *Reorienting the East: Jewish Travelers to the Medieval Muslim World*, University of Pennsylvania Press, 2014.

Katz, David S., *The Jews in the History of England, 1485–1850*, Clarendon, 1997.

Marcus, Jacob Rader, and Saperstein, Marc, *The Jew in the Medieval World: A Source Book, 315–1791*, Hebrew Union College Press, 1999.

Mundill, Robin R., *The King's Jews: Money, Massacre and Exodus in Medieval England*, Continuum, 2010.

Pessah, Tom, 'When the Sultan took in Jewish refugees', *972 Magazine*, 25 January 2018.

Sherwood, Harriet, 'Eight centuries after the pogrom, pride flickers again in York's Jewish community', *Guardian*, 13 December 2015.

Amba (mango pickle)

Bhogal, Ravinder, *Jikoni: Proudly Inauthentic Recipes from an Immigrant Kitchen*, Bloomsbury, 2020.

Hu, Joanna, and Kaul, Rosheen, *Chinese-ish: Home cooking, not quite authentic, 100 % delicious*, Murdoch Books, 2022.

Krishna, Priya, *Indian-ish: Recipes and Antics from a Modern American Family*, Harvest, 2019.

Roth, Cecil, *The Sassoon Dynasty*, Robert Hale Ltd, 1941.

Somekh, Sasson, 'Forever Amba', *Haaretz*, 8 May 2002.

Twitty, Michael, *Koshersoul: The Faith and Food Journey of an African American Jew*, Amistad, 2022.

Zhang, Jenny G., '"Always Be My Maybe" and the Trap of "Authentic Cooking"', *Eater*, 4 June 2019.

The Shoes of Tanboury

Levy, Lital, *Poetic Trespass: Writing between Hebrew and Arabic in Israel and Palestine*, Princeton University Press, 2014.

Babel

Kellman, Steven G., 'The Secret Jewish History of Esperanto', *Forward*, 30 August 2016.

Nabug

Adamczeski, Vida, and Tynan, Deirdre, 'Good Food Again: the story of post-war English food told through the arts', *Vittles*, 27 February 2023.

Blyton, Enid. *The Enchanted Wood*, George Newnes Limited, 1939.

Chaney, Lisa, *Elizabeth David: A Biography*, Macmillan, 1998.

David, Elizabeth, *Spices, Salt and Aromatics in the English Kitchen*, Penguin Books, 1970.

Denny, Roz, *The Tudor Kitchens Cookery Book*, Hampton Court Palace, 1994.

Godoy, Maria, 'Dining After "Downton Abbey": Why British Food Was So Bad For So Long', NPR, 19 February 2012.

Leyel, C. F., and Hartley, Olga, *The Gentle Art of Cookery: With 750 Recipes*, Chatto & Windus, 1925.

Nasrallah, Nawal, *Delights from the Garden of Eden: A Cookbook and History of the Iraqi Cuisine*, Equinox, 2013.

Nunn, Jonathan, 'First, Catch Your Peasant: A Critical History of the Peasantry in British Food Writing via John Berger, Elizabeth David and Patience Gray', *Critical Quarterly*, 27 April 2023.

Purkiss, Diane, *English Food: A People's History*, William Collins, 2022.

Pym, Barbara, *Excellent Women*, Jonathan Cape, 1952.

Pym, Barbara, *A Glass of Blessings*, Jonathan Cape, 1958.

Roden, Claudia, *A Book of Middle Eastern Food*, Nelson, 1968.

Rodinson, Maxine, and Perry, Charles, and Arberry, Arthur, *Medieval Arab Cookery*, Prospect, 2006.

Stivers, Valerie, 'Cooking with Barbara Pym', *Paris Review*, 27 October 2017.

There and then

Murad, Aaron, and Murad Rehany, Orit, *A River of Tears, the River of Hope: The Saga of Two Torah Scrolls*, AuthorHouse, 2013.

Rodriguez, Tori, 'Descendants of Holocaust Survivors Have Altered Stress Hormones', *Scientific American*, 1 March 2015.

Recipes for outwitting death

Galer, Sophia Smith, 'The Aladdin Controversy Disney Can't Escape', BBC website, 14 July 2017.

Khatchadourian, Raffi, 'Michael Rakowitz's Art of Return', *New Yorker*, 17 August 2020.

Rakowitz, Michael, and Friends, *A House with a Date Palm Will Never Starve: Cooking with Date Syrup: Forty Chefs and an Artist Create New and Classic Dishes with a Traditional Middle Eastern Ingredient*, Art/Books, 2019.

Rakowitz, Michael, *The Invisible Enemy Should Not Exist*, https://artuk.org/discover/artworks/the-invisible-enemy-should-not-exist-310263.

Samuel, Sigal, and Mintzi, Vali, *Osnat and Her Dove: The True Story of the World's First Female Rabbi*, Levine Querido, 2021.

Shaheen, Jack G., *Reel Bad Arabs: How Hollywood Vilifies a People*, Arris, 2003.

Tharoor, Kanishk, and Maruf, Maryam, 'Museum of Lost Objects: The Winged Bull of Nineveh', BBC News, 29 February 2016.

Trilling, Daniel, 'Salvage value: the rescue missions of Michael Rakowitz', *Apollo*, 23 May 2021.

Voon, Claire, 'Slick Replica of Palmyra's Triumphal Arch Arrives in New York, Prompting Questions', *Hyperallergic*, 20 September 2016.

Evil Eye Guy

Behar, Ruth, *Travelling Heavy: A Memoir in between Journeys*, Duke University Press, 2013.

Hawthorn, Ainsley, 'Middle Eastern Dance and What We Call It', *Dance Research*, Issue 1, Vol. 37, 2019, 1–17.

Mizrahi Dance Archive, https://www.mizrahidancearchive.com/.

Acknowledgements

Thank you to everyone who generously shared their stories, knowledge and expertise with me. I am especially grateful to: Eli Timan, Assaf Bar-Moshe and all at the Oxford School of Rare Jewish Languages, Mark Turin, Sara Manasseh, Jackie Barzvi, Ruth Timan, Lilac Yosiphon, James Barr, Rebecca Hughes, Claire Warrior, Christopher de Bellaigue, John Curtis, Mike Pitts, Jeffrey Spurr, Martin Worthington, Jonathan Nunn, Rachel Rose Reid, Gabriel Kanter-Webber, Oded Amit, Gaby Glassman, Patrick Matthews, Kriti Kumar, Patrick Wagstaff, Lea Misan, Alex Eisenberg, Daniel Eisenberg, Ross Perlin and Héloïse Sénéchal.

This is the third book I've been lucky enough to work on with my agent Judith Murray and editor Becky Hardie and I am so grateful to them and to Asia Choudhry for their encouragement, wisdom and rigour, and for believing in this book from the start. And thank you to Jules Rogers for taking my picture.

Thank you to my friends and family for support and conversation which hugely enriched the book: Laith Elzubaidi and all at the British Arab Writers' Group; my Royal Court Theatre Jewish Study Group comrades Rachel Mars, Nick Cassenbaum, Jess Latowicki and Eve Leigh; Helen Kedourie, Maddy Costa, Stephen Brown, Lucy Michaels; my brother Edmund, and my cousins Karen and Michelle, Philip Arditti, Hassan Abdulrazzak, Emma Ayech, Helen McColl, Sophie Heawood, Amy Rosenthal, Emily Rhodes, Joel Morris, Michael Leventhal, Tom Secretan, Sarah Slotover and Jude Cook. Thank you to

Marina Benjamin and Rachel Shabi, my Iraqi Jewish Women Writers' Support Group, for nourishment of all kinds.

Most importantly, thank you to my mother Amanda who didn't just teach me most of the words and recipes in the first place but generously and patiently went over them with me for this book and only sometimes laughed at my terrible pronunciation. Thank you to my father Ezra for trusting me with his stories, and also to my grandmother Aida, who died as this book was going to print. May her memory be a blessing. Thank you most of all to my son, inspiration and co-pilot.

Index

SE indicates Samantha Ellis.